THE ART OF IMAGINATION

Srdjan Bogicevic

This is a work of fiction. Conversations are either the product of the author's imagination or are used fictitiously.

For permissions contact:

contact@theartofimagination.info

ISBN: 978-1-9994944-1-4 (ebook)
ISBN: 978-1-9994944-4-5 (hardcover)
ISBN: 978-1-9994944-2-1 (paperback)

www.theartofimagination.info

I want to dedicate this book to our *Creator*. Without *His* help, I could never do anything in my life. Although it is only an imaginary character, I want to thank my *Future Self* as well for giving me the answers I needed at the time of writing this book. Last, but not least, I want to thank my soulmate Aleksandra. Your love, support, and help mean to me more than you can imagine!

This piece of art is for my family, who hasn't seen me for years. I want you to know while I was writing this book I was thinking about you all the time. Although there are thousands of miles between us, I will always be looking your way. I will always be watching over you. You mean more to me than you will ever know! I love you!

Contents

Introduction

Hello, my name is *Srdjan Bogicevic*, or you can call me *Serge* - the preference of my Canadian friends. What you are about to read is a full interview with my **Future Self** (from this point forward, I'll refer to it simply as **Future**). Yes, you read it correctly. I know it may sound impossible to have an interview with your *Future*, but that's exactly what I was doing - interviewing my *Future* or maybe it's better to say I had a strange conversation with my *Future*. Let me explain something; it has been said that we are created in the image and likeness of our *Creator*. Whether you call it God, Buddha, Jesus, Universe, Shiva, Source, you name it. The label may be different, but the essence is the same. We are created by a Creator, which means that we have the divine qualities and the same power as our Creator. You may not know it because you haven't experienced it, at least not yet. I am here to tell you that your greatest power is your **Imagination**.

"We can create anything we can imagine."

In your *Imagination*, you can live the life you really and truly desire. First, put enough belief into your thoughts, then strengthen this belief by putting your thoughts into words, and finally, put these words into action. If you persevere and don't give up, you will live your dream life precisely as the initial thought you imagined. The most powerful tool that you have right now in your life is your *Imagination*. That's how I was able to go to the future and talk with my *Future Self*, in my *Imagination*. That's the *purpose of this book*: **to stimulate your thoughts. To make you think about your life and the future you want to create.** I started writing this book to keep my mind positive at all times and to remind myself that I can create whatever I want. The idea seemed good and I decided to follow it.

But while writing, I realized that there was much more than this; there are people in this world who still need answers to the many questions they have. I decided to ask my *Future* some of the questions that will have the greatest benefits for you.

When I was using my *Imagination* to go into the future (in my mind, my future), sometimes I was afraid that I would lose touch with the present moment. I was so inspired by this idea that sometimes, for example, when I was with my friends in a restaurant, I caught myself thinking about the future instead of being present, because that's the only moment that truly exists – *now*. However, somehow I managed to separate these two things and what I discovered is, when you think about your future and imagine how you would like to live, the whole *Universe* then works in alignment to fulfill the dream that you have. You'll notice that people, events, resources, books, and every other conceivable force will work to help you achieve your goals.

By the time I started writing this book, I had already achieved many things I had dreamed about, and that's how I know that we can do, be or have anything we truly want if we put our *Imagination* to work for us together with our thoughts, words, feelings, and actions. I didn't have any order at which to ask the questions. I was asking, and in the end, put it together in a way that I believe would be most useful for you to read. I must note that these questions are not new. They were asked by the first people of this planet, and they have been answered time and time again. For whatever reason people didn't receive these messages, and that's why I believe that our *Creator* will send them in perpetuity through people, places, events, circumstances, songs, books until we understand the message.

I want to clarify something. Everything that you're about to read is what you already know. It's inside of you. It's a part of who you are. You wouldn't be attracted to this book, and you definitely wouldn't invest your money, time and energy into buying and reading it, if this did not represent at least a part of who you are that's in alignment with your value system and your philosophy of life. Also, some of the topics that you're about to read, you've probably read or heard before in some other great books or from other great people that had walked on this planet. This is just one more unique way of delivering the message for you to remember who you really are. That's why I believe that God will send you the same message over and over again through different sources that will translate that message in their unique way until you receive it. Don't get the wrong idea, I don't consider myself as a messenger from God or anything like that. I believe that perhaps, this book serves as another way for you to receive the message you need to hear at this moment.

You'll see in the text that during this interview, the roles were reversed. Instead of having my *Future Self* to answer my questions, I was the one who did the answering. I think that my Imagination was playing some interesting tricks on me. The whole idea of speaking to my *Future* seemed good, so I decided to follow the flow of my thoughts.

I didn't go to some quiet place and try to meditate or visualize this interview. I've simply done it by taking my headphones; turn on some good music, grabbed my laptop, and started writing. I was asking myself questions, and I was looking for the answers in my *Imagination* by imagining how my *Future Self* would answer the questions that I had. It was fun. This whole idea and concept inspired me to put all my efforts and energy into writing everything down to provide the highest possible value to you - my readers, and my dear human beings.

My hope for you is that you'll find what you're searching for by engaging in such a conversation with your own imagined *Future Self*. The words you're about to read will stimulate your *Imagination* to work in your best interest, and you'll be inspired to do something with your life because I know for sure that we deserve to live the spiritually abundant life in all areas.

Now let's go to the interview.

My First Meeting with My Future

Middle of August 2018, it was a beautiful summer evening when I decided to open my laptop, turned on some beautiful epic music and used my *Imagination* to go into the future to talk with my *Future Self*. Although I didn't know in what way this interview would go and what would be the outcome. I was inspired to give all my effort and use my Imagination to talk with the *Future* that would provide me with all the answers that I needed. I asked these questions because I wanted to improve my present situation. However, as these questions evolved, I realized that there are so many people in this world that would want to know how to improve their lives in every area. So I started this interview:

Serge: I see that you're surprised to see me, but I've come to you because I need some answers to improve my life. Would you be interested in having an interview with me?

Future: Wow, first of all, I'm glad that you came to me. It brings me memories of how I looked back then. Damn, I was handsome and a very athletic young man at that age (laugh).

Serge: Haha do not flatter yourself too much.

Future: Just a little, it feels good. Anyway, you came to me because you're seeking some answers. Why now? What is the purpose of this surprise visit? You know that this is only your *Imagination* and that your *Future*, as you call me, is only an imaginary character that you're using to expand your wisdom and knowledge.

Serge: Well, to be honest, I want to write a book that will provide some answers that today's people need and still don't know who they are or where they want to go. Even young teenagers that are about to jump to adult life needs to know in order to live the life they desire. Why now? I don't know. Probably because *now* is the right time to do this. If I wanted to do it 3 or 5 or 10 years ago, I would probably not be ready for it.

"The reason why you didn't do something you wanted before is that you were not ready back then. If that thing you want had happened a few years before, you probably couldn't handle it. However, I believe that everything will happen at the right time, in the right place, with the right people." - **Srdjan Bogicevic**

So yes, I wanted to write a book four years ago. I had this idea, but now I know why I didn't. Simply put, I wasn't ready for it. Now I feel I am. I feel happy now. A few months ago, for no reason, I realized that I became happy and started to appreciate everything I have in my life. I've started to enjoy life itself. Probably that's one of the reasons why I felt ready to write this book now.

"Logic will take you from A to B. Imagination will take you everywhere."
- Albert Einstein

Also, I'm well aware that this is only my *Imagination* at work, but that's exactly what I want to do for my readers. To stimulate their thoughts and use their *Imagination* as the most powerful tool to create a life they want to live. As **Albert Einstein** said, – **"Imagination can take you everywhere!"**

Future: That seems like a good reason to have this interview. I can see that you're excited about this book, and you're giving your all to use your *Imagination* as best as you can.

Serge: Trust me; I'm dying to be of service! I want to contribute to this world. I know so many different ways to do it, but I believe that this book can be one of the greatest tools to use to change other people's lives.

Future: That's very noble of you. I'm inspired to hear your questions, and I'll give my best to provide you with the most valuable answers so every reader will find something that will improve their life at once through the application of some principles that we'll discuss here. Where do you want to start?

Serge: Hah now we're coming to the hardest part.

Future: Are you telling me that you don't know what you are going to ask me?

Serge: Actually, I know what I want to talk about. It's just that I don't know where to start.

Future: Your problem is that you're thinking of what order to ask the questions so it may be logical to your readers and easier for them to consume.

Serge: How did you know that?

Future: Have you forgotten that this is only your *Imagination*?

Serge: Oh yeah. Well, that's true. I want to make these questions in particular order, but it seems that I have no idea how to put them in that way.

Future: Do not try to do it in that way because you'll lose the flow of the ideas. Listen to your heart and go one question at a time, and in the end, everything will fall into place. In the beginning, you stated that you believe everything is happening at the right time, right place, with the right people, am I right?

Serge: Yes, you are. Thanks for reminding me. I'll follow your advice, but the other problem is that I have a million questions.

Future: Well since you decided to use your *Imagination* and come here, in this (let's call it) dimension, I'll cooperate with you and provide you with all the answers that I can. I want to clarify that no one can give all the answers at one time, because even if you're 70, 80 or 90 years old, there are still some things that you can learn. Learning, or better say remembering can last forever. Very few people will remember who they are during their lifetime.

Serge: There are so many other great books that teach people about eternal life, God, or similar matters. So, if you don't mind, let's talk about subjects that I believe will be of great benefit to everyone that will read this.

Future: Oh, boy! You're impatient to hear some answers.

Serge: Just like you were many years ago.

Future: True, I can't deny that. You are me, and I am you. Okay, so where do you want to start?

Serge: I'm curious about you or better still, my *Future Self*, can you please tell me something about yourself? Like whom you are now?

Future: I believe that you know a lot about me at least until your age.

Serge: Yes, I do, but somehow, I want to know what happens later in my life. Although I'm fully aware that if I want to experience your story, I'll have to put my whole heart and soul to live the life I want. I guess I'm curious about what I've become.

Future: I think that's a good starting point. Let's start from there. I'll mention one more time that this is your *Imagination* and it doesn't mean that what I'm about to say now will happen in your real life. It's what your heart and your *Imagination* desire to be when you're 80 or so years old.

Note: This was the first moment when I imagined my future, and it felt so good that I could feel as if the future is already here. While you're reading these words, I would like you to stop for a moment and imagine what your *Future Self* will tell you about whom you'll become and what you have achieved. Just close your eyes and imagine yourself as a 70-80-year-old and see what your life will be about and feel it. You can call this your first task; to put yourself in the position of your *Future Self.*

My name is Srdjan; I'm from a small town in Serbia called Pozega. I'm 84 years old, and this is a small portion of my story, which I hope will inspire you to be who you are and to live the life you desire. With gratitude and happiness, I can say that I've lived my life fulfilled every single day. I've experienced the joy of achieving all of my dreams and the full blessing of this gift called *life* that our dear God gave to us. I dedicated this story to our dear God because without His help; I would never achieve anything in my life. I assume that what you'll read in this book is a true masterpiece, and because of that, I want to share something with you that unfortunately, most people don't realize during their lifetime. However, I'm sure you will and that you will accept the principles that this book will provide you to help you remember who you are and that you are never alone! I spent more than 50 years with the love of my life (I know that my *Present Self* would like to know who she is, but it's something that he will soon discover), who gave me two beautiful kids and they provided me with even more joy with my grandchildren. I was travelling around the world, more than 100 countries. I have been to places that most people dream of, ate all kinds of different foods, enjoyed all sorts of adventures and most importantly, wherever I was, my main goal was always to make the most positive impact on that community and change other people's lives for the better.

My main business was never a business because I was working with all my heart and passion. My desire to help others was greater than receiving a personal benefit from it. That passion can't be described with words. I'm delighted and grateful that I've changed millions of lives through inspirational speeches, books, projects, and daily work with all kinds of people from 6 to 86 years old. I must note, I didn't do that alone! I've been able to do all of this thanks to my best friend! Thanks to Him who always was there to open the doors, to help me when I needed help the most, raised me up when I fell, cheer me up when I was losing hope, being my friend even when I thought that I was alone. You can say that this is another message of this book; *you are not alone.* Never! God is always there. You can name it whatever you want; I call it God. Everything I did and the person I become was thanks to Him. To some, only this part of the book will be enough to go and start changing themselves for the better; it will make you remember who you are and that you are not alone. To others, this is not enough, and I can fully understand that. So keep reading, and I'm sure that this interview will be enough to change the way you think; to change the way you function; to change the way you feel; to change the way you deal with life.

As you read, I've lived a happy and fulfilled life. However, it wasn't always like that, as my *Present* knows. Like most of you reading this book, I was alone at one point in my life. Alone in my thoughts. Alone in my feelings. Alone in all the constant battles that I had to fight. Alone in everything! My heart was empty. I was lonely. I thought that I would never achieve anything meaningful; always be alone, and would never find the love of my life, have kids, make my parents proud. I thought I was going to be forever miserable, unhappy, and many other negative things.

One thing that I firmly believe is that if anyone wants a real change to take over their lives, and they ask God for help, they will succeed in that intention. So somebody asks the question: Where did this all start? When did I get these miserable and negative thoughts? When did I lose my confidence, hope, and faith? When was the time I started to think that I'm unworthy? That I'll never be able to do anything with my life? That I'm alone? That nobody loves me? That I don't belong anywhere?

I still clearly remember the moment (I was about 15 years old) when my lovely grandma told me, *"If you don't finish university, you'll never do anything meaningful in your life."* Oh boy! I wish she knew how much she was wrong. These words *"You'll never do anything meaningful in your life"* were so deeply engraved in my mind that I've said to myself *"I'm going to succeed without my university degree no matter what."* I did finish university, but I've never used that diploma because I was sure that I'd never need it, which is a truth you'll see throughout the book. Of course, I've never used that as a negative thing but rather as a motivation to do something extraordinary with my life. Whenever I was going through rough times and I wanted to give up, when I didn't know what to do, where to go, how to deal with the situations that I've been in or deal with issues of life; somehow, her words always found a way into my mind. I truly believe that from this perspective, these words, *"You'll never do anything meaningful in your life"* were a blessing. At the same time, these words could have had an opposite effect on my life if I had accepted them as the truth. For now, I'll stop talking about my life because here we're coming to one critical subject that you want to talk about and that is **"the power of words,"** am I right?

Serge: Yes, you are! I must admit I was amazed that you still remember everything from your childhood, and actually, you call my mind back to some of these things. However, let's not lose the flow of the conversation. I want you to explain everything you know about this subject and give us some steps or insights that our readers can use immediately to their benefit. So please keep going.

The Power of Words

Future: No problem. As I said, these words, *"You'll never do anything meaningful in your life"* could have had a different effect on me if I didn't use it as motivation. Let me explain what I mean by that. I'll use perhaps one of the most famous stories about the power of words. It goes like this:

It was the year 1855. A young child came home from school and gave a paper to his mother. He said to her, *"Mom, my teacher gave this paper to me and told me that only you should read it. What does it say?"* Her eyes welled with tears as she read the letter out loud to her child. She said, *"Your son is a genius. This school is too small for him and doesn't have good enough teachers to train him. Please teach him yourself."* Many years later, his mother died. One day he was going through a closet, and he found the folded letter that his old teacher wrote his mother on *"that day."* He opened it. The written message on the letter was: *"Your son is mentally deficient. We can't let him attend our school anymore; he's expelled."* The name of this boy was ***Thomas A. Edison!***

This compelling story is perhaps the best example of *the power of words*. Imagine if his mother had told him what was written in the letter that day. How would that message affect him? What impact would it leave on him? Although we can't predict the future, somehow I'm sure that if she told him the truth, we might never have heard about his great inventions and what kind of genius he was. Fortunately, she did exactly what I believe that we all have to do; and that is to **encourage people around us to be who they are and share their genius with the world.**

"Do everything you can to share your genius with the world. The world needs your message!" - **Srdjan Bogicevic**

Your word is the gift that comes directly from your *Source*. Whatever you're thinking right now, whatever you dream about, the feelings that you have inside, everything will be manifested through words. *The word is not just a sound or a symbol. It's the power you have to express yourself and communicate and to create the events in your life. It's one of the most powerful tools for creation.* Depending on how they are used, words can set you free, or they can enslave you more than you know. Words can change someone's life or even destroy it. In the case of Thomas Edison, the words his mother told him had a positive impact on his life.

You have to be careful about the words you choose to say; especially in critical or crucial situations where you're in the middle of an argument, or in the moment of making some big decisions. Words create beliefs.

If I tell you that you're stupid and you're not strong enough in your mind, you may start to believe that you are really stupid. Maybe we were in the middle of some silly argument about something completely irrelevant, and for no reason, I've told you that you're stupid (even if I didn't think that). As a consequence, you start to think about it. Due to the constant thoughts you held about it, you've started believing it. Although my intention wasn't to hurt or insult you, my unconscious use of these words affected you and had an impact on your thoughts, which led you to believe those words. So now, whenever you do something wrong, make a mistake, or don't understand something, you'll remind yourself over and over again that you're stupid until you break your patterns and change your beliefs. In this example, my words had a negative impact on your life.

When you catch yourself in that kind of situations where another person is saying these kinds of words, the first thing you should do is to be aware of the moment; to be present and not respond with similar words. You have to understand that whatever that person is telling you, it's nothing personal (even if you think it is) and don't take those words to heart. If you know who you are, you'll have no problem hearing bad things other people say about you. If you don't know who you are, somebody can ascribe any identity unto you and then you'll become whomever they want you to be. You'll pretend to be someone whom you are not, and when they leave you, you become confused because you don't have a real understanding of who you are. And that will be your reality until you finally discover who you are.

I remember when I was very young; I tried to learn how to play the guitar. I started to listen to rock & metal when I was about 11 years old (my first and one of my favourite bands was Iron Maiden). Whenever I heard great melodies, I wanted to learn how to play the guitar so the one day I could perhaps have my band. My dad played guitar for years, and my grandpa also did. When I started, I knew I didn't have the talent at all, but I didn't care, I wanted to learn. One day when I was practicing, my father came to see and heard what I was doing. He saw how much I was struggling, and I'll never forget his words that he would later repeat several times, which became my belief. Those words were, *"That's not for you; you should give up. You're not talented enough."* He said this so many times when I was young that it took me years to change those false beliefs. I think that he still doesn't know how badly I wanted to kick him in the face back then. He told me that I was not good enough for guitar, for folklore, soccer, and handball… But honestly, I don't blame or judge him. He just didn't know what my potentials were. What talents and abilities I have. As you can see, his words had a significant effect and negative impact on me at that time.

> *"Wisdom is found only in truth."*
> **- Johann Wolfgang von Goethe**

The clearest words are words that contain the truth. One thing that I genuinely believe is that we always have to say what we mean. You may say that it is better to lie if you think that someone close to you will not be able to accept the truth. In the end, a lie would hurt more than the truth. Also, if we all say what we really mean, we can avoid potential unpleasant situations, solve some problems we have between us and someone we care about. We have to be careful about how we say them. Words can hurt more than any other physical pain. I believe that we all experienced this at some point in our life.

Let me give you another example. You wake up in the morning, and you feel thrilled. You feel so wonderful. You stay for one or two hours in front of the mirror, making yourself beautiful. Then you go to school, and one of the girls from your class comes to you and says, *"What the hell happened to you? You look so ugly. Look at how you are dressed! It's ridiculous."* This is enough to put you all the way down in hell. Maybe this girl just said this to hurt you. And she did. She gave you opinion with all the power of her words behind it. If you accept the opinion, it becomes your belief, and when you put all your energy into that opinion it becomes your reality. This belief can only be broken by adopting a new belief. Tell yourself that you're beautiful and how great you are. Tell yourself how much you love yourself. Use the power of your words to break these false beliefs that cause you to suffer.

How many times have you caught yourself in a devastating situation until your best friend came to you with words of hope and encouraged you to move on? How many times have you seen on TV the power of words when someone saves a person who wanted to commit suicide? How many times have you failed in life, and your mother came to you with words like, *"don't worry baby; everything will be okay?"* I can't describe just how powerful words are. When I had the idea about my first company, one of my friends told me that it was a great idea to follow my passion back then and he encouraged me to take action immediately. That helped me a lot because it's always a good feeling when you have support. He didn't just encourage me to do something; he helped me to build a website and gave some fantastic marketing tools about promoting my company and business. I feel grateful to have him all these years as my friend and particularly for hearing these words of encouragement when I needed them most.

You don't know the power of words until you develop your mind and your consciousness enough to realize and be aware of it. Now I'll let my *Present* tell you how negative words can affect you through personal example.

Serge: Can you help me understand what specific example you want me to talk about? Why don't you speak about it since you're the one who's providing the answers?

Future: It doesn't matter who speaks. This is a mutual interview, get used to it. I want you to talk about the *"event"* that happened when you were in the 4th grade; that shaped your childhood.

Serge: That's one of the most painful things that ever happened to me. Do I need to talk about that?

Future: You want to help your readers; right? So yes, you have to. Please continue.

Serge: Okay, this is something that I am not particularly eager to talk about, but I know how many people are currently going through or passed through similar experiences, so, to help somebody else, I'll speak about it.

In the 4th grade, I experienced an event that changed my life entirely and set the theme for my life for years to come. It was the first of my big life challenges. It was my introduction to bullying. I was labelled as (what is translated to) a *stinky boy* by one of the kids who wanted to pick on me. What started as a joke changed everything; for that moment was where my life started to fall apart. How? Although I was only 11 years old at that time, that *"stinky boy"* soon became a *"famous"* nickname that haunted me for the next 11 years. I became labelled, and from then, all the kids that I knew teased me and kept calling me all kinds of different names. The bullying caused me to begin to separate myself from my peers. I struggled to find someone whom I could call a friend, and I felt as though I didn't belong *"there."* I was thinking of ways to leave town and find a place where I would be accepted for who I was.

My first opportunity for *"escape"* came in the 6th grade in the form of a computer game called Counter-Strike. For the first time, I found *"friends."* I say *"friends"* tentatively because they were all virtual friends. I know that may sound crazy, but it was the first time I had a *"feeling of belonging."* However, in the real world, I struggled to find a girlfriend because of my nickname. I had many problems with kids who abused me whenever they saw me. Although I had virtual friends, deep inside, my heart yearned to find a *"real"* friend and girlfriend. As the years went and the saga continued, I would ask myself over and over *"What have I done to deserve this? What do I need to do to show others who I truly am and find any relationship?"* Back then, my parents were still in the situation of struggling with their lives and their problems. As far as I can remember, they were always too busy working and worrying about how to make ends meet, to pay bills, provide food and clothes, etc. Trust me when I say that there was no one who understood me, listened long enough to attempt to help me overcome these challenges and show me the way to start to love myself and accept myself as a valuable person in this society, in this world.

I changed towns again when I started high school. Guess what? Nothing has changed. It got worse. I had no idea what to do but to hope and pray that one day, this nightmare would come to an end. Time went on, and in 2012, I finally had an opportunity to move far away to where I could start all over again, and eventually be who I was. I moved to another city, in another country, and on another continent. New life, new people, YES! I'll finally get to be myself for the first time in my life (or at least I thought so). A few months in my *"new"* life had passed, and there I was again. I had the same problems with people. It seemed as though people didn't even need to know my past. I couldn't find friends, I didn't feel any more love than I did before, and now I was even more lonely because not only did I have no friends, I was on the other side of the world and was completely different from everyone. But there is an underlying reason for this; it was the years of killing myself with negative thoughts and saying that I wasn't worthy; I wasn't good enough; and that nobody liked me; all of this translated my nightmares into reality. The reason why everything continued was because of the things that filled the inside of my head! I was angry and resentful. The word "love" wasn't even in my vocabulary, so how could I expect it from others? Can you see how HUGE the impact words can have?

I decided to move back to my home country, and then something happened. Accidental or not, I was looking for a job, and when I was at the interview for one company, I got introduced to something called *"personal development."* It triggered something in my head, and for the first time, I started to read books on self-growth. In the company I was part of; I met with people who were interested in learning about me! I remember saying to myself, *"I found it!"* I found my *"sense of belonging,"* and I found friends! I couldn't be any happier! That was just the beginning of my new journey or what I like to call my *"new life."* It wasn't easy. I had many challenges along the way; much attributed to my state of mind, which was conditioned by past events/beliefs. It took me five years of full-time hard work on myself to finally, finally, yes, finally start to feel, really feel love for myself. At that moment, I became open for the rest of the world to love me.

"The word "responsibility" means that you can change your response. It's one thing when something happens to you, and you may not have control over it, but you have full control over your attitude and how you will respond to that depends only on you!" - **Srdjan Bogicevic**

As I said earlier, my life was a living hell for 11 years or so. Only when I took responsibility for my thoughts, words, and actions, I was able to change my reality. So that's the *first step* if you want to change your life. ***Take full control of your thoughts, words, and actions****.* Since we're talking about the power of words in this section, what else can you do to improve not just your life but the lives of others too?

Be kind to all people and speak words that are beacons of inspiration, enthusiasm, and encouragement to all. Discipline yourself to speak in a way that conveys respect, gentleness, and humility. Always speak the truth. Avoid lies. Avoid double standards in addressing people. Be impeccable with your words. Don't use your words to manipulate others, to insult or belittle anyone. Don't forget that we all want to hear kind and sweet words because they are music to our ears.

Yehuda Berg said, ***"Words have energy and power with the ability to help, to heal, to hinder, to harm, to humiliate and to humble."*** Always say the words that you want to hear.

Future: Nice, you've said it perfectly.

Serge: Well, it's going to take me a while to realize that I said these words. Sometimes I can't believe that I'm speaking in this kind of way. It feels good!

Future: Don't let your ego get too high now and don't forget that these words are yours.

Serge: Don't worry, it will not, and yes, I know that, but still it's hard to believe that they are coming from my mind. When you said what others could do to change the way they talk immediately, I realized that it is easier said than done.

Future: It may be like that at first. With practice, you will get more aware of what you are speaking and how. However, just by reading these words, your readers will not accomplish anything. They need to practice, and they can do that by starting to be aware of what they are saying.

Serge: I see. So one must be present at the moment and always aware of the words he's choosing. I like it!

Future: Does that mean you're satisfied with this story about the power of words? Do you have any questions about it?

Serge: Yes, I do. I mentioned that when we take full control of our thoughts, words, and actions, then we'll be able to change our reality and our lives. Can you expand on that?

Future: It's imperative to review the thoughts you have throughout the day and observe what you think about yourself and your life overall. Be aware of the words that you use when you speak about yourself and the images that you hold inside your mind about your relationships and life. Have you ever asked yourself the question, *"How do I see myself?"* Do you see yourself as someone who is not worthy? As someone who always fails in whatever he does? Have you become cynical and critical toward others, miserable and without purpose? Are you struggling with how to change your life?

Serge: Well, in the last few weeks, I had these thoughts about writing this book, doubting if that was really me who was speaking and questioning whether I'm supposed to write?

How do you see Yourself?

Future: That's normal. In every action you take towards your dream, there are always moments of doubt. However, do not allow your negative voice to tell you that you're not worthy of writing the book. You're worthy, and you have the message that you're about to share. Let's continue. All these questions above are essential because:

"Your view of the world is a reflection of the way you see yourself!"

What would happen if you changed these thoughts and started to see yourself as a worthy and valuable person? As someone who is gentle, smart, responsible, and authentic? A human being who is always growing and expanding? What if you saw yourself as someone who wanted to help others, inspire change, and share your love? Why am I asking you all of these questions? The reason is straightforward – *your view of the world is a reflection of the way you view yourself!*

I want you to realize that you have the power of choice. You have complete control of the thoughts you think, the words you speak and the way you behave. Why is this important? You'll always have two voices inside your mind that will tell you contradicting things. One will say to you that you can do something; the other that you can't. One will say that you're beautiful, while the other you're not, etc. The good thing is that you can choose which voice to listen to. You can choose what words you'll say at any moment in time and the behavior you will demonstrate in every situation you encounter throughout the day.

The Thoughts You Think

What your life will look like soon pretty much depends on the thoughts that you think about yourself, and on how you view your life at every moment of every day. It can only benefit you if you start thinking positive and encouraging thoughts about yourself. I remember years ago when I was young; my ex-girlfriend told me that it was time to end our relationship. I felt like the whole world was falling apart. I'll never forget the thoughts I had about myself. They destroyed me; and for the subsequent few months, those words ruined my confidence in finding a new partner. It was like I forgot who I was. I thought that I'm one of the worst guys in the world. I felt like I wasn't good enough, that I was unworthy and that I didn't deserve anyone. Some of you reading this might have shared a similar experience.

It took nearly 2.5 years for me to come to peace with myself about my past relationship and finally forgive myself. Doing so gave me a chance to start thinking differently in ways that would help me find a new relationship and improve the relationship I had with myself. What I learned was, *"**your thoughts about yourself can affect your whole body.**"* Negative thoughts can cause your body to feel pain even when it's not there; because the body and mind are connected, creating a confusing difference between imagination and reality. It is the same reason why negative thoughts can weaken your body and cause you to feel tired and without energy.

I'm suggesting that you to start monitoring the thoughts you have about yourself, and when you catch yourself having negative thoughts, change the mental subject. Find something that will encourage your mind to immediately start thinking about something that you love; something that fills you with positive emotions.

An example of a way that I deal with this is when I was your age, whenever I was at home and caught myself with negative thoughts; I turned on YouTube and searched for an inspirational speech to listen to or turned on some music and listened to a few of my favorite songs. There were times I started singing to change my thoughts and mood. You can find out what works best for you. Try a few things. If you keep putting the effort in finding a way to replace negative thoughts with positive ones, the thoughts you have about yourself will slowly begin to change, and your life will start to improve by becoming more joyful.

I want to take this opportunity to recommend a fantastic book to read, which I believe can significantly improve your thoughts, it's called *"The power of positive thinking"* by *Norman Vincent Peale*. That book helped me to change the way I look at things, and I believe that book, as well as this one, will improve the way you think about yourself.

The Words You Speak

I have already said a lot about the power of words; but because thoughts and words are part of the creation process, I'll say a few more things about it.

I joined *Toastmasters* (it was the year 2014, I believe) to improve my communication and public speaking skills. One of the things we learned was how to speak in front of an audience (large or small) and how to lose the fear of public speaking. They task you with all kinds of projects that will take you to step by step on how to organize your speech; get to the point, use your voice and body language, and the likes. Of course, the most important thing is to practice. Practice! And guess what? – Practice! It is essential to do this as much as you can because **with practice comes mastery**. Some of my first speeches (in my opinion) weren't as good as I wanted them to be. I'll never forget when I had a speech titled *"Sense of belonging"* and how bad it was. As soon as I finished, I immediately started to judge myself and began to tell myself some words that were the opposite of positive; *"Srdjan, you were terrible man! You suck! You didn't even know what you were saying. You looked miserable and sounded awful! You'll never be a speaker; this is not for you!"* etc. (believe me, I said a lot more than that, but I think you get the essence). Although I had all of these thoughts, I had also received encouraging feedback from people that told me that it was a good speech. I didn't believe them. It took me a while to reverse my thoughts and started speaking differently to myself.

*"Better than a thousand hollow words, is one word that brings peace." – **Buddha***

Your thoughts about yourself affect your words. Don't underestimate the power of words. The words you tell yourself can either lift you and inspire you to do what you like to do and be who you want to be or as they did to me at the time can put you entirely down; causing you to need some time to get back on your feet. How you talk to yourself after you do something wrong, make mistakes, or say something terrible to others is a critical decision. You have to be aware of the words you say to yourself at that moment; and with enough practice and constant selection of empowering words opposing negativity, you will eventually start to discover yourself naturally choosing the alternative (positive words) when an uncomfortable situation occurs.

The Behaviour You Demonstrate

*"If you don't learn to control your thoughts, you'll never learn how to control your behavior." – **Joyce Meyer***

I like this quote because it's so true. ***You have to learn to control your thoughts first, your words next and then together they will dictate your behavior.*** Think of it like building a house; you can't expect the roof to be stable and strong if the foundation and walls aren't built properly. Try to remember a time when you had negative thoughts and backed it up with using all kinds of bad words about yourself. Was your behavior positive back then? Did these negative thoughts and words support a positive reaction that made you take any action toward your goals or dreams? I believe they didn't, and it was because being in that bad/negative emotional state disabled you from taking any positive action.

When my first business started to drown, I didn't know what to do. At that time, I didn't work on myself, didn't know how to handle things that happened to me. I had so many issues that my head was exploding by thinking about them, let alone dealing with them. Together with my drowning business, my personal life started to derail. Although I changed my behavior and was trying to do something about it, the real problem was that my actions weren't in alignment with my thoughts and words. I was having negative thoughts about myself, using and thinking words that weren't positive at all; so of course, my actions failed. My belief system was wrong; I didn't believe that what I was thinking would help me to get out of the situation. It took me some time to calm myself; and little by little, I started having better thoughts, speaking positive words of hope, and after a few months, I got back on my feet. Only this time, my belief structure was aligned! I was different in my thoughts. I spoke different words, and I took actions that were in alignment with who I was at that time. Naturally, my life changed.

In every situation where you have full control of your behavior, you have to be present at the moment and consciously choose how you are going to think, speak, and react in that situation.

It's imperative to start having positive thoughts about yourself because you are perfect just as you are right now, and you have to understand that. Think of yourself as someone beautiful, humorous, always smiling, and positive; one who gives compliments and inspires others to be the best version of themselves. Think of yourself as someone who is capable of doing and being whatever you want. Focus your emotions on those thoughts because it will create a positive belief within you and put you in a positive state of being that will eventually cause you to start living by those thoughts.

When you start having the thoughts that please you, translate them into words that will represent who you are; start telling yourself that you can do, be and have whatever you desire and believe in those words. If you can believe in your thoughts, you will not have any problems in believing your words. Imagine what your life will look like shortly if you start vocalizing what you want to do, whom you want to become, and what you want to have. Speak!

Finally, when you put your thoughts and words in alignment with who you are, you'll be inspired and guided from within to take an action that will produce the results that you want because your thoughts are creative, and your words are productive. Your thoughts and words will set the stage for your action, which will be magnificently effective. You'll manifest all of your desires, and this my friend is *the process of creation*. Behave in a way that will represent your thoughts and words about yourself.

Serge: I'm already in the process of changing myself, for the past five years or so. I consistently worked on developing my mind, body, and consciousness;

but for whatever reason, it always seems that I cannot manifest what I want. No matter how hard I try to apply all the principles I've learned till now, it still seems that I'm not doing something right. At the end of the last paragraph, you've mentioned the creation process. I intellectually know how it works but not experientially. To be more specific, I've used this process to attract so many things in my life, but it seems much harder to do it now than it was before. Since you are me and I am you, you know exactly what I'm talking about, and I'm sure there are so many people who will read this and are in the same situation as I am. Can you explain why that is?

Future: Do you remember the very first time you used the creative process to attract what you want?

Serge: Yes I do, it was January 2014 after I read the book *"The Law of Attraction"* *(by Esther & Jerry Hicks)* and applied the principles described in that book.

Future: Nice, now explain to your readers what the principles were and how the *Creation process* works.

Serge:: I was hoping that you're going to talk about that.

Future: Why would I, when you know it perfectly? Let's make a deal, you are going to explain the process and how it worked for you, and I'll tell you exactly why you are struggling now to do the same. Is that fair?

What is your Vision?

Serge: I think it is. Well, what I know is the very first thing you have to do is to **decide what you want to do, be and have.** We have to stop and see what our vision is; although most people don't even know what their **Vision** is.

Future: I'm sorry for interrupting but this is a very critical subject, and I know that you know something about it.

Serge: You mean about **Vision**?

Future: Yes. Tell your readers something about that subject because it's critical to clarify it, and then we'll be back to the *Creation process* because without a *Vision* you'll probably not be able to manifest anything you want.

Serge: That's true. Well, I know for sure that everyone has a dream, a vision, a calling, and an inspiration inside of them.

Vision is all about who you have decided to be. It is something that you love, excited about, gives you energy, and makes you feel passionate enough to commit yourself to it. When you have a clear vision, magnetic things occur, and you draw into your life amazing synchronicity – people, places, things, ideas, and events start to synchronize in your life to help you fulfill your dreams. If you can dream and commit your whole being to that vision and give all your energy, you can become successful in achieving all of your desires.

When you set a goal, you should be able to **visualize** (it will be described in the following chapter) it as if it has already been achieved. You must see it powerfully. Clear vision does not necessarily come from your head. Sometimes you need to listen to your heart. The problem is that most people don't have that clear vision. They always feel that they are not allowed to have a vision, and they need to live someone else's dream and vision. You need to silence your restless thoughts and stop to ask yourself: *"What do I want? How do I really feel? Where do I want to go?"*

We should live from inspiration. That is something that should guide us and help us create our vision. If you want to achieve your goal quickly, you need to have clarity of why you want it and why you need it in your life. The stronger and more important your *why* is, the more power you will have to pursue that goal.

If you want to know what your vision is, you need to take the time to think about it. Discover what makes you happy and gives you energy. Fish out what you feel passionate about and search for 'that thing' that you can't stop thinking about before you go to bed because you can't wait to wake up and start doing it. It will be a good idea to take one day, maybe a whole week or even a month to think about what it is that you would like to be. Ask the people around you who love you; your friends, family, or soul mate, to help you ascertain what it is that you're good at. Ask if they ever noticed any unique talent that you even don't know you have; something unique in which you are gifted with. I remember when I was talking with my friend about starting a new business, and one part of the company was speaking at events and training. He told me that he was always amazed at how good of a communicator I was and how well I spoke in front of people. This came as a shock because I never noticed and nobody ever told me that I was a good speaker. I'm not saying that you have to listen to other people about what your vision should be, but just ask them because sometimes you can't see what others can.

When you finally decide what you want, write that down on a paper or the vision board. Write it in the present tense, like it's already happening. Put it somewhere where you can continuously see it because you want to impress your subconscious mind to think about your goal all the time. Make your vision big, because there's no difference in an effort for the mind to think about small dreams than to think about big dreams. You have to dream about *impossible* goals because they are exciting; they can stretch your brain, encourage your *Imagination* to find resources for your dream, etc. When I decided to change my life, I put my goals in a magic notebook that I created. I put the pictures of the city and country where I wanted to live, the car I wanted to drive, the person who I wanted to become, the image of my ideal soulmate, the kind of people I wanted to be surrounded with, where I wanted to go on vacations, etc. Also, below the pictures, I wrote the text in the present tense as if it already happened. Be specific and put as many details about your goals as you can, because the subconscious will automatically start to search for ways to attract what you need to achieve that goal.

Here's a good thing! If you can envision it, it doesn't matter how small or how big your vision is, that means that there's a resource to achieve it and all you need to do is, allow yourself access to these resources. Everything that the mind can conceive, it can achieve. How that will happen is not yours to think about. The **how** will show up in the process. I never thought about how I'm going to do it. You have to believe that you can do it and that you'll find a way on how to do it.

Everything that exists on this planet (except the water and earth) is created twice; first in human thoughts, then in physical reality. If you want anything in your life, you need a vision first and fall in love with it so that you can begin to attract not necessarily a house (for example), but the books, resources, people, seminars, etc. that will help you achieve that goal; and eventually, you will do it.

You can discover your vision at an early age or later, it doesn't matter when you are going to discover it. It doesn't matter how young or how old you might be. The only thing that matters is that you start living your vision and believe that whatever that vision is, you can do it! I know this because you and I are here to do magnificent and magnanimous things.

Future: That's good. You have described many things. And you've mentioned that to achieve something; it would be great to create something called **Vision boards**. Can you expand on that because I believe that your readers will want to know more about it?

Serge: I thought that you're supposed to be interviewed by me and not vice versa.

Future: Why? You don't like to talk? As far as my memory serves me when I was you at your age, I wanted to speak and write a lot. Am I right?

Serge: Yes, you are, but it would be better for you to talk about it since you're a more accomplished person than I am at this moment.

Future: It has nothing to do with the accomplishment. Your *Imagination* makes you believe that I'm more accomplished, but your heart says that soon, you'll be much more successful than you ever thought. You already know a lot about it because you've used that tool to attract what you wanted before. Anyone who has experienced something like you have can talk and teach about it. So speak freely. Please explain to us what you mean by ***Vision boards.***

Vision boards

Serge: I guess I have no choice.

Future: This is YOUR book. Right?

Serge: I got your point.

"The man who has no imagination has no wings."

– Muhammad Ali

A **Vision board** is any board on which you display images, thoughts, and texts that represent whatever you want to be, do, or have in your life.

When I heard about vision boards in the movie *"The Secret"* a few years ago, I remember thinking, *"What the hell are these guys talking about?"* I wondered how this board could ever help me change my life and get what I wanted. It looked too easy, so I couldn't believe that something so simple could have a significant (if any) impact on my life. At that time, my ego was so huge that I thought I already knew everything there was to know; and because of this, I was a close-minded person. My ignorance didn't allow me to learn anything about the subconscious and the principles of how we could influence it. I was negative. In fact, I had thought that all of this information about vision boards was simply BS. (Boy, was I wrong!)

A few years later, life had me knocked down. Sometimes that's exactly what you need to get to the point where you'll listen and be willing to learn something new. When life knocks you down, and you lose everything, what else is there? When you are alone, without a job, without money, friends, family, without any support, what can you do? You can choose to give up and feel sorry for yourself, be negative, sad or depressed (which will not change anything but put you in an even worse state of being). On the contrary, you can decide to do something about it and try to change your life no matter how hard, or crazy ways to do it may seem. As for me, I decided not to give up and gave myself a chance to change my life.

Pretty soon after my decision was made, I decided to try the idea I was once so ignorant about. I was going to make my vision board where I would put pictures of my goals and dreams which I wanted to attract and achieve in my life. I wanted to put the board somewhere I could see it all the time. It took me a few days to think about what it was that I wanted to do, be, and have in my life. I began to find pictures on the internet and began to print them and put them all up on my vision board. Some of the goals I put up on the board were:

- The city and country where I wanted to live
- The body that I wanted to have
- The car that I want to buy
- An ideal girl that I want to find
- The kinds of people that I wanted to be surrounded by
- The ideal house that I wanted to have
- The person that I wanted to become
- How much money I wanted to have in my bank account
- What I wanted to give to the world
- What legacy I wanted to leave etc.

I put up the pictures, and below them, I wrote a short text as if I already had all of these things. Then, every day I would spend some time in my room and wait till there was silence in the house or I would go out and find a quiet place in nature. I would turn on some music (not the same song every time nor the same type of music), relax and put myself in a beautiful positive state of being. Music was the best tool that I used for putting myself in that *higher* state; you may find out that something different works better for you. Some people find it by taking a walk or even petting their pets. Whatever it is, use what works best for you to put you in a higher state where you'll feel happy and positive for no reason. When you feel comfortable and positive, that is the time to start the visualization process.

What I mean by that is, simply turn off the music or stop doing what you're doing and look at your vision board (If you're outside, make sure you have a picture of it at hand). Observe your dreams. Notice every detail and after a few minutes of observing, close your eyes and start visualizing your dreams as if they are already there; as if you have achieved them. Try to touch it, feel it, smell it, and you'll begin to enjoy yourself because it can feel so real at that moment. You feel happy, and your body reacts, then you feel the positive emotions of having those things even if you don't already have them. Do this for ten to fifteen minutes daily but don't force yourself to do it, because the most important thing is to feel good when you imagine your dreams as if they are here already. For me, this exercise was so powerful that I'm still doing it every day. It's one of my favorite tools to attract my goals.

Since the first time I started visualizing my goals on my vision board up until now (five years), I'm happy and grateful to say that many of the things from that board I've achieved. However, it hasn't stopped; I am now working on the remaining as well as new goals that I set up on my *Vision Board*. Now don't get me wrong. I'm not saying that just by visualizing your dreams, they will show up. That process is a little bit different, and I hope that my *Future* will explain it eventually, but this is one of the most powerful tools to use toward achieving your dreams. Think of it as your first steps. You must first learn to walk before you can run.

Many of the friends who have seen the transformation of my life and what I have achieved in a short period always thought that I am just *"lucky."* I'm not saying that I didn't have a little bit of luck during that process, but what they didn't see was the time I've spent reading, writing my goals down, meditating, visualizing and doing what is necessary to change my life. They didn't see how many hours I've spent just looking at my vision board and imagining the kind of life I wanted to live. This tool has made a big difference in my life and has had a significant impact on it.

This was just a short portion of my story and how this one tool helped me. So now let me break it down and give you a recap of how you can begin your *Vision Board*:

1. *Think about what you would like to be, do and have*

2. *Find pictures (or create them) of what you want to have, be, and do (GET CREATIVE!)*

3. *Find a board (maybe 32×32 or 40×40) and put the pictures on it*

4. *Put the vision board up on your wall so you can see it first thing in the morning when you wake up!*

Make multiple vision boards so you can put them in a few places like your room, bathroom, car, office, kitchen, etc. **You want to think about your goals all the time!**

Your subconscious works on images. When you think about your dreams, and you feel inspired, it will give you ideas on how to be closer to them or achieve them immediately. And when you receive it, you have to believe and act on that idea, or it will go away.

Remember the **purpose of vision boards** is to bring to reality everything you want into your life. You can decide what your goal is, but when you put it on the vision board, it becomes a vision. Vision boards serve as reminders of your dreams. Whenever you look at a vision board, it will remind you why you are doing whatever you're doing. They can get you fired up and motivate you to do more than you've planned. They can inspire you to keep on going when you feel stuck or when you are losing hope; and perhaps, the most important is that they keep you focused and excited!

Future: I told you that you already know a lot about it.

Serge: Maybe I think that I'm not supposed to write about it yet, and for sure you know a lot more about this.

Future: Trust me, this is more than enough for now. As you can see, you have almost described the full *process of Creation* and bringing things into life, or better say, to attract what you want. So I'll do my part and explain it as clearly as I can.

How to get what you want

> *"I've come to know that what we want in life is the greatest indication of who we really are." - **Richard Paul Evans***

There are a few steps that you have to take to get what you want.

The first step is to **decide what it is that you want**. You've said it perfectly, so I'll not go deeper into that. The **second step** will be to describe that (what you want) with as many words as possible; put it on a piece of paper and write it in the present tense like it's already happening. The more specific you are, the more details you put into that thought. These details make you develop more feelings that will enable you to be more open to getting what you want. When you put that on paper, find the pictures of your goals and do what my *Present* has said, make a **Vision board** and put it somewhere you will be able to see it all day long. You can have it in your room, your bathroom, on your phone, in your office, put it everywhere because you want to think about them all day long. It has been said that *"man becomes what he thinks about all day long."* To visualize it clearly and powerfully, you must **FEEL IT**! I can't even express how much important this is. The only reason why my Present was able to transform his life was that he felt it before it happened. There's one ultimate truth that most people don't realize, and it is that you don't get what you want in life - you get what you are! That's why feelings are essential when you think about your goals and dreams.

When you decide on what you want, and you create your vision board or put that on the piece of paper, there's a very critical step to take - it's to **believe**.

You have to convince yourself that whatever you want is already on its way towards you. This is the step where most people get stuck because the last stage of getting what you want is to **take action and be open to receive it**. I'll come back a little later about *believing* step but the last step to get what you want is to go out and do something about that dream.

Yes, you can have a dream about getting that fit, summer and sexy body. You can find a picture of how exactly you would like to look, visualize it all day long and even believe that you'll get it. But if you don't take your butts off the bed and go to the gym and workout hard, what do you think will happen?

Let's say that you're dreaming about that girl that you want to ask out; you know her, and you know that you want her. You're always foreseeing you two together, but you might miss the chance to be with her unless you take action when you see her and do something about it. Yes, there's always a possibility that you won't get exactly what you hope for, but that's the beauty of life. You'll get exactly what you are at that moment. At the same time, that's the beauty and mystery of life, because you were hoping for something but got something entirely different. You may be disappointed only to realize later that it was even better than what you were hoping for.

Let me tell you a story about how my *Present* did set a goal to move into one city in Canada but ended up in another and the miracle that happened along the way. Or, maybe you (my *Present*) would want to tell us about it.

Serge: I think it doesn't matter who will talk about it since we both had the same experience.

Future: Exactly! Now could you please be kind and tell us that story.

Serge: I guess it's pointless trying to argue with myself.

Future: (Laughs) Come on, right now, your readers already discovered that you love to talk and write a lot. The stage is yours.

Serge: Thank you, my dear *Future*. I want to mention that you'll probably hear the same story twice throughout the book, but it will be told in such a way that will describe the principle that I'm about to teach you or to illustrate. So this is the story that my *Future* want me to tell you.

It was June 6th, 2014 (exactly six months after I decided to move to Canada) when I arrived in Montreal. I went through the security check, and came down to pick my luggage. I found out that it didn't arrive with my airplane and I was asked to tell them the address of where I was going to be so they could deliver it within two days. I gave them the address of the hostel where I took a room in Ottawa because for whatever reason; I decided to spend seven days there before I go to my planned (final) destination - Calgary, in Alberta. But let me tell you something before I continue.

Earlier, to be precise six months before I came to Canada, I had this thought that I wanted to move here; for a reason unknown, I decided to go to Calgary. I didn't have any family there, neither anywhere else in Canada, and I didn't have a job, and don't even mention of having enough money to stay for long. The only information I had was, the oil industry in Alberta is in expansion and that they needed many workers over there and I thought that someone would give me a job no matter what. That's a true story. I had no idea of neither where I was going to live nor of whom to ask for help; let alone where to look for a job. But somehow I wasn't worried at all because I had this strange faith inside of me that pushed me to believe that everything would be okay. I decided to stay in Ottawa simply because I wanted to prepare myself mentally for what I thought was coming. That's the only explanation about my decision to move to Calgary. My friends still believe that I was the craziest person at that time. I believe that too.

To get back from where I stopped earlier, I came in that night to Ottawa and checked into the hostel; and two days later, my luggage arrived. After two days of walking around and enjoying the peaceful atmosphere in Ottawa, the time has come for me to leave. I bought a ticket to Calgary. I went to Greyhound bus station (because the bus ticket was around 170$, and airplane ticket was 420$, and I had only 2000$ with me which made me wanted to save money. Although, it was supposed to be a two - day ride LOL), and for whatever reason I wanted to stay in Ottawa just a little longer. So, I bought the ticket for Monday which allowed me six more days to stay in Ottawa. Now for the first time, I was thinking about what to do and where to go when I get to Calgary. I must admit it was scary. I began to experience a little bit of fear. One day passed, the second day, a third day, fourth, and I was still thinking of what I was going to do when I arrived. I was scared. I really was. But every time I experienced this feeling of being afraid, I had this invisible voice inside my head that was telling me, *"don't worry, everything will be just fine."*

"Life has a strange way of surprising you and taking you to a whole new route that you didn't even know existed!"

Sunday evening, I believe it was around 9:00 pm. My phone rang, and it was a message received on Viber. It was from my childhood friend. The message was, *"You lucky bastard; I can't believe that doors are opening for you even if you just came to Canada!"* I was looking at the message confused and replied: *"Brother, what the hell are you talking about?"* He said, *"I really can't believe how lucky you are!"* I replied, *"I still don't know what you are talking about. Can you please explain it to me?"* He wrote, *"We found you a job in Toronto. I'll call you tomorrow to explain everything."*

My heart started to pump fast. I was shocked and confused because I knew he wasn't joking. I called him immediately and asked, *"Yo, what's going on? What job? What the hell are you talking about?"* I was nervous, didn't know what was going on. He said *"Brother I met a guy today in the bar and he told us to tell you to go to Toronto, and you can work in his company. I don't know all the details, and I'm tired because it's 4 am and we just closed the bar, but I'll call you tomorrow when I find out all the information and let you know exactly what's going on. I'll ask my friend, his niece, to give me his number so you can call him too. I'll call you in the morning, don't worry. You lucky bastard! (laugh)."* And he hung the phone. I knew that he wasn't joking. He was serious, but I had so many questions like *"Who told him that I have a job? Is that even true? What's going on? What am I supposed to do now?"* etc.

I was full of questions, I tried to call my parents, but they were offline because it was 4:00 am, and they were sleeping. I sent them a text to call me the moment they saw the message. It was 4:00 am in Serbia but around 10:00 pm in Ottawa. In all that confusion, I checked on Google until when the Greyhound will be opened, and it said until 2:00 am. I ran to the bus station immediately. I decided to go and change my ticket to Toronto! I had a feeling that it was exactly what I needed to do. I've put all my faith in my instinct, or you may say *"sixth sense"* and said, *"I hope this is true!"* When I got to the bus station, I asked them,

"*Could I change my ticket for Toronto instead of Calgary?*" and they said yes. So they changed it, and the journey was scheduled for Monday at 7:00 am.

I took the ticket, and on my way back to the hostel I was thinking, "*What the hell am I doing. Is this the right thing when I don't even know if this is all possible…?*" But I had a gut feeling that everything would be okay. I came to the hostel, and you would be right to assume that I didn't sleep at all that night. I was looking at my phone the whole time waiting for my dad or mom to call me. All of a sudden, I'm not going to a place that I had prepared myself mentally for in the past six months. I started laughing at myself, thinking about how life can surprise you when you don't expect it.

Finally around 1:30 am (it was 7:30 am in Serbia) my dad texted me "*Hey I'm awake, are you okay? What's going on?*" I called him immediately and said "*Dad, please call Marinko (my childhood friend who told me about Toronto and the job) immediately and ask him to tell you everything about the guy who apparently lives in Toronto but now he's in Pozega; give me a call as soon as you can. I'm not going to Calgary. I'm going to Toronto in the morning.*" Dad was shocked and didn't understand what was going on; but he said: "*Okay son, don't worry, I'll call you as soon as I find out what's going on.*" I replied, "*Call me until I wake up. I can't sleep, but if I fall asleep, call me until I respond.*" Dad said, "*Take a rest son, and I'll call you, don't worry.*" Peace came to my mind, and I fell asleep. My alarm clock was ringing at 5:30 am, and I got up from the bed, checked my phone, nothing happened.

I went to take a quick shower, put all my stuff in the luggage, and was ready to go to the bus station. Just before I was about to leave the hostel, my dad called me and said, "*Son, go to Toronto. I called Marinko, and he explained everything to me. Yes, you have a job there. I'll give you all the information later but for now, don't worry. Just go there and text me when you get there. By then, I'll know everything you need.*" So I did.

I was excited. I was happy. I couldn't believe that I was lucky to have doors open that quickly. I've arrived in Toronto and WOW! I was amazed by how big this city is. I couldn't believe that I was actually in Toronto! The moment I stepped into the hostel, I turned on the WiFi and called my dad who explained to me who that person was, where to go for a job and whom to call. It was a job in the construction company in Mississauga. But I'm sure you want to know how this happened. So, I'll go back to the story my friend told me and you'll see *how the Universe works to deliver to you everything you truly want and dream for.*

My friend was working the night shift in the bar in my hometown. He and a few other friends were sitting in the bar and talking about how crazy I was to go to Canada without anyone there, with zero English (I didn't know how to put one sentence together), without a job, not enough money, etc. The guy who offered me a job is actually from my hometown that I didn't know he exists, let alone lives in Toronto! He came for vacation, and it happened that he was in the bar behind my friends, heard the story and told them to let me know that I have a job in Mississauga if I'm interested. I believe it is a miracle! I mean, what were the chances that he'll be there in that bar, at that time, sitting behind my friends and hear my story? Sometimes, *luck* comes to those who believe in what they are doing. It's a part of life, part of the process, and I truly believe that you have to deserve it.

I went to that company the next day and started working there two days later. A week after that, my boss came back to Mississauga. We met each other, and we were laughing about the possibility of this kind of thing to happen. This is my story on how life can play with you. Sometimes, it can give you what you want in a different form, far better than the one you would expect.

Future: I'm sure that many of you who read this will realize that something similar has happened to you if you look deeper into your life. There is one *thing* that I as well as my *Present*, were holding inside us during this period, and that *thing* is the *key* to getting what you want. It's called *belief.* So let's move to that subject for now.

Belief

I've already said that you have to decide what you want, create a vision board, and every day, visualize that goal as if it is already achieved. Take action towards it, and you'll be on the way to getting it. However, if you don't believe in what you're doing, you may delay the manifestation of your dreams. Belief is a very important thing.

Belief *is a thought that you keep thinking over and over again.* **It's a habit of thinking.** It's a philosophy that you live by. It's important to know that when you want something and you don't believe that you can have it; what are the odds that you'll get it without belief?

I'll ask you to say something *right now*, and that is **"I can do all things!"**

Serge: I CAN DO ALL THINGS!

Future: Did you really say that?

Serge: I did.

Future: How does that feel?

Serge: It feels fantastic! I've said it with power and conviction.

Future: Did you put your emotions into it while you were saying it?

Serge: Yes, I did. That's why it felt so good.

Future: I'm glad to hear that. We'll discuss later in this book about the importance of using your feelings when you're thinking about something or speaking about it. For now, let's keep talking on this subject (belief).

Also, I want you (reader) to say it now with power and conviction – *"I can do all things!"*

Did you say it? If you did, say it one more time, say it aloud, *"I can do all things!"* Wouldn't it be amazing if you believe that? Would you sleep good tonight if you believe that?

Imagine if you were taught that from the time you were born into the world. The first thing your mother told you when she looked at you was: *"Baby, I want you to know that whatever you decide to do or be in this life, you can do it!"* Imagine the first time when you made a mistake or you failed, and your parents came to you with their arms on your shoulder and said to you *"Don't worry baby, just get up and keep going because you can do all things."* Imagine the first time you failed miserably in your relationship; your marriage; job; business; or in your life; but you have this thought, you have this belief, that no matter how many times you fall; failed; get rejected; you will get up. You will keep going. You will breakthrough. You will never give up because you know and believe that *you can do all things!*

You have to understand that no matter how young or how old you are right now, no matter what your circumstances are, no matter the predicament that you're in, no matter what is happening in your life right now, it *does not define who you are*! The reason you didn't change some of the things that are happening in your life right now is that you didn't change your beliefs!

Whatever happened until now is over. It's in the past. *What will happen in the future depends on the beliefs you hold in your mind right now.* Now is the time to change those false beliefs that you have. You have the power to do that. You can do it! The beliefs that you hold in your mind will dictate your behavior. If you want to get a job, and you go for the job interview; but in yourself, you don't believe that you'll get that job, what do you think will happen? Or, imagine if you go on a job interview and they ask you what you can do, and you reply *"I can do all things!"* Would you walk with your head up and your back straight if you believe that? Let me ask you again; do your current beliefs serve you? If not, change them!

You didn't believe that you're dumb until you heard that you're dumb. You didn't believe that you can learn until you heard that you could. You didn't believe that you're unattractive until you heard that! You didn't believe that you can't do it until you heard that you couldn't! Whenever you hear those voices, whether they are coming from people around you, or they are coming from your mind, you have to talk back to them and say *SHUT UP!*

Talk to yourself! Talk to your mind! Talk to your childhood! Talk to your dilemma! Talk to your crisis! Change your story! Say to yourself that you are smart enough! Brave enough! Worthy! That you have all that you need to get what you want! Do you know why? *Because it's true!*

You are smart! You are brave! You are beautiful! You are worthy! You have everything that you need! Say that to yourself every day! In the morning, when you wake up. In the evening before you go to bed. Look at the mirror and say it loud! You have to do all of these things if you want to change your beliefs, first about yourself then about everything else! Remember, **belief is a thought that you continually think of!**

What else can you do to change your beliefs? Let me give you a few suggestions:

- **Affirmations**
- **Mental pictures**
- **Mirror technique**
- **Books**
- **Audiobooks**

Affirmations became so popular in this new age philosophy that I'm sure that most of you already know what they are and what their purposes are. It's merely a sentence; you can write something that you want to believe in, and by repeating those words that you write over and over again, you'll impress the subconscious mind that will lead you to create a belief. Although I'm in my late 80s, I still have a few affirmations that I'm repeating every day to remind myself while I'm still alive. There is one affirmation that I want to share with you that I'm still keeping in my wallet and I believe that my *Present* have it with himself right now and it's about starting your day on track. It simply says:

"I believe this is going to be a wonderful and blissful day. I believe I can successfully handle all the challenges that will arise today. I feel good physically, mentally, emotionally. Being alive is wonderful. I am grateful for all that I have had, for all that I now have, and for all that I shall have. God is here, and He is with me. He will see me through. I know that I can do all things through Christ, which strengthens me. Keep your heart free from hate, your mind from worry. Live simply, expect little, give much. Fill your day and life with love. Forget self, think of others. Do as you would be done to. God is great. With God, all things are possible. And never forget: Every day you wake up in the morning, it's a sign - the best is yet to come!"

This is just an example of how you can write an affirmation. I believe that some of you want to write an affirmation about attracting money. The one that I used to say was taken from probably the best book ever written on the subject of Personal Development, and that is **"Think and Grow Rich"** by *Napoleon Hill* (if you didn't read that book I suggest to you to run to the closest bookstore and buy a copy), that says:

"By the first day of January 20___, I will have in my possession $1 million which will come to me in various amounts from time to time during the interim. In return for this money, I will give the most efficient service of which I am capable, rendering the fullest possible quantity and the best possible quality of service as a (and here you describe the service you will provide, for example, I wrote: inspirational speaker and writer). I believe that I will have this money in my possession. My faith is so strong that I can now see this money before my eyes. I can touch it with my hands. It is now awaiting transfer to me in time and proportion that I deliver the service I intend to render in return for it. I am awaiting a plan by which to accumulate this money, and I will follow this plan when it is received."

I had a few more affirmations on my wall like *"Believe that you can, and you'll do it,"* or *"Yes, you can,"* etc. but you can create your own. Here is the tricky part. It's not enough to say those affirmations. I want to explain this because it is crucial, and with affirmations, three ingredients are necessary:

1. ***Consciously choose the positive words***

2. ***Clear visualization***

3. ***Use your feelings***

This is what most people don't understand about affirmations; they speak the words with no visualization nor feelings. Let me give you an example; if you say *"I love apples,"* that's a concise choice of positive words. When I say the word *"I,"* my mind knows that I'm talking about me. When I say the word *"love"* my mind knows that I like it, and I enjoy it. But when I say the word *"apples"* my mind gets confused because it's searching my entire hard drive, my subconsciousness from the day I was born for every occurrence of the word *"apple"* like red apple, green apple, granny apple, red delicious, Apple iPhone, Apple MacBook, etc. *"What apples was he talking about?"* My mind has no idea. The above analogy means **'words alone are not enough.'** That's why we have **visualization**. So when I say *"I love apples"* and visualize the bright green apple, my mind goes *"Ahh! That's what he was talking about. He loves bright green apples."* Words and visualization are essential and then comes **feeling.**

Feeling is emotion, and emotion is energy. Everything is made up of energy in this Universe that is vibrating at a particular frequency. What I believe is that, when your subconscious is filled with patterns that are vibrating at a specific frequency, for example; anger could be vibrating at 20 kHz, happiness at 40 kHz, I don't know what the numbers are, I'm just making stuff in terms of numbers, but everything is vibrating at a certain frequency. If you can go to your subconscious and create a pattern, infusing it with energy that is vibrating at a particular frequency, then you can attract things of a similar nature to it.

So if you go to your subconscious and repeat an affirmation which has a concise choice of positive words, clear visualization and you infuse a feeling into it; now you're at the same frequency of what it is you want to attract in your life.

That's why the vision boards are such a powerful tool to attract what you want. If you combine your affirmations with your vision boards, you'll be on track to manifest your goals.

There's no need to speak about the vision boards again since it's already documented.

Mirror technique is a potent tool to change your beliefs. You can lie to your colleagues, you can lie to your friends, to your family, but you can never lie to the person you see in the mirror. Look at yourself in the mirror every single day and make eye contact with yourself and say what you want to believe from now on. But look for a few seconds, look clearly, and feel your whole being. Feel the confidence that is rising inside of you. Say, *"I CAN DO ALL THINGS!"* Say it with power and conviction. When you wake up, and you go to brush your teeth, look in the mirror, and say, *"I love you."* Say *"I'm happy and grateful to be alive, and today will be the best day of my life."* Do it for the next 30 days, and you'll see what will happen. You'll be surprised when you catch yourself with a different belief system.

Books and *audiobooks* are potent tools to impress your subconscious mind. We'll talk about them a bit more in separate chapters but for now; read the books that can inspire you to change your thoughts and your belief system. Listen to audiobooks that will motivate you to do what you think is impossible.

Whatever you choose to do, no matter if it is mirror technique or affirmation, or reading books, commit yourself to do it for at least 30 days because that's how long it will take your mind to adopt these things as a habit. You want to make a habit of thinking differently. Say now; *I CAN DO ALL THINGS! I know and believe that!*

The enemy within

Of course, you'll have to face that small negative voice inside of you telling you all of the reasons why you can't do certain things. Why you can't have whatever you want. Everyone has this voice inside their mind. That's why it may feel like a lie when you're saying the affirmations. You may feel that you're lying to yourself. You may say *"But you just spoke about the positive affirmations, vision boards and beliefs and how we can do, be and have anything we want if we just believe that, and now you're saying that it actually may not be as easy as it sounds at all,"* and that is correct. I'm sure that my *Present* knows what I'm talking about.

Serge: I do. I'm well aware of these two voices.

Future: Would you like to tell us something about the only enemy that exists in your life?

Serge: I would instead give you that delicate task to speak about it since you're much more experienced than I am.

Future: I'm your *Imagination*. Don't lose sight of that.

Serge: I know. Speaking of the voices, what side do you represent since I can look at you as a *voice*?

Future: The side you want me to be.

Serge: So you're a good voice?

Future: If that's what you believe.

Serge: Well, you're helping me with writing this book and providing all this wisdom. So I believe that you're a good one. Keep going, please.

Future: Do you have any major goal in your life that you want to achieve?

Serge: Yes, I do.

Future: What is it?

Serge: To become an inspirational speaker and best-selling author. To teach others everything I know and share my knowledge, especially with young and upcoming generations in every area that our school system has failed them. To be of service to this world.

Future: If you could live your life over again, what would you do differently?

Serge: Is there any purpose behind these questions? I mean, you know all my answers, and I'm trying to figure out where you are going with them.

Future: I'm asking because I want to expand on that invisible negative voice that each one of us has to face in almost every critical moment of our lives when we have to make a tough decision. So I know that you have something to say; and although you would like me to speak, I'll leave it to you because you can give your readers all they need to know.

Serge: I get it. Well, I know is that my goals were different throughout the last few years because I was trying to figure out who I am and what my purpose is in this journey of life. In the past, the meaning of the word *goal* had an entirely different definition to me. I thought that my purpose in life was to finish university, find a job, become a boss, and do that for the rest of my life. Not to mention, get married, have kids, and go on vacation once every year only to finally retire and wait until life was over.

Future: I assure you and your readers that life is not meant to be imagined that way.

Serge: Well, now I know that life does not need to be imagined that way. A few years ago I didn't know that, and I'm sure that most people still don't know that. Unfortunately because we are conditioned with the idea of what a happy life should be, we create barriers within ourselves that make it harder to go outside of these *"normal"* goals. I remember, immediately after I set my real goals for the first time, I heard that invisible voice inside my head saying *"You can't do it, you are not worthy, nor do you have the skills you need to achieve these goals."* I also remember thinking, *"What does this voice know about me, and why does he keep telling me that I can't do what I want?"* After some time this voice would go quiet, but as soon as I would start working on my dreams or take any action, the voice would immediately come back to me with all kinds of discouraging words, *"Stop doing this! It's not for you! Go back to your old job and earn just enough to pay your bills. You can't do this!"*, but a second voice, formerly quiet, persuaded me to stay consistent and always replied, *"You don't know what I can nor can't I do, so shut up!"*

"The only enemy that you have in your life is your very own negative voice..."

Have you ever experienced this inner conflict between these two voices? Have you ever noticed that the only enemy you have in your life is your own bad voice? I remember working in a network marketing company; we had a monthly seminar about growing our business, but we also had big annual events and leadership development weekends. At these events, the company gives recognition to the best achievers of the month or year, etc., and I would look towards these giants in our industry and say to myself *"I can do that! I can be like them! I can have a large organization, become a speaker, and be successful just like them!"* I always got fired up at these events. During these moments, I was convincing myself that I was able to do the same things that our company leaders did. But as soon as I left the events, my inner voice started to haunt me telling me, *"Serge, you can't do that. You don't have that kind of knowledge and experience to achieve what they did. What makes you think that you can earn 50 thousand, 200 - 300 thousand a month when you barely earn five hundred now..."* and because I was so weak at the time, it would immediately put me in a bad and frustrated mood.

One of the greatest weapons that the enemy from within use is **procrastination**. Every human will sooner or later have to face this enemy. When do you think is the first time that enemy attacks you? You're right. When you hear the alarm, and your first thoughts are *"I want to sleep five more* *minutes,"* and then you hit that famous snooze button. Your very first decision in the morning, and you immediately fail to make it the right way. Believe it or not, if you can break this habit and stop snoozing every morning you wake up, it will change your day and life. Because if you get up immediately after your alarm sounds, you've beaten the enemy early and now you're ready to face it throughout the day. There's a good trick to fight procrastination that I've learned from *Mel Robbins*; it's about counting backward whenever you catch yourself wanting to delay something. For example, when you hear the alarm and you hear this voice that says, *"sleep a little more,"* even though you know that you have to wake up, count 5, 4, 3, 2, 1 and get up immediately. It's called *"rule of 5,"* which means that you have exactly 5 seconds to decide before your mind destroys you. If you don't reach a decision, you'll hear the voice that will send you thoughts of doubt, low confidence, fear, anxiety, stress, etc.

Also, one of the things the enemy within is determined to do when you find yourself at the breaking point in your life is, to isolate you. Do you realize that the more you're overwhelmed by life, the more you want to separate yourself from others? This is especially true for men. The more things are bothering him, the more he isolates himself.

Women have a different approach to this. When something is bothering her, she wants to talk and verbalize that, but men don't verbalize, they internalize it. I know so many times when I was overwhelmed by something; the first thing I wanted to do was to lock myself in my room and not talk or see anyone. But you have to understand that ***every time you isolate yourself, you terminate your dreams.*** That's precisely what the enemy wants you to do. Don't isolate yourself for too long.

It's okay to be alone and take the time to think on your own but don't separate yourself from the rest of the world just because you don't know how to handle temporary problems. Put your clothes on, get out, and enjoy the moments that you have in front of you. Every day is a blessing if you learn how to appreciate life. Your friends want to help you, your parents, your spouse, your son, your daughter. Some people want to help you to overcome any temporary adversities. So don't isolate yourself. If you don't isolate yourself, you will shut down that voice telling you to go in the dark place.

"What can I do to shut this voice down!?"

Whenever I want to do something, by default, this bad voice would come to me reminding me of all the reasons why I couldn't do it. I asked myself so many times, *"What can I do to shut this voice down!?"* This voice will always be there. Haven't you noticed when waking up on a gloomy day seeing the weather through the window, it immediately cause you to hear your negative voice saying, *"Well, the weather is miserable today, so you should probably be miserable too."* How many times have you wanted to go introduce yourself to that person you have had your eye on, but you didn't because the voices in your head kept saying *"You can't do it?"* No matter how much money you make, no matter what you accomplish, this voice will never leave you. So, what can you do?

What I did and would suggest you do - **ignore this voice and choose to listen to the good voice** that says, **"You can do it! You deserve to live the life you want."** However, to do this, you have to work on yourself every single day. It's constant monitoring of your thoughts, words and actions every moment, every minute, every hour, every day, and consciously choosing the thoughts, words, and actions that make you feel good and inspire the best in you. It will not be easy in the beginning, but with practice and persistence, you'll eventually come to the point that you'll know naturally what thoughts and words to choose because it will become second nature.

Future: I'm sorry for interrupting, but won't constant monitoring of your thoughts exhaust you?

Serge: It may look like that in the beginning, but I assure every reader that after some time, it will become second nature. You'll be able to instinctively choose which thoughts you'll allow flowing in your mind and which you'll simply let go of or erase.

Future: Perfect. Please keep going.

Serge: I encourage you to start reading books like this one that will stimulate your mind to think positive thoughts. Start verbalizing words that will inspire and empower others and you. Say what represents you for who you are. Lastly, start behaving like the person you want to become! Meditation also helps to silent this inner bad voice and allows you to focus on continually reminding yourself that you have a good voice inside of you which you can choose to listen to. There are so many different methods that you can use to develop your mind and your consciousness to shut the negative voices out. We all have the freedom to make a choice! Choose a good voice to listen to!

If you look carefully, it's never about what happens on the outside; it's never about the circumstances or people around you. It is always about what's happening in your head. *The battleground is in YOUR MIND!* That's the real battlefield. All your problems are coming from your mind. The bad voice does not have to tie you up externally; it just has to tie up your head. With stress, worry, doubt, anger, rebellion, self-doubt, fear, and low self-esteem. It can make you physically sick because your mind is sick. But my question is, do you have a mind to change?

The most powerful tools you have right now in your life, in your body are your mind and your **Imagination**. If you can change your mind, you can change your life. If you can have a new mind, you will have a new perspective; you will have a new way of looking at your situation, you will have a new way of looking at your circumstances. You don't have to get out of trouble; you just have to get your mind out of trouble. With a new mind comes; a new, better and more positive voice.

"You can't lie to yourself..."

What I know and have experienced until now is that you'll have a lot of lonely times in your life. You can lie to your friends; you can lie to your kids, your family about why you didn't do something, but there's one person that you'll never be able to lie to, and that's the person you see in the mirror. The only emotion you don't want to have when you're 70, 80, or 90 years old is the emotion of regret. Every single morning when you wake up, you have a choice of which voice to listen to. I encourage you to listen to the voice that inspires you, that tells you that you can do it, that you deserve it, and that you are a worthy and valuable person. The voice that says you can do and have whatever you want.

Future: I'll add that sometimes people need to ***abort every voice*** that says *"you can't do it," "you can't be it," "you can't have it," "you'll never get up"* etc.they need to abort that voice and to push it out. Do you still hear this voice in your head?

Serge: For sure. Almost every day. The only difference is that as soon as I hear it, I try not to give a second thought to it. Immediately, I search for a positive choice of words or force myself to take some actions that will change the physiology of my body and put me in a good mood no matter what this negative voice has to say.

Future: That's interesting.

Serge: What is it?

Future: You've mentioned that by taking action, you can change the physiology of your body, and you can put yourself in a good mood. How can you do that?

Serge: I use some methods or tools that help me keep my mind positive at all times, especially when this negative voice wants to take charge.

Future: Go ahead and describe these methods.

Serge: It seems that this interview is going a different direction than I was hoping it would go..

Future: In what direction were you hoping it will go?

Serge: You know, I'll ask questions, and you'll provide answers. Not vice versa.

Future: I thought we are one, right? And let's be clear because I want your readers to know something about you. Deep down inside of your heart, you want to write this book. You want to find a way to write because you believe that your book will be life-changing. And it will be! You love to write. You love to talk. You love and enjoy it so much that you can do it all day long. It's your passion. You indeed came to me to look for the answers you need, but still, this whole conversation is happening in your *Imagination*. If you observe, your *Imagination* is an infinite field of unlimited resources to think about and create whatever you want. You chose to come to me and ask for guidance. The truth is, you don't need me to write this material. You have all the answers inside of you. You just have to look for them. So keep going. Keep writing and talking. I don't want to talk about this anymore because, by the time you finish this book, this interview will be mutual. Now, would you be kind enough to tell us the methods of putting yourself in a positive frame of mind whenever you want to?

Serge: Yes, I know what you are talking about, and you are right. I do love to speak and write, but I still have this thought that I'm not somebody that people will listen to, or read anything I write. Although my confidence is on a high level, I still have these thoughts of doubts, insecurities, or worthlessness.

Future: That's what makes you human. And it's okay. It really is. I'm sure that most readers will relate to you. No matter the level of confidence you have, there's always going to be this voice of doubt, fear, insecurity but like you said, you have a choice, and I know that you're always choosing the thoughts that will serve you the best. So let's get back to the current subject of our interview.

Serge: Okay, let's talk about putting yourself in a good mood.

How to change your mood instantly

D o you ever wake up in the morning only to see through the window that the weather is miserable, and for no reason, you also began to feel miserable? Throughout the day, you kept talking about how miserable the weather was and telling people that you felt miserable. Even events in the news were miserable, making everything else more miserable. I believe that we have all experienced this at one point or another.

There are always going to be situations during our day that can impact and sometimes even ruin our good mood, but you have to understand that you can choose how you are going to respond to these situations. Maybe you can't do it every time, but with practice and consistency in making the conscious choice that every time you face a challenge during the day you'll (no matter what!) stay in a good mood.

Personally, every morning when I wake up, I make it a clear intention that **"I want to feel good"** and every single day I stick to that intention. You can say the same thing to yourself, or make up an affirmation that will immediately put you in the right state of being. Of course, I am only human, and I still catch myself sometimes in a bad mood throughout the day. So let me tell you how I deal with these moments to get me feeling positive again:

- **Workout** – Do you exercise? As part of my healthy lifestyle, I have my exercise program, and I go to the gym at least five times a week. I do cardio and weight lifting; it makes me feel so good once I'm done (although it is painful during the workout). If you don't like going to the gym, you can make a plan to exercise at home or outside. Just do some exercise, it will keep you healthy, in good shape, and form.

- **Eat healthily** – If you're going to the gym or doing any exercise, then you know the importance of healthy eating. Even if you don't work out, you have to eat healthy to avoid facing some negative consequences later in your life. If you want to have more energy during the day, a healthy meal plan can help you a lot. There's so much information on the internet about healthy food and meal plans. So don't be lazy! Do the research and make yourself a meal plan that best fits your budget and will make you happy.

- **Reframe negative thoughts** – My way to do this is through reading personal development books and listening to audiobooks or inspirational speeches. There are so many negative people and so much negative information that you're facing every day. You have to find a way to always put some positive input in your mind – that will help you to stay in a good mood.

- **Smile** – Scientists have discovered that if you put a smile on your face for no reason and keep it for two minutes, it will change your mood instantly! Not to mention that you never know how your smile can impact someone else's day and mood.

- **Listen to music** – You probably already know how good music can affect you and put you into a fantastic state of being. It's one of the most effective ways to change your mood.

- **Meditation or silence** – Practicing meditation made a dramatic difference in my life. After a few months of practicing, I noticed how calm I became and how immune I was to all negative news, people, and events that came my way. Meditation can create a long-term positive impact if you give it a try. If you don't like meditation, then you can practice silence. Spend some time in silence every day. It can calm you, help you think clearly, focus on the bright side of things and can change your mood for the better.

- **Service** – In previous jobs, I had the privilege of serving people in restaurants, and I learned not only how to serve them properly, but also how to make their day. With a short conversation, a few words or even a simple smile, I was able to change their mood. Now, I'm helping others to find their sense of belonging and purpose in life. When you make others happy, it will make you even happier. Serving others will improve your mood and life dramatically.

- **Join an organization** – I'm a member of a non-profit organization called *Toastmasters* whose goal is to *"empower individuals to become more effective communicators and leaders"* through their supportive atmosphere and programs. When I'm in that environment, I feel amazing because I'm learning, expanding, and meeting all kinds of interesting people. The thing about joining an organization is, you never know when or how you might help someone or how someone might help you. You can volunteer in churches, community centers, or wherever you like. Trust me; it will give you a way of looking at life. It will make you happy, and it will improve your character and personality.

- **Be kind** – Nothing can change your mood like an act of kindness. Even if you're the observer of an act of kindness, it will touch your heart and change your state of being. Do something kind every day. Say to your friend how kind they are. Buy someone a flower. When you're interacting with a stranger, put on a smile, and give him a silent prayer.

There are so many ways to improve your state of being, and these are the steps that I take when I want to put myself in a good mood. The mood is an emotional state, and feeling good is the most important gift you give to yourself every day. Make the conscious choice to feel good every single moment. I know that you can do it so, start now. Say to yourself, *"Today, no matter what happens, no matter whom I encounter, I will feel good."*

These are my tips for putting myself in a good mood whenever I feel that I'm not at my best. Of course, sometimes no matter what I do, it seems that it doesn't work, especially if I have negative thoughts that are so dominant at that moment. In that case, I try to take a deep breath and go into the conscious part of my mind and ask myself, *"Where are these thoughts coming from?"* I expand these questions until I found when I picked up those thoughts, and then I ask why I am feeling negative about it. If I'm honest with myself, I'll find the answer, and once I know when and why I have these thoughts, I'll be open to reverse them and change my mood immediately.

Future: These are interesting methods. Believe it or not, I've been using them all my life, and they never failed me.

Serge: Glad to hear that I'm going to use them all my life and that they work. Do you have anything to add to this?

Future: I think this is enough to help your readers immediately. It's essential to build or create a rapport with yourself.

Serge: It is. If you don't have rapport with yourself, how can you expect to have it with anyone else? Since I mentioned rapport, would you tell us something about it? I want to take a little break and let you talk a bit.

Future: It will be my pleasure. I'm glad you asked about it because I believe this subject will be of great value. I will also describe techniques that anyone who reads this can use immediately to create a rapport with anyone. So let's talk about it.

How to build rapport with anyone

"*Trust and rapport are the heartbeat of the business, the backbone of high performing teams, and the secret sauce for healthy relationships.*"
- *Susan C. Young*

When you look at relationships between people, you'll see that people quickly get in rapport with people who are similar to themselves but don't bond with those who are not. The reason for this is that most people put most of their attention only on the words they speak rather than other relevant variables. However, words don't always create rapport. In reality, words only account for 7% of communication, which means that 93% of communication depends on your skills or what we call nonverbal communication.

Imagine you go to a local bar, and you meet someone (waiter, some random guest), and suddenly you get engaged in a conversation. What are you going to do? You probably start with questions like *"Hi, how are you?" "What's your name?" "Where are you from?"*, and then out of nowhere, you don't know what to say or ask next, and just as quickly as the conversation started, the conversation is over. You're left feeling awkward, stupid, whatever word you want to use. If questions or words don't create rapport, then what does? There's something called *"matching and mirroring."*

I first heard about matching and mirroring years ago when I was at a seminar by *Tony Robbins*, and it caught my attention. I believe it was in October 2016. Am I right?

Serge: Yes, you are. You have a good memory!

Future: These things you can never forget because it has an everlasting impression on you. To be clear, your *Imagination has an infinite memory!* Therefore, I'll share with you this knowledge that I've gained from one of the best in the field. I must mention that most of the things that I'm going to say in this post were notes taken from that seminar, and not all the words or ideas are mine.

Note: These words are not from my imaginary *Future*. My *Imagination* had just put it in the simplest possible way so everyone can have a picture of these techniques inside his or her mind that he or she can apply immediately.

Matching and mirroring came in 1981, and the person who pointed it out was *Dr. Milton Erickson,* who was a medical doctor, as well as a psychologist and hypnotherapist. Dr. Erickson had many clients who came to him with all kinds of problems which he was able to solve with just one session. How? Dr. Erickson understood that we have both a conscious and subconscious mind, and he knows that the subconscious mind is more powerful. Therefore, he knew that if he could influence a patient's subconscious mind, he could change everything. We naturally do matching and mirroring our entire life, but what Dr. Erickson observed is that when two people come together, and if they get in rapport, they became like one another in a variety of ways; what he called "*mirroring*" each other.

The way he solved their problems was by mirroring them. Whichever body language people showed to him, he responded with the same body language, connecting them to him. I'll give you examples so that you can better understand what I'm talking about.

Let's say that you want to mirror someone on the phone. What are some aspects of voice that you can mirror that will make them immediately and subconsciously connect with you?

- *The tone of voice* – This is huge! If you mirror someone's tone of voice, they will feel connected to you and won't even know why. It works even better when you're outside with somebody and whenever you want to connect with them, try to mirror the tone of their voices. Surely, if the person you're talking to is having a low tone of voice, you'll not create a rapport with your louder tone. So, put your tone a little bit lower and be connected with the person on a subconscious level and trust me; that person will not know why you are in rapport.

- **Tempo** – Naturally, I speak a little bit faster than most of the people I know. For years people would always ask me to slow down so they could understand me. Although it was annoying for me, eventually I slowed down. That experience taught me how to speak with people at the same speed they talk, and now I can always feel a rapport.

- **Volume** – How many times have you heard of a mismatch between two people when one speaks loudly while the other so quietly that you can't even hear what they said? That's a perfect example of how you can break rapport in one second.

- **Terminology** – Keywords! There are certain words people use again and again. I have a friend who uses the word *"excellent"* more than any other word, and if I reply with *"amazing,"* it may sound the same to me, but that word may not have the same meaning to him, therefore, causing a loss of rapport. If you mirror someone's words which they use most often, they will feel heard, understood, and they will also think that you are as smart as they are.

Let's go to another example. If you're with somebody face to face, what could you do to mirror their body language?

- **Posture** – When you mirror a person's body, you begin to understand more about them. Is that person sitting, standing or relaxing? It would be best if you did the same. If that person's legs are crossed or if they have placed their hands on a table, wait for few seconds and then match what are they doing in the same way.

- **Gestures** – People often use gestures along with posture to give insight on how they categorize their experiences. If someone gestures with hands in a particular way, wait a few seconds and make the same gestures they use.

- ***Facial expression*** – If someone tells you a story and they're really into it, they will make subtle faces. Are you going to look at them with a serious look while they're smiling? Of course not! You'll look at them with the same happy, stupid, crazy, weird, or whatever face they've made.

- ***Eye contact*** – I've heard so many times (especially in business) when people say that if you want to influence someone, you have to look directly into their eyes for a certain period and not break eye contact. This way, they will know you mean what you are saying. There's only one problem with that. If you speak with someone and that person keeps staring into your eyes without blinking, it can sometimes freak you out. So when you are looking at someone's eyes, and they blink, give them pause and move your look away.

- ***Breathing*** – Very powerful. One of the most powerful tools to mirror someone. If you breathe in the same pace as another person, you'll feel what they are feeling; you'll feel connected with that person.

- ***Proximity*** – It means that everybody has a certain amount of space that they need to be comfortable. It's different for everyone. I know many people who need to be so close to you with their face that they almost stick it with yours (and sometimes they have bad breath, right?). That can piss you off, but if you want to build rapport, you have to *"hang in there,"* because that's what they need to feel comfortable.

- ***Touch*** – You can build rapport with this more than with anything you can ever say. You can see that when you shake someone's hand, and you have those people who want to show you how strong they are (like, I'm a real man), and you also have people with *"fish hand."* Just mirror their handshake, and you'll immediately be connected with them.

Now, you may ask, do I need to do all of this to build rapport? The answer is no. It's important to understand that you can build rapport with your leg position, the tone of voice, maybe with one simple gesture or with breathing or touch. You'll be surprised what you can mirror and not even be noticed. I challenge you to try these techniques consciously, and with enough practice, you'll be able to build rapport with every person that comes your way.

(The conversation went "on hold" for a moment because Serge got out of the "Imagination mode")

Serge: I ran away for a second.

Future: Yes, I noticed. Where did you go?

Serge: To find a book where I've taken these notes and check them, and I'm shocked that you still remember almost everything I wrote in that seminar. I applaud you for that.

Future: Don't forget that you're using your *Imagination* and that we're having this interview in your subconscious mind. That's why I know all this stuff. By the way, can you see how powerful *Imagination* is?

Serge: Of course I see. In my *Imagination*, I had some of the most pleasant experiences, as well as some of the most painful. I can imagine how many people in this world who are not using their *Imagination* for the good of themselves. They're using it to relive the pain they suffered a long time ago over and over again. I wish I can help them let go of past hurts. Can you help me with that?

Future: I'm deeply humbled by your desire to serve humanity. You must know that you'll probably not end the pain in this world because people are choosing for themselves how they are going to feel, but you can at least help some of them that are searching for guidance or ways to let go of the past hurts.

Serge: I have, or better say we have been through a lot! It took us years to overcome the pain that we've suffered.

Future: Indeed. Now we have the experience that we can share with the world to help those who need to let go of everything that weighs them down once and for all. So let's talk about the ways to let go of past hurts. I will talk about the four ways that helped us to overcome wounds from the past.

Four ways to let go of past hurts

It might help to remember that there's nothing you can do to change your past. However, you can change the present and create your future as already stated in a creative process. It doesn't do any good to worry about something that you have no control over. I know it hurts. We've all been hurt at one point in our lives; we all have experienced some emotional pains. What can you do about that? If you know your past is still nipping at your heels, now is the time to change that. Why? Because you'll discover keys that can unlock the door to your full, unbridled, joyful, and infinitely rational expression of you.

How do I know? You remember the story that my *Present* was telling about the time when I was labeled "*stinky boy?*" Well, it took 11 long years, but I finally did it. I finally let go of all the anger and resentment that I kept in my heart for years. In one moment of insight, I took responsibility for my happiness. I stopped feeding my mind with angry thoughts. I stopped telling stories about what should have been. At that moment for the first time, I experienced peace.

I believe the only way you can accept new joy and happiness in your life is to open your heart to it. If your heart is filled with pain and anger, how can you be open to anything new?

1. Decision! – Let it go

My moment of insight was the moment when I decided to stop focusing on the past and start living in the present. You have to decide that! No one can do that for you. Make a conscious choice that you'll face your past and accept it as it is and find a way to learn from it. Everything in life starts with a ***decision***! That's a starting point if you want to change anything. Don't be fooled that it will be easy because it won't. You have to give your best to focus your thoughts and feelings to restructure your thinking. Because you'll have a lot of moments or situations that will remind you of your past; and that's the moment you have to be conscious and make a decision then and there that you'll let it go; that you'll not react emotionally but rather rationally because you know how powerful your thoughts and words are. Like everything in life, it will become easier with practice, and eventually, you'll let it go. But you have to decide that you want it. So please do it. And do it now! Now is the right time! Now is the right moment to make that decision. Write it on a piece of paper and read it every day until it becomes a part of your belief system, a part of your subconscious mind.

2. Stop blaming others

You can imagine how many people I blamed for my unhappiness. Guess what I discovered? All blame is a waste of time and energy! No matter how much fault you find with another, and regardless of how much you blame them, it will not change you. You only hurt yourself by being a prisoner to your bitterness and resentment. I was blaming everyone for my unhappiness. The people around me, the city that I was living, the whole country, even God, because he allowed others to hurt me. I didn't know why I had to go through all of that; but then, life was preparing me so one day I can teach others how to overcome these things. Take responsibility for your life, and stop blaming others. Focus on what you can change to make your past a bygone.

3. Forgive them – and Yourself

Forgiving others often takes time. It took me a lot of courage to forgive every bad word that was said to me and all the abuse that I experienced during the years. We may not forget another person's bad behaviors, but virtually everybody deserves our forgiveness. If you want to move forward and welcome joy, love, and happiness into your life, you have to find a way to forgive them. Although, the more critical part is to forgive yourself, because sometimes we may end up blaming ourselves for a situation. Remind yourself that everyone makes mistakes and that you too deserve to be forgiven. When I've taken that step and forgave myself, I was open to receive the love that we all want to experience. Forgiveness is one of the most powerful tools for having a peaceful mind. I genuinely believe that, and definitely, it's a way of letting go of your past hurts.

4. Focus on the Present and what you can do Now

You can't change your past, but you can create your future. *You can make today the best day of your life.* When I realized what my mission and purpose were, I was immediately so focused on doing what I'm supposed to do towards my dreams that I didn't have the time to think of my past. Find out what it is that you love to do. Focus on your dreams and get active, and I can guarantee that you'll be so busy doing what's needed for your goals that your past will have a hard time occupying your mind.

I know how it feels to be hurt. It's hard to let go of one's pain. But you have to do whatever you can to let it go. It's not healthy. It adds to our stress, hurts our ability to focus, and impacts every relationship that we have.

Make a decision. Do it now!

I'm sure that these four principles can help anyone who's dealing with past hurts. One step to get over it is a *strong desire.* If you don't want something badly, probably you'll not do everything you can to get over it. Do you have anything to add to this?

Serge: I don't. You said it all.

Future: Then we can move to the next subject.

Serge: The problem is that I don't know what next to talk about.

Future: Don't try to fit in all these subjects at once. Listen to your heart and ask.

Serge: That's it!

Future: What is it?

Serge: You just said something that I think we should talk about.

Future: And that is?

Serge: Don't try to fit in! I know for a fact that so many people in this world wants to be accepted and to fit in somewhere. They're afraid to be alone, and they will do anything to be accepted. Can you talk about that?

Future: For sure. I think that's a great subject to talk about. And you're right, so many people are not who they are because they want to please others to be accepted; and in that process, they lose themselves and become even more unhappy. So let's expand on this a little.

Don't try to fit in - Be who you are!

> *"Be who you are and say what you feel because those who mind don't matter, and those who matter don't mind."* – **Bernard M. Baruch**

How many times have you caught yourself in a situation where you said something to please someone? Or you did something because you wanted to be accepted by others? Have you ever felt that you were not perfect and you didn't fit in anywhere? How did you feel after you said or did something that did not represent who you are or what you were thinking? What questions did you ask yourself in those moments?

When I was growing up, I had a hard time finding a group of people that would accept me for who I was. I couldn't find a friend; that one person who will always be there for me and accept me with all of my shortcomings. I remember when I was about eight years old, never having someone who would walk to and from school with me caused me sadness at that time. You may say, *"but you were just a kid back then."* The truth is that from a young age, we can start to feel something that is called *separation*, which occurs from not having someone around us.

Growing up in a family where your parents don't have time for you or even when they do have time, they would rather watch TV than spend at least ten minutes of their day with you, and being only eight, ten or twelve years old and all the while having trouble finding a friend in school or your neighbourhood; what else can you expect than to feel alone and secluded from everyone else? This, in essence, is what happened to me, and it initially prompted me to think that there was something wrong with me. So what I started doing as you can assume was to act like someone who I was not. I began with speaking words and behaving in ways that would please others.

This is a problem that can start at home. If you don't behave in a way your parents like, then they say you are bad. They later try to *"motivate"* you to act in the way they seem appropriate. If you please them, they will provide you with all kinds of *"rewards."* With that being said, being busy trying to please your parents first can also reflect the behavior you exhibit outside of your home. You begin to try to please everybody else to feel noticed and to fit in.

You can see the connection here. It starts at an early age, and if you don't find a way to break the patterns, you'll feel separated from everyone else all your life, and you'll always think that something is wrong with you. When you feel isolated from everyone, you start to feel that you're separated from God. I know that my words can't change your beliefs about you just by reading them, but I encourage you to change the story you're writing about yourself.

When you look at yourself in the mirror, what do you see? Do you see yourself as a perfect manifestation of your Source or as an imperfect being that doesn't belong here? Change your story! You have to start by telling yourself that you are perfect as you are right now; that you are in the right place, at the right time. There's nothing wrong with you. If you're not surrounded by people who accept you as you are, change it. Find new friends. You're always attracted to those who are like you. I'm sure that you've heard a quote *"birds of the same feather flock together"* which means that you are surrounded with people who are exactly like you. It's the same with everything else in your life.

"You don't attract in your life what you want; you attract what you are!"

All my life, I was trying to please everybody except myself! When I finally decided to stop doing that, I was open to new people to come into my life. When I started to value myself and feel the love, I began to remember who I was, and I became attracted to others who were just like me. Guess what? I found people who accepted me as I was! I found friends! Not the fake ones who want you to be what they want. Not the ones who like you only when you behave in a way that pleases them. I mean friends who will accept you for who you truly are. People who will encourage you to be whoever you want to be, and who will be there no matter what.

Now, I'm blessed to be surrounded by people who love me, appreciate me, and are grateful for having me in their lives. I'm not trying to pretend that I'm somebody that I don't believe in. If someone doesn't like me, I'm okay with that. I don't try to convince them to change the story they have about me, because I'm aware that **what you see in others is just a mirror of what you see in yourself**. When somebody says something negative of me, I don't judge them. I silently wish them all the happiness, and I'm able to be at peace with that. On a deeper level, whenever you say something about someone (bad things), you aren't labeling them with your words, you're labeling yourself as someone who needs to say those kinds of things. My suggestion is never to judge anyone and never say anything negative even if you're right.

It's not easy rewriting the story you have about yourself overnight, nor is it to change your "*friends*," but you have to find a way to do it. If you can't do it alone, find help. I'm sure that there will always be someone who wants to help you become who you want to be. Of course, you can be better than you are right now, but you have to work on yourself every single day. Remember, don't try to fit in. Be who you are!

Serge: Very powerful and truthful as well. The moment you begin to be *you*, you'll see others who will be shocked by the "*new you.*" What they don't know is that there is nothing "new" about you. You just started to behave in a way that represents who you truly are, and they have this image of you that is not anymore what they want from you.

Future: And suddenly, the people you cannot please any longer start disappearing from your life.

Serge: That's true. Moreover, it can be scary too. Because all your fears about being alone become a reality, and unfortunately, most people think about loneliness as something terrible, but it is not.

Future: So why don't you tell us about it and explain how loneliness does not necessarily have to be a bad thing.

Serge: That's one of my favourite subjects to talk about. It is something that I'm passionate about sharing with others to help them overcome it.

Future: Because you mastered it, and I know how passionate you are about helping others to understand and learn it too. Tell us about it.

Serge: I will gladly do.

Loneliness

> *"Loneliness adds beauty to life. It puts a special burn on sunsets and makes night air smell better."* – **Henry Rollins**

We have all been alone at some point in our lives. Alone in our thoughts. Alone in our feelings. Alone in all the internal battles, we had to fight. I too had that feeling all my life. Even now, I still feel that way sometimes; although I have amazing people in my life that I'm happy to call my friends. What is your story? Do you have a feeling that you are alone? That you have to fight all the battles all by yourself? That you have to go through life alone? Let me tell you one thing. I believe that you are not alone, and you don't have to go alone through your journey toward a greater life.

Loneliness is a state of mind. Therefore, like any state of mind, it can be developed, cultivated, or changed depending on your needs or what you want to accomplish. You can change it by changing your mind *first. There's nothing as powerful as a changed mind. TD Jakes said, "You can change your hair, your clothes, your phone number, your address, your spouse, your residence, but nothing will change in your life until you change your mind."* Let me explain what I mean by that through personal experience.

I'll not repeat my story since you can find it all over this book, but I'll tell you one part that is relevant to this subject. I had a belief that when I change my friends, address, company, and country, I would be happy. I thought when I find new friends, a new job and better opportunities, I was never going to feel lonely again. Well, as you can guess, it didn't work that way. Nothing changed until I started to change my mind. I knew that until I changed my inside world, nothing would change on the outside. When I figured out that loneliness is only a state of mind and that I have full control over my attitudes towards it, everything started to fall into place; slowly but at least the progress has been made.

Now you may want to know how I came to that point. Firstly, I still haven't come to the point where I feel that I'm not completely alone, but I can surely say that I'm getting closer to it. I always believed in God. In the last twelve months (it was August 2018 when this book was in the process of being written, but this "*conversation*" with God started a year before, in March 2017) I started talking to God more than I ever did before. I didn't have any particular reason, but I felt that I needed to do it. And what I discovered (I repeat this is only my experience, you don't have to believe in it or accept it as truth) was that *you are never alone because God is always with you*. ALWAYS! I heard in one of *Dr. Wayne Dyer's* speeches that he read something in *"A Course in Miracles"* that really got me, and it is this – *"If you knew who walks beside you at all times on this path that you have chosen, you'd never experience doubt or fear again."* That means if we have this understanding and faith that we are never alone and there is someone who always walks with us side by side, we'll never feel that we are alone and we'll never be afraid of anything.

If we want to come to that point where we'll feel the presence of God in every moment, one of the main things that I believe we have to do is to *develop faith*. So let's go through briefly because I think it's very crucial to talk about it.

Sometimes, because the lack of faith affects your attitude when you stop believing that God is going to operate in the newness of your life, you become bitter, and you don't allow any help that will restore your faith. You gave up too soon and what you want is the anointing of God, and bring that anointing to that troubled place in your life where you find it hard to believe that things will ever work out.

Because we lost faith, we started to be afraid. We fear that we'll not have enough money, enough friends, enough love, that we'll be alone for the rest of our lives, etc. I can tell you theoretically about many techniques for developing faith that I've learned, but practically I've been developing faith only through positive affirmations that I've written on the board in my bedroom, and a piece of paper I have in my wallet.

Faith is also a state of mind that may be induced or created by affirmation or repeated instructions to the subconscious mind. Honestly, the method by which one develops faith (where it doesn't already exist) is really difficult to describe, but I genuinely believe that the best way for developing the emotion of faith is by every day constantly repeating affirmations to your subconscious mind like *"With God all things are possible"* (or you can write something that you like).

You can create your own affirmations and repeat them every day several times until it becomes memorized and part of your subconscious mind. By developing faith, you'll start to see things differently, and you'll never see loneliness as something tragic or sad or whatever you want to describe it. You'll never be scared or bored to be alone. Most people are afraid to be alone in their room. They are scared of their thoughts. They have this need to call or text someone to go anywhere just to run from themselves. But being alone can benefit you beyond your *Imagination*. You need time to be alone. You need time to be still. To be quiet. To be silent. To meditate. Even to talk to yourself and sometimes the conversation that you're having with yourself can be the only intelligent conversation you'll ever have.

When you're alone, when you get still, when you clear your mind, the flow of ideas are coming into your mind. You feel refreshed, inspired, clear in what you want, etc. Now, I'm not suggesting that you have to be alone all day, but you need *"your time."* Just to be you! I have a question for you – Do you like who you are when you are alone? Do you enjoy your own company? If you don't enjoy your own company, how can you expect for someone else to enjoy it? Everything starts from within.

There are so many single people in this world, and maybe you are one of them. Some of you are single again. Now if you think being single is tough, try being single again. Dealing with issues that come along with being single is different from dealing with issues that come along when you're married or in a relationship. Singleness has to be managed; and when it is managed appropriately and effectively, singleness becomes a gift. What you must realize is that if you're single, it means that you are a whole person and if you don't understand that, you'll think that you are a fractioned individual which means that you need somebody to complete you. However, you must understand that you're a whole person waiting for another whole person to complement you. Not to complete you, and God knows not to compete with you, but to complement you. You want to find someone with whom you might share your completeness. I'll not get deeper into this subject about being single, which will be described in the next chapter, but my point is that being alone is a gift if you recognize it.

Trust me, I know what it means to be alone. It's not easy going on alone, but if you keep going, stay true to yourself. It will be worth it in the end. The hardest walk you can make is the walk you make alone, but that is the walk that makes you the strongest. That is the walk that builds your character the most. To all of you fighting battles alone, stay strong, keep going. This walk is hard, but the hardest walks lead to the greatest destinations. The toughest climbs always lead to the best views. It will be worth it in the end. And if you show what you're made of, the right people will show up in your life, and you won't be alone forever. You have qualities only few can admire because most don't possess. You have strength only few can understand because most have never experienced. So don't give in. You're stronger than you can imagine.

Don't make permanent decisions over temporary situations. Loneliness will pass; you'll get another opportunity. There are no permanent conditions in this Universe. Everything is temporary. Stay strong. And please, don't forget that ***YOU ARE NEVER ALONE!***

Future: Trust me when I say that with this subject, you'll inspire millions of people to change the way they look at this.

Serge: I hope I will.

Future: You've mentioned something about singleness. What do you mean by that?

Serge: Most people think that being alone is the same as being single. There's a huge difference. Loneliness is a state of mind that can be changed. Singleness is a temporary situation that you are experiencing because of the expectations you had when you wanted to get into a relationship. Singleness has to be managed.

Future: Would you please tell us how to do that?

Serge: You know, I was thinking about the name of this book.

Future: And what names appeared in your mind?

Serge: Only one name and that is **"Interview with my Future Self."** However, after these questions that you have for me, it seems that I'll have to rename it because I'm not sure who is interviewing whom.

Future: I like it. That's a good name for this book. Although, I think that you should rename it to **"The Art of Imagination"** since you're using your *Imagination* this whole time and keep the "**Interview with my Future**" as a subpart of the title.

Serge: WOW that's a perfect title. I'm definitely going to take that one!

Future: I've said many times, we are one, and it doesn't matter who is talking as long as we are providing value to your readers. Am I right?

Serge: Yes, you are.

Future: Now let's go back to the next subject where you will explain how singleness can be managed.

Serge: I would rather change the subject to: *"Singleness as a Gift."*

Singleness as a Gift

First of all, you must realize, to be single implies that you are whole. Being single is not being alone. On the contrary, being single suggests that you are a whole person.

I know that there are many single persons in this world. Maybe you are one of them. Some of you are single again. I said in the previous subject that if you think being single is tough, try being single again. From personal experience, I know that being single is not easy at all, especially if you're single for an extended period, and when we talk about these people or ourselves, often we feel sorry for them or ourselves because we believe that they are unhappy. We associate being single with loneliness and sadness. We assume that they are sad, depressed, frustrated, dark, etc. However, is that true?

If we change our perspective on these things, we might be able to see a completely different picture. Being single can be beneficial beyond belief. What I mean by that is, when you're single, you can discover some things that could improve your life dramatically. It may sound odd, but when we manage to be single appropriately and effectively, it can truly be a gift.

When you're single you have the freedom to seek God; you have the freedom to go back to school; you have the freedom to explore different talents and gifts you might have; you have the freedom to plan a future for yourself. If your time is managed effectively, you will have time and energy to do things that married people or people in a long-term relationship often don't have time or energy to do because of the commitment that lifestyle requires. It is unlikely that you could have a spouse and not alter your lifestyle; because when you are committed to that relationship, you have to be prepared to feed that relationship. What I'm trying to say is, dealing with all of the issues that come with being single is a bit different from dealing with the issues that come with being married. Being married can affect you in many positive ways but also being single can have even a greater impact on your life. You can rediscover or remember your relationship with God. You can also rediscover who you are. You can discover what type of lifestyle suits you; what interests you have; what dreams you want to pursue; what is that you want to do for the rest of your life and what changes you need to make to get you there. Being single is being committed to a relationship with yourself.

If you want to discover these things, you need to spend some time alone. The reason people are fighting being alone instead of embracing it is that they are scared to be single or to be alone. They have this need or urgency to call someone or text somebody even if they don't like them; just to make a connection. People are uncomfortable being alone in their room. They may be afraid of their thoughts or struggling with their lives. But time spent alone should be embraced because only then can you truly discover some things that you couldn't before. When this time is savoured, you can develop your relationship with God, you can develop a relationship with yourself, and you can see what you want from life, what your passion is and what your purpose is. So let's talk about these things.

On deepening your relationship with God

Deepening your relationship with God (or with your Source or Universe, or whatever you call it) is basically coming to a point in your life and your walk with God at which you're comfortable enough, to be honest with Him, to reveal and come to terms with who you are, and to finally recognize that God knows and accepts who you are. God invites each of us to travel with him along the highway of life, and he extends his hand to us for guidance along the journey. Along the way, we'll deepen our understanding of God and discover the kind of life he desires for us. But in the process of living, we experience some challenging and difficult situations that made us forget not just who God is, but also who we are.

When you are in a dark place, when you feel overwhelmed by life, it's easy to forget that God is there and also to forget who you are. He will never leave you or forsake you or forget about you. He's always there, standing with you by your side at all times and waiting for you to take your life into your hands and live it to the fullest. If you devote some time to develop your relationship with God, I'm sure that you'll notice that He has always been there and your life will immediately start to improve on every level. I must admit that I'm still in the process of developing my relationship with God, and I haven't gotten to the point that I feel the presence of God in every moment, but I'm improving on it every day. I'm at the point where I feel comfortable, to be honest with God, to talk openly about everything knowing that He already knows everything and that He knows who I am.

You should be able to talk to God. You must be honest with Him because He's your Source. There's nothing that He doesn't know about you or He can't understand about you and your life. You may ask, *"How can I talk to God?"* Well, you can have a conversation with God in the same way you have a conversation with anyone via any medium. You can communicate through your thoughts and with your words. Probably the best communication is through feelings because feelings are the language of the *Soul*. You can talk to God through prayer. Now, we may speak to God and still ask, *"Will God give a response to us?"* I believe that God always responds to us in the form of thought or even spoken word; through some other signs that we must train our mind to see because they're easy to miss when we don't pay attention to them.

Use the time that you have as a single person to deepen your relationship with God. No matter who you are or where you are in your relationship with God, find a way to allow Him to speak to your heart, and help you change yourself from the inside out. God is eager to walk with you. Learn how to listen to Him. He will speak to you when you don't expect it. While you're cooking, driving, exercising, working, standing in line at the market, try to open yourself up to listening to the Holy Spirit within you. Trust that you will be interested in everything God has to say to you. Listen to that voice that's inside of you. Think and feel; sometimes about who you are, about who any human is in comparison to God. Appreciate that. Let that understanding grow within you. Let it overwhelm you.

The ultimate truth is that if we all come here from our Source, that means we have the same power that our Creator has, and we are able at any moment to have access to it if we deepen our relationship with Him.

On embracing who you are

How can you remember who you are if you don't spend some time alone and try to understand yourself better? You need time alone to just simply be you. To experience self-discovery, you need to have privacy. Sometimes life can be so overwhelming that you forget your name. It is easy to forget who you are. From an early age, as early as the day you came to this world as a perfect reflection of your Source, some people go above and beyond to point out all of your imperfections. Sometimes it starts from the home where well-meaning parents were strict about regular behavior that they found strange. Some parents used punishment to encourage the behavior they wanted to see. Outside of the home, there may have been bullying from other kids for no reason. These are the first moments in which we easily start to forget who we are.

There may be countless situations where we start to forget who we are, but my point is that it happens when we are least aware of it. Suddenly, you may catch yourself pretending to be someone who you are not to fit in or get along. You may alter your behavior to please others even if you don't like it and know that is not something that you want to do. However, you continue doing it to be accepted. You may catch yourself saying words that are not reflective of who you are. Soon afterward, you may even become trapped in the habit of speaking and behaving in a way that does not reflect who you are. Words stimulate thoughts, and as a result, you may start thinking all kinds of thoughts about yourself that are not true. Inevitably, those thoughts build a false and distorted reality of who you are.

In some cases, years may have passed, and you could find yourself in your 20s, 30s, 40s, or maybe even older and you still don't know who you are. However, the more time passed, the more you come to see that perhaps you never took the time to rediscover and embrace who you are. You never spent time alone enough to think about it. To try to remember it. By now, you may notice how often I repeat the word *remember*. The reason is that I genuinely believe that in the first nine months of our lives, from the moment of our conception to the moment of our birth, everything was handled for us. We didn't have to worry about how tall we would be, what kind of hair we would have, how our bodies would look like... When you're a baby, everybody sees you as a perfect human being. Then, when you start to grow up, for whatever reason, we start losing that perspective on ourselves, and that makes me think... If in the first nine months, our outlook on ourselves was not an issue, why couldn't that be true for the next 90 or 100 years? It's because we interfere. We forget. That's why I urge you to take your time alone and remember who you are.

Start now. Start today. Start thinking differently. Start thinking only of thoughts that will serve you. *The highest thought is the thought that contains joy.* Speak only the words that will reflect who you are. *The clearest words are those words that contain the truth*. Above all, you must feel. Feel the thoughts, feel the words, feel yourself overcome the overwhelming urge to be dishonest about what makes you happy! *Because the grandest feeling is that feeling which we call love! Joy, truth, and love. These are the principles that you want to live by.* When you think only of thoughts that serve you, when you speak the words and take actions that reflect who you are, then you'll be able to experience the true glory of being alive.

In case you have trouble remembering who you really are, let me begin to remind you. *You are the most beautiful, the most remarkable, the most perfect being God has ever created.* You can trust that this is true, for who can reject such a perfection?

On pursuing what suits you

When you're single, you have enough time to think about yourself, those things you would like to do, have, and be. You have enough time to plan a future for yourself. You have more than enough energy to do all kinds of things. If you haven't yet found the lifestyle that suits you, now is the right time to go looking for it.

Finding your passion is not hard at all. ***Where your heart is, there will be your passion.*** It will always be found in serving others in one way or the other because service to others is the highest purpose you can discover. It helps if you go a few years back when you were a young kid to try to remember what your biggest dream was and to awaken that dream again. See what's inside of you and build on that. Start thinking again about that dream that you have forgotten and even if it seems impossible now, remove those thoughts and choose the ones that will serve you better. Choose the thoughts that will keep you on the path to achieving that dream until the emotion that you feel while you think about it grows too big and strong for any doubt to linger in your mind.

I'm not talking about your dreams only, but also about your interests, talents, skills, and abilities that you probably don't know you possess. What interests do you have right now? Interests make you an interesting person. You can agree that there's nothing worse than when you go out with somebody and ask for their thoughts on something, and that person replies, *"Nothing. What do you think about it?"* or something similar. It can be awkward going out with somebody who has nothing to say. If you don't have any interests yet, now you can develop some. Deepening your knowledge can help you to do just that. Is your interest in basketball, world affairs, wars, politics, history, technology, writing, communication, or marketing? Whatever you are interested in, find what you like to talk about and seek out people and places that foster these interests.

What talents do you have? I started writing recently (March 2017 was the first time I started writing). For 28 years, I didn't know that I had this talent. If someone had told me five, ten, or fifteen years ago that one day, I would write inspirational blogs or even a book, I would laugh. What talents do you have? Try to discover them and try not to listen when others say you are good or bad at something. Everything requires practice. In the beginning, we must overcome being bad at something to become good at it. Every talent needs time for development. I've noticed that the more I write, the better I get at it. Discover it within you. Find those talents and unleash them.

What else? What skills and abilities do you have that you underutilized or not used at all? What else do you like to do? Do you like to go hiking? Maybe biking? Swimming? Flying? Discover those things, they are all already inside of you; you just have to discover them and go do them. Time alone will help you to discover what suits you best, and if you use this time properly, you will be more than ready for something bigger in your life like deep and meaningful relationships.

In conclusion, time spent alone helps us to see who God is, it lets us know who we are, and it frees us to find a lifestyle that best suits our interests and dreams. Use the time you have wisely before you get into a relationship because when you discover who God is, who you are and what suits you, you will also become a more wholesome person looking for another wholesome person to complement you instead of to complete you.

This is not to suggest that you should spend years or more being single, but instead use the time you have to discover for yourself everything that I've mentioned. If you're single again or if you've just gotten out of a relationship or marriage, before you jump into a new one, it may be wise to find out why it didn't work the first time and reflect on what happened. Perhaps you are certain of their faults and mistakes, but we must take responsibility for our part in any mess. My suggestion is to seek a more wholesome life as a single person. See who God is. See who you are. See what sort of life truly suits you. Then, when you remember or discover all of these things, you'll become a whole person, ready to get into a relationship or marriage in which you will truly share your completeness.

> *"If you change the way you look at things, the things you look at change"* – **Wayne Dyer**

I hope you'll change the way you look at being single because if you learn how to manage your time with yourself, you'll soon realize it to be an invaluable gift.

Future: Very powerfully said.

Serge: How can you know who you are until you take some time for yourself and try to figure it out?

Future: That's true. Most people don't like to spend time alone, and what that means in a deeper sense is that they don't like who they are. Because when you're alone, all things that are inside of you starts to show up in your mind and you actually see how much you don't enjoy your own company. To change that, they try to go out with somebody that they don't even like just to feel better about themselves, which is not in alignment of who they are.

Serge: That's a sad thing. So many people are forty, fifty, sixty, and even older, yet, they still don't know who they are. I said a few times, thank God that I've realized who I am before I die.

Future: When did that happen?

Serge: It happened exactly when I decided to spend time with myself and thought seriously about what I would like to do, be and have, and the kind of person I want to become. I think the moment you decide all of that, after some time if you put effort into manifesting your goals you'll instinctively remember who you are. It will suddenly pop into your mind, and you'll be awakened into who you are.

Future: I remember clearly that moment when the awakening happened to us. But still, we don't want to judge these people. We should allow them to be who they choose to be no matter what and believe that they will sooner or later remember who they are.

Serge: I'm not judging anyone. I learned a few years ago that we should not judge anyone or anything.

Future: That's true.

Serge: I would like you to tell us about not judging people.

Future: For sure. What would you like me to talk about specifically?

Serge: Why we need to stop judging others, how to practice that, and whatever else you can add to it.

Future: Sounds good. Let's talk about non-judgment.

No judgments

Judgment is a constant evaluation of things as good or bad, right or wrong. We live in a world full of judgments. How many times do you catch yourself judging others by the way they look? Talk? Walk? Dress? Behave? We don't only judge people; we judge everything else like events, circumstances, animals, whatever we see or hear about them. We even judge ourselves more than anything or anyone. When we are constantly evaluating, classifying, labeling, analyzing, we create a lot of turbulence in our internal dialogue. So let's talk about practicing **non–judgment** and how that can help us to see people and things differently.

There's a prayer in *"A course in miracles"* that states, **"Today I shall judge nothing that occurs."** This statement helped me a lot to start thinking differently and to remind myself not to judge anything or anyone no matter what happens. When I read that, I began to think about it. I realized that we are so quick to judge everything that happens. We see someone who is dressed the way we don't like – judgment is there! We hear someone laughing, and for no reason, we feel annoyed or offended, and we immediately judge them. We see a beautiful girl, but we don't have the courage to go and meet her, what is the first thing we do? We judge ourselves. We say that we are not good enough, that we don't have courage, that we are never able to find true love, etc. All these evaluations are nothing more than false statements that we made about ourselves.

We go to jobs that we don't like most of the time, what are we doing? We judge ourselves because we're not happy to work there; we judge the work itself, and the people in that company. If your boss is an asshole (by your own opinion), you judge him, and you spend a lot of time judging. The problem is that with all of these judgments, we only create inner turbulence that doesn't want to leave us because, with your frustration, anger, resentment, you feed your ego, and that's exactly what ego needs to feel alive. However, with practicing non-judgment, you can create a blissful silence in your mind that will help you look at things and people differently.

This is what I did; first thing in the morning when I wake up; I have a routine to read a few affirmations, to be grateful for what I have, to set a clear intention for that day and I say aloud that whatever happens today, I won't judge. I started saying aloud *"no judgments"* every time I catch myself if I'm about to judge something or someone. In the beginning, it was hard, of course, but the more I told myself, the more I saw the results in the form of less judgement. I remember I was in a restaurant with friends, and they were talking about one situation and the people involved in that situation, and they were arguing on and on; and then they turned around to me to ask for my opinion because I didn't say one word, I replied to them, *"Sorry guys, I have no judgments."* They were confused and didn't believe what I just said. They asked me again, and I replied with the same message. I believe that night was the turning point for me because since then, I continuously remind myself of not judging anything. I believe that I came to this point because of constantly repeating a statement *"no judgments"* over and over again, and I impressed my subconscious mind with those words and they have become my second nature.

Trust me, I did this so often that people around me become so annoyed with my words, but I didn't care. It worked for me and helped me to change my view of the world and the people in it. Why is this important? Why is it so important to stop judging others and events? Because we all don't want to be judged in the first place! How many times have you said to someone, *"Don't judge me."* How many times did you do something and say to someone, *"Don't judge what I'm doing because you don't know why I am doing this?"* Well, the truth is, even if you stop judging others, you'll still be judged. Only this time, you'll not care about that, because you know who you are and that's all that matters. You don't need to explain yourself or your actions because you don't need anyone's approval and that will bring the peace of mind that we all want.

What I've discovered is that when you stop judging others, you'll not only see others from a different perspective, but you'll start to see them as who they are, and you'll notice the love that you feel toward them. Even if they judge you, you'll not take that as something negative and fire back. Instead, you'll send them a silent blessing or prayer because you know that whatever they say is nothing personal, it's just a reflection of their state of being. When negative events or adversities occur, you'll not judge them and classify them as negative, you'll see them as a sign for you to grow or as an opportunity to see and be who you are. I believe that only by practicing *non-judgment,* you can transform your life and change it for the better.

Serge: That's exactly what I did. It worked perfectly for me. I was saying these words *"no judgments"* over and over and over again until I realized that I've stopped judging others.

Future: That's one more step closer to the perfect reflection and manifestation of your Creator.

Serge: You make me feel good.

Future: Well, the truth is you make yourself feel good.

Serge: Haha, true! I wonder for years why we don't teach our kids these things while they are still young, especially in school.

Future: Because the school is not meant to teach kids these things. It will take a long time before somebody brave takes a leap and opens a private school that will teach kids all these things they will need in life. Only then the public schools will consider putting programs that will benefit upcoming generations.

Serge: There are a few things that I wished I learned in school.

Future: Like what for example?

Few things I wished I learned in school

S *erge:* I was talking to a friend about the educational system, not just in Canada or Serbia, but all over the world. We had an interesting conversation because he told me all the reasons somebody has to go to school and go to college or university, and I gave him all the reasons why all of that is not necessary at all. Of course, we were arguing, and somehow I believe that both of us were *"right"* about it, depending on how you look at it. I want to share with you some of the reasons why I believe the current school system is not good at all (it's my personal opinion) and few things I wished I learned while I was in school.

I must say that I'm not entirely against the school system, but honestly, I'm not a fan of what's going on, especially in today's time. I mean it is 2018, and we still have the same educational system that was 50 years ago! It didn't evolve at all! Our kids are learning things they will not use in everyday life. I don't know so many people that use Pythagoras formula in daily activity. Also, they bother our kids with unimportant things they don't need because, today, every kid has a cell phone and whatever information they need, they can easily find on Google in a few seconds. School teaches you how to memorize knowledge but not how to use that knowledge practically so you can reap the benefits after you finish school. But let's get back to the topic. Here are a few things I wished I learned in school.

Don't be afraid to make mistakes

Unfortunately, in school, they teach us that we are not supposed to make any mistakes. Because if we make them, they will punish us. The punishment usually comes in the form of an *F* on the tests or calling us out in front of the whole class if we don't know something. Of course, there are (but very few) teachers who encourage kids to make mistakes, because they understand they are necessary for kids to learn from them to become better than before. Whenever you do something *"wrong"* in your teacher's eyes, they will punish you. And when you're told so many times at an early age that you can't make a mistake, you become afraid because you know that you'll be punished. What happens then? You become scared of making mistakes in life.

In reality, making mistakes is not a bad thing at all. How else will you learn if you don't make mistakes? How else will you grow? Life is a big experiment. Sometimes you will succeed in whatever you want to do; sometimes you'll not. If you open a business, it's normal in the beginning that you'll make some mistakes. That doesn't mean after the first one you should give up on it, or you aren't good or talented enough for that. It merely means that you need to change your strategy and try something different, and if required, change it a few times until you discover what works. Thomas Edison failed almost ten thousand times before he invented the light bulb. I genuinely believe that we have to make mistakes to find out what will or will not work when we make it. It gives us feedback about what we need to change. I must say, I rarely learn from just one mistake, sometimes I make the same mistakes two or three times before I learn, but that's okay. I'm willing to make a mistake to achieve something.

I wish school had taught me that making mistakes will only help and benefit me and not been punished and making me afraid of doing whatever I wanted.

How to dream and set goals

I never heard any teacher that said to anyone from my generation how to dream or set goals in life. Now I know how important it is to have a goal or dream because if you don't have one, you're not going anywhere. What is your direction in life? How do you know what you want to do or be, if you don't set goals and put it on paper? Yes, you may have it in your mind, but you need a practical step that will enable you to come closer to your dream. I wish my teachers encouraged me to dream and taught me to set short and long-term goals. I wish they taught me how to visualize my goals and how to impress the subconscious mind to think all the time about that goal. First time I ever heard something about "goals" was in 2012 when I was already 23 years old. I'm not saying that was a wrong time, but I wish I heard that at an earlier age. I wish they taught me the importance of taking action towards my goals.

Money

I genuinely wish I learned in school how to work with money. Like a simple rule of 70/30 that I'm using in my life, which means that from 100% of my income, I'm able to spend only 70% and live with that. 10% goes to a saving account, 10% to the investment account, and 10% is for giving back. Nobody taught us how to spend money. The importance of saving money and even greater importance of how to invest money. School system has not done a pretty job at preparing us for the real world and the rules about money. Especially in Canada, I see so many people that are in huge debt and almost broke because they didn't learn how to work with money. Nobody taught us how to sell, to make a transaction, the importance of taxes, why we pay them, etc.

The reason why I'm telling you this is because the first time I started earning a bit of a serious amount of money, I didn't know what to do and how to work with it. I thought that I could spend as much as I want without thinking that something bad can happen. Guess what? At the age of 23, I found myself completely broke with several thousands of dollars in debt, without a job and even without food to eat. It was tough for me. When I came to Canada, I had already learned a few principles that will make my life more comfortable, and those principles like 70/30 rule helped me to manage my money correctly. You have to know how much you spend every month, where your money is going, and also how much you're earning, so you can make a plan on how to spend or invest money properly.

How to work on myself

What I mean by this is, I wish I learned in school how to build self-confidence and learn ways to deal with situations in real life. I know that everything depends on the situation you find yourself in, but at least the school system could teach us some useful tips to overcome fears of failure or disappointment. As a kid, you're trying to fit in, you're trying to please everybody, and if you're not cool or beautiful or smart, you can hit the wall. Teachers are also not doing a very good job at this. If a teacher tells you to stand up in front of all kids in your class and ask you "*What is the capital city of Canada?*" and you don't know, they may punish you with bad mark or even worse, they can laugh at you or bully you in front of all the kids. Teachers can even start yelling at you and asking you how possible is it that you do not know that. And other kids can make fun of you. But what teachers fail to understand is that all of these things can destroy your self-confidence and change your story about yourself. You start feeling that you're not smart, that you are not good, etc.

I had several experiences during junior high school when I was embarrassed by the teacher, and I even ran out of class once. To make things worse, I was also punished for running away from class. I didn't want to go to school for days. I remember how much I lied to my parents that I was sick just not to go to school. It destroyed my self-confidence. I'm not saying that all teachers are bad or anything similar, but basically, they are not so good at teaching kids how to build self-esteem, trust, and belief in themselves. I wish that I had someone who can teach me how to work on myself back in those days so I can efficiently deal with today's challenges.

I genuinely believe is that today's teachers have to work more with kids than ever before. The world is changing rapidly. Everything new today will be old tomorrow. The school system has to evolve together with technology and changes that are coming into the world. Today's kids are all concerned about social media, and how many *likes* they have or don't have (unfortunately it become a standard to determine whether they are cool or attractive which we will talk more about in the topic ***"Popularity based identity"***) on Facebook or Instagram, and all the technology that is coming, we will have more distractions than ever. I truly desire that teachers in school can start teaching kids how to be who they really are, creative, how to love and appreciate everyone around them, be brave, courageous, not scared of making mistakes, to dream, to work with money and build their self-esteem.

I believe that if our kids can learn these few things in school today, it will make them better prepared for the world that is coming and evolving.

Your kids will imitate you

Future: I believe that kids of your generation should learn these things and more in schools. I'm sure this book is not just for adults but even for teenagers. Every parent should read this book. Why? First, to improve their own life. Then, to teach their children the skills to be independent and intentional in creating their lives.

Serge: There are so many other things that our current school system needs to fix to provide real value to our kids.

Future: Like?

Serge: I don't know if I should speak about it, it may cause some controversy for some readers.

Future: Since when you're worried about controversy?

Serge: I'm not worried at all. I'm still considering whether to include some things in this book.

Future: Do it. People will think that it is insane to be talking to your *Imagination*. So don't worry about it. If you believe that your words will inspire change, then speak. Don't hold back at all.

Serge: I'm not holding back anything. There are so many things that we need to teach our kids, but not just we as individuals, but the school system should do that first!

Like I said, the school system endeavors to teach children how to memorize facts instead of teaching them how to use their minds. We need to give our children the privilege of leading in their schools. They should be able to learn by doing and to be engaged in some form of practical labor connected with the daily problems of life.

Schools should teach them how to use and budget their time as the most valuable asset they have! They should teach them what to eat and how, to be definite in all things, to decide what their major purpose in life is. Kids should be taught how to form good habits that will lead them to a greater life, the difference between temporary defeats and failures. They should be taught how to express their thoughts fearlessly and to accept or reject the ideas of others and also, the value of harmony in relationships. They should learn not to accept others opinions unless they are formed from facts. They must be taught to think for themselves, the power of independent thought; that there is no problem which does not have an appropriate solution. That the only limitations they have are in their minds. Kids should be taught to be true to themselves at all times and not try to please everybody else; and learn to be who they are, and many other things.

Future: I can feel the anger there.

Serge: I'm frustrated. I still can't believe that our kids are learning the same stuff that previous generations used to learn 50-60 years ago. I know so many things now that I believe will benefit our kids if they start learning them at a young age.

Future: And how would you make them learn these things?

Serge: There are a million ways to do it; through fun games, through sports, through some other activities. There are so many creative ways to teach them all these skills. I believe that kids would enjoy going to school instead of being bored in classes waiting to be over as soon as they get there.

Future: Do you have any plans to do something about it?

Serge: Of course I do. I have a specific goal and plan on how to do it. I have a full project that I believe will soon be realized.

Future: Don't you think that all these things that you've mentioned should be learned at home?

Serge: Absolutely! But how can we expect parents to teach kids something they don't know? Maybe in the families where parents have this knowledge, their kids could be taught, but there are very few such families. Probably 98% of parents have no idea what I'm talking about. They're not aware that their kids are (more often than not) the reflection of them! Do you know parents who are heavy smokers but restrict their kids from smoking?

Future: For sure, like our parents, for example.

Serge: That's an example that I'll use here. When I was young, I used to hate smokers because smoking stinks! It is polluting the air and gives bad breath. You can't breathe normally and not to mention how bad it is for the health overall. During our family lunches, I was always the one who was eating slower than my parents and sister. Usually, my mom and dad finished first, while my sister and I were still eating. Immediately they finished their lunch; they would take a cigar and start smoking even if my sister and I were still eating. I hated them because of that. What a terrible habit! I was telling them to stop doing it, but they have always shut me out. I was about 12 years old when I decided not to eat with them. I would take my lunch and eat in my room. Years passed, and they still didn't realize how bad that habit was. Also, I clearly remember when they were *"teaching"* my sister and me to never smoke.

Because of the smoking during lunch hours, I decided to never smoke in my life. I've tried once and said that it's not for me. My sister didn't make that decision. She became a smoker, and I believe that was mostly because of our parents.

Future: Don't be so harsh on our parents. Don't you think that our sister started smoking because of the environment?

Serge: You could argue that our environment has a significant impact on our behavior, and that is true, but most of the habits we have are picked at home. Let me explain what I mean by that.

When we were born, I truly believe that we picked up the vibrations of our parents. That we can feel everything they feel. Our mind is total blank till the time we reach the first sign of consciousness, and we begin to recognize the objects around us, people, our parents, etc. The first thing we do is start to imitate others, and naturally, the people we begin to imitate first are our parents! Imitation becomes a habit. Then we started to imitate others like relatives, school teachers, peers around us. That imitation extends not necessarily to the physical expression but also thought expression. Like I said, if our parents have a fear of something and they express their fear within the range of our hearing, we pick up the fear through the habit of imitation and store it away as a part of our subconscious mind. It's the same with other things. We see our parents drink; we want to drink too. We see the food they eat; we want to eat the same food. We see them smoking, guess what? Most likely we would want to try it too!

You see, your parents act in a certain way; what do you think you will do when you get into a similar situation? If your dad is yelling at your mom, and you're a boy, you'll do it too with women. Also, if you're a girl, you'll be afraid that one day some man will yell at you. Later in life, you'll hear these words going your way from somebody like *"he's just like his father"* or *"she's just like her mother"* or similar comments because you became a reflection of your mom or dad.

Future: But we didn't become anything like our parents. How can you explain that?

Serge: Like I said, more often than not, we are either the reflection of our parents or as you've argued the products of our environment. But there are always exceptions. For me, the turning point about smoking was the day I got so pissed off and decided not to have lunch with my parents anymore because of their smoking habit while we were eating. My sister went a different way. She's doing the same thing. As soon as she finishes her meal, she takes a cigar.

Future: That's an example; the smoking, what about the rest of your life? Like being different from them, doing some things that they have never done?

Serge: Because I went through many disappointments early in my life, and because I was growing up believing I was alone and that all my life I'll be a failure; I believe that there was something inside of me that wanted me to make a change. I had this thought all my life that I'm somehow different from the people around me. Deep down, I knew that I don't want to be like my parents, to follow in their footsteps and live life in the same manner that they were living. Now, don't get me wrong. Somebody can think that I'm criticizing my parents or that I still hold a grudge towards them; that is not true.

I love my parents! I really do! I love them more than they will ever know. And I'm aware that they didn't know some things and probably still don't know anything about who I am, and what I'm talking about. And that's okay. A few years ago, I realized that I'm at peace with that. I'm not judging them anymore; I know it's their life and they can do whatever they choose; whether it is good or bad for them. The only thing I can do is to be the example and hope that one day, they will be inspired by my own life and decide to change their thoughts, beliefs, and life.

The reason I'm talking about them in this (somebody can say negative but truly is not) context is that it is a perfect example of what I'm trying to explain the relationship between kids and parents.

To get back on track, I knew that I wanted more from life. I'm sure that most people know some families where parents were addicted to alcohol, and they had two kids. One became an alcoholic also and the other one a completely successful and happy person. What was the difference? They were growing up under the same circumstances, the same parents, same roof but one became just like them and the other one something entirely different. Do you know why that is?

Future: Because one didn't know how to be something different and the other decided at some point just like you did that he will never be like his parents.

Serge: Exactly. Why that happened to one and not the other is a mystery of life, I believe.

Future: What is your solution to that "*problem*"?

Serge: What most parents don't know is that they need to be aware of what they are doing, how they talk in front of their kids and of course to be aware that their kids will imitate them. Also, they have to realize that they are leaders in their family. And by leading the family, they should be an example. But I think I have dived too deep into this. So let me jump to a question that is related to this subject. Why do you think most people fail to recognize themselves as leaders? I am not referring to parents here but everyone?

Future: Because most people believe that being a **leader** is only a title reserved for chosen ones in their community, in their job, in their school, in their sports team, etc., but every person in this world is born as a leader. They just don't know that.

Serge: I'm sure you know something about that. Can you expand? What you mean by being a leader? And what do you mean by leadership?

Becoming a true Leader

> *"A leader is one who knows the way, goes the way, and shows the way." - **John C. Maxwell***

Future: If you're looking for leadership, you don't have to look ahead to find it. Great leadership often starts at the back. It does not begin when you're the President of a country, Manager, or the CEO of a company, Co-owner of business, Mayor of the city. Sometimes, it is possible for life to lead you faster than your mind is prepared to handle. I believe that every promotion comes really from God. God can put you in a place that you're placed in a position of leadership, but mentally and emotionally, you really haven't got a grip on what life has handed you; and if you don't know what you have, you won't know how to take care of it. And if you don't know how to take care of it, you may mess around and lose it. The truth is that leaders come from ordinary places.

Serge: If I may interrupt you for a second, you said that sometimes you could be placed in a position but not be prepared mentally, and I can relate to that. When I joined a network marketing company, I came to a situation where all of a sudden I had to lead other distributors and help them reach their goals, but mentally I didn't know how to do it. I was stuck; I thought I was a leader, but that wasn't the case. And as a result of that, I messed up and lost all my distributors and clients too. I didn't know how to take care of them.

Future: That's a good example of how you wanted to become a leader before you were mentally and emotionally prepared to be one. I was about to explain how to prepare yourself to become a true leader.

Serge: Please, go ahead.

Future: Thank you. First of all, when you say that you want to become a great leader and you want to do what needs to be done, willing to work harder than anyone, more than anyone, be the example, willing to go the extra mile, and many more. I'll tell you right away, you're asking for trouble! To take your case, at this moment you're working in a construction company as a store manager. Aren't you?

Serge: Well you can say that I'm taking care of the company when the owner is not there and although I don't like to use that title, you may say that I'm the manager.

Future: Good. Like in every business, the more you go to a higher position the more you get paid because your duties and responsibilities become higher and greater and you have to deal with problems and issues on another level than you have when you were just a worker. And the truth is, your owner is paying you for conflict.

Serge: For conflict?

Future: Yes, for conflict. Like in every business, it doesn't matter if it is big or small, you are paid to manage conflicts, pressure, and struggles. In other words, the more money that is placed in your hands, the more you have to be able to handle, to deal with, and manage conflict appropriately. Let me tell you one more thing; all of us are leaders in one way or the other, whether you're leading your children or leading your family or even leading yourself. It's sometimes hard to lead yourself to act right.

When you're in a higher position, you will face different issues, higher pressure, and new opportunities. And if you don't like where you are right now in your life, and you say, *"I can't take this anymore,"* or *"I don't want this,"* what you're saying is that you don't want to go any higher because to go higher, you must face different issues, problems, and pressures. You're rejecting a call to move forward; to move higher not just in your company but in your life. And moving up means more problems to manage. In fact, the issues that you're dealing with right now may be the training that you need to go through in order to be prepared for the next level in your business, your life, and role as a leader.

If you don't allow your current issues, pressure and stress you're dealing with to break you, if you keep on going straight through the storms that you're facing, the doors will be opened for you to go to the next level.

When I mention the conflicts, I didn't just mean the external conflicts; sometimes, you have to manage the internal conflicts. When you start going all the way from the bottom, and start moving up further and further, every step takes you to a different level of life and living. Sometimes your life is moving faster than your mentality (like in the example of my *Present*). You can have that dream job or that position that you always wanted, and everything moved in your life except your perception of yourself. What you have to understand is when God moves you along in life, it's not a sprint; it's more like a marathon, a step by step process. You probably know from your example as well as from others that so many people want to move forward in a rapid motion. They want to go from being a security guard to the Presidential suite in one step and trust me, that's not what you want. If you take the elevator and move on too fast, you'll not be able to handle it. You can't handle the pressure, the conflicts, the criticism, the problems and opposition on that level because your mind is not there yet. That's why you want to go through a step by step process.

Serge: That is why 99% of people who win a lottery go bankrupt after a few years because they don't know how to manage the money. In other words, they earned it, but their mindset wasn't prepared for everything that comes with it? Or like the athletes who lose all their money after they finish their respective careers and in a short period, lose everything they had earned?

Future: That is correct. You know some people are still hoping to hit the jackpot or win a lottery. What all of them have in common is that they know how they will spend that money, and almost all of them say the same thing. They'll invest in real estate, hotels, restaurants, even the whole buildings but still, they end up losing all that money sooner or later because their minds are not prepared for everything that comes with it, although it is possible for one to learn how to deal with the new situation and eventually develop his mindset. That will happen with only less than 1% of people who earn a considerable amount of money too fast.

Serge: That's why it has been said that if you take all the money from the richest people in the world who have learned how to earn it, and you give all that money equally to every person that exists, after some time all the money will be returned to the pocket from which it has been taken. It's because every *true millionaire* had developed their mind so powerfully that they possessed the knowledge that is necessary to acquire wealth.

Future: You know that almost every millionaire lost all of their money at least once, and some of them even more times? But when they lost their money, they didn't lose their mindset. Take all the money from a *true millionaire*, and soon they'll earn it again because they have the knowledge to earn it again.

Serge: Well said. I don't want you to lose the flow of thoughts about leadership, so can we get back on the track, please.

Future: Of course. Don't worry about it; we'll not go on a different route, sometimes it is good to break the pattern and ask the right questions as you did with this one. But let's keep going about leadership.

As I said, you want to move forward in life through steps. When you get to the next level, you need to learn how to balance yourself, how to handle the opposition, and criticism on that level. When you're about to feel comfortable at that level, you take another step, and you're at the next level. Then you have to start all over again. You have to learn new things; you are going to be hit in places you would never expect to be hit. You have to deal with life on another level, and that happens whether you're in a corporation, sports, organization, or even in a family like when you have another child, for example. You finally learn everything you need to know with the first one, and you have the second one, and everything that was working for the first is not working for the second, and you have to figure it out all over again. That's life! That's what you want. That's how you grow.

What you must know is, as soon as you start moving forward, others will be jealous and envious of you. They don't understand that you still perceive yourself as if you were where you started, but the steps are leading you higher and further than you've ever been before. God has many blessings and good promises in store for you. All you have to do is stop complaining about where you are right now, because God has placed you in that position so you can go through training and grow your consciousness for the next level. If you don't quit, and you keep going and even be grateful for all of the conflicts you have to manage, the problems you have to solve, you'll go to another dimension that you've never dreamed of, and when you get there, you'll be grateful for all the things you have been through to get where you are right now.

Now, let's talk a little bit about external conflicts because you will have them. There's no way that you can go up and not have the external conflicts. If you want to get to where other leaders went before you, there's no way you can get there and not face some forms of obstacles. Of course, that's only if you are a leader. If you are a follower, you don't have to read this. You can jump to the next subject because whomever you're following will clear a path for you and you just have to go through the path behind your leader. However, if you're a leader, you'll have to encounter thorns along the way and what you're actually doing is clearing a path for the next generation.

You're supposed to have external conflicts because you're doing something that has never been done before and whenever you're doing something new, be aware that people will reject it at first. They will not understand you. So you'll have to confront the conflict in a strategic, non-emotional way. ***Leaders have to be the voice of reason. Your detachment from conflicts emotionally is an expression of faith that you can handle it.*** That's why you have to be rational. Don't be afraid to do something that needs to be done. If you want to become a leader, you'll have to accept that you will have external conflicts along the way.

Next thing that is stopping people from taking the lead is fear. Fear of failure but also fear of success. What if things don't work, right? What if I fail? What if I lose this position and even this job because I wanted to become a leader? Because of the fear of failing, most people will not take the risk to move forward. They don't have the faith that they can do it. They don't want to buy a new house because they might lose it. They don't want to get into another relationship because they might end up hurt again. They don't want to apply for that position because they *"know"* they will not get it. That's why they stay unhappy and comfortable, but become jealous when somebody else takes that step and do what they wanted to do, but simply didn't have the courage.

You'll see in your environment. When you take a step ahead, people will try to sabotage and envy you because they know that they're as smart as you, they're as educated as you, they know you your whole life, but all of a sudden you took that step further and they are one step behind. You become a mirror to them. When they look at you, they see themselves; only they are not where you are. I know it's hard to take that first step, but you have to do it to take the lead and have faith that God will be with you along the way, and will make sure that you'll be strong enough to endure it and go through everything to get you where you want to be.

> *"Take the first step in faith. You don't have to see the whole staircase; just take the first step." - **Martin Luther King, Jr.***

The next fear is a fear of success. What if I succeed and can't handle it? You're afraid that you'll reach your goal, but some disaster will happen. You want it, but you don't want all of the stuff that comes with it. It's like you want to build that dream body with all the muscles and look extraordinarily good, but you don't want to go to the gym, to work your butt off, to feel the pain, to eat properly, to keep the discipline, to be consistent and everything else that comes along with it. If you miss the opportunity because you were afraid, you'll always be where you are right now and feel miserable. Deep down inside of you, you'll feel disappointment and regret because you knew that you should take that chance and go after it. You have to find that courage inside of you and take the first step to become a true leader.

Now, tell me, do you want to become a true leader?

Serge: Of course I do. But now that you've said all this stuff I can't believe how everything is related. Everything that I've been through up until now was preparing me for what is coming. I'm truly grateful for all the conflicts, oppositions, and fights that I have gone through to become who I am right now, and for taking the step to become a true leader. But I never knew before now what it means to be a leader.

Future: I know you didn't know.

Serge: It was only when I joined a network marketing company a few years ago that I found out the true meaning of leadership and what it takes to become a leader.

Future: Tell us about that experience.

Characteristics of Good Leaders

Serge: A few years ago, I had joined a network marketing company, where I found my first mentor. One of the first things he mentioned when we started working together was to go out and educate myself on learning how to grow a business and become a leader. I remember asking myself what he meant by, *"become a leader."*

At that time, I thought that being a leader meant to be what most of us call *"a boss."* To be someone who drives employees through fear, depending on authority, blame others when things go wrong, using people to get ahead, taking credit for ideas he didn't create, giving commands, etc. Fortunately, through educating myself and talking to successful people from within the company, I started to learn what he truly meant by *"become a leader,"* and of course everything my *Future* has said is a confirmation about everything I've learned back then.

As my *Future* said, a leader is someone who is a good role model with regards to knowing how to inspire others to act upon the same goal. Now, leaders come in all shapes and sizes, but there are certain things that all good leaders have in common; which is what I want to share with you. Here are some of the characteristics of the most successful leaders that I've met and learned from:

They give compliments

As you have probably experienced before, (almost) every boss finds fault, but never gives a compliment to their employee. What I saw in leaders is; they give compliments whenever they can, and they always look for the positive aspects of every person in their company/team.

They forgive

A leader always forgives when someone does something wrong or say something inappropriate. I remember when I had an unpleasant interaction with my mentor, and I used some bad words in that argument. He didn't respond with the same message. Instead, he just smiled, calmed me and with a soft voice told me, *"we'll talk tomorrow."* I felt so bad that night I couldn't sleep, but the next day we had an enjoyable conversation, and after everything was sorted out, we continued to have an even more successful relationship.

Leaders take responsibility for their failures

Followers are the ones who never take responsibility for what they do. They always blame others or events for their failures or unsuccessful life. They never say, *"I didn't do what was necessary to make that happen."* Instead, they blame others; they say they didn't have enough resources, weren't lucky, etc. They would say anything to have an excuse for the failure. Leaders, on the other hand, take full responsibility not just for their failures, but the failure of their team. It's because leaders understand at the end of the day they are the ones who have failed. Leaders embrace the defeat and accept it as something positive that they can learn from and don't use it as an excuse for not achieving predetermined objectives.

Leaders want success for others

Every leader knows that the more they are happy and grateful for what others accomplish, the more they will have a chance to be even more successful and happier in their own life (this is because your team is getting stronger). You would want to stay in that frame of mind that wants everyone to be successful, and that's how you too will grow and become the best person you can be.

Goals

If you're taking action every single day, but you don't have a goal(s), how will you know if you've reached them? Do you even know where you are going? You must have goals; every leader has them. Goals are exciting. They keep you on track and expand your Imagination. If you have them and you're already taking steps in the direction of results, when you get there, don't stop. Set new goals that will keep you focused and continuously excited not just about that goal, but about life too!

They read and learn every day

Almost any great leader that you can think of, no matter how much they know, they continue to learn and read every single day. Leaders do this because they are aware that there's always something new to learn or develop some skills that may help them achieve a specific goal. A book might be able to elevate them to the next step or expand their consciousness and awareness. It's a habit you should want to develop; to learn and read every single day.

Leaders accept change

When a leader sees that something doesn't work, they change it. Most people are afraid of change, because change can put you outside of your comfort zone, which makes most people fearful of taking a potential risk. However, leaders are those who embrace the change and are willing to get out of their comfort zones. Change allows leaders to grow and expand. To take a risk is to know that there's no such thing as failure, only a temporary defeat. Change is inevitable in today's world, and if you want to be a leader, you have to find a way to love and embrace the changes that come.

TO – DO List

Two years ago, I saw a picture on Facebook with a board where someone had written, *"Things to do today,"* and he had about 35–40 things that he wanted to do that day. I found out later that the man who posted the picture was one of the most successful people in the world. If you want to be a leader, you have to plan your day, week, month, and even year. Sometimes you won't finish doing everything that you write down, but just having a daily list can keep you focused on priorities in your day. It keeps you on track toward your dream.

They share information

Have you ever worked in a company where you feel that your boss doesn't want to share any information with you or to help you because they don't want you to be better than them because they were afraid that you might take their position? A true leader is not scared of that. Leaders want to help and serve you. They want to share information because they know that information will help you grow. If you pay attention early enough, when your team grows, as a leader, you grow too!

Leaders talk about ideas

Every leader is open to talking about new ideas with their employees because they don't have an "*ego problem.*" Leaders don't think that they are the smartest or they know everything. Instead, they encourage the people in the organization to think about new ideas so that everyone can make progress and be more successful. I remember I was working for one person who had a construction company. He saw himself as the smartest person in the world who knew everything and anything. Whenever employees came with new ideas, he rejected them and looked at us as if we were far below him. There was no way we could come up with good ideas. Later on, he would use some of the ideas that we gave him, claiming them as his own and never gave credit where it was due. As you might have guessed, I didn't stay with him for a long time.

Leaders give recognition to others

When you work in a company, you want to feel worthy and valuable, and you want to be recognized for your hard work. A leader is one who always gives recognition to his employees. It doesn't matter if it's just a kind word, applause for achieving something, or maybe hold an event where the best workers are recognized. A leader knows that everyone looks for some recognition and always makes sure to give it.

Attitude of gratitude

Gratitude is something that every leader on this planet possesses. They are always grateful for what they have, for the people that are part of their team or company, and they work on teaching others how to be thankful in life.

Anyone can be a leader, but not anyone will do what is necessary to become a leader. All leaders are charismatic people who radiate positive energy and spread the love around them. They embrace everyone and treat workers/teammates with respect as their equal. A leader will encourage you to try new things that you haven't tried before, inspire you to move towards your goal, motivate you to grow and learn when you may have failed. Give a helping hand when a mistake is made, take time to talk when needed, share the information which could lead you to work better, or even become a leader yourself. A leader will encourage you to be a better you through motivation, experiences, and information which could also help you become a leader yourself. Leaders empower you to be who you really are and many more beautiful things.

Is there anything that you would like to add?

Future: There's one more thing. ***Leaders are committed***. What I mean by that is, a true leader has to be the last to leave the ship if things are starting to fall apart. Some people own a company and don't have enough money to pay themselves sometimes. However, as true leaders, they pay every employee and every bill that comes first. They are always the last to be paid for what they are doing. You have to be committed to not giving up no matter how bad things get. Also, you have to be committed to not letting your ego stand in your way when things work perfectly for you.

Everything else you mentioned is precisely the characteristics of a true leader.

Serge: I'm glad that we've talked about this important subject. I'm feeling it. I believe that I'm on the right path and that if I keep going, soon I'll become a true leader and successful in every facet of my life.

Future: Keep doing what you're doing. You're on the right path! I know that, and deep down in your heart, you know it too! Your book will inspire your readers; you know that?

Serge: I hope so! That's why I'm writing this material with your help. I've put a lot of effort to go into my Imagination to be able to talk with you and create something special like this book.

Future: You've mentioned that leaders read every day. That's an interesting topic to venture into. Since you're writing a book, can you tell us why someone should read?

Serge: For sure, there are plenty of reasons why everyone should read.

Why are you reading books?

"You're never alone when you're reading a book." – **Susan Wiggs**

Have you ever asked yourself why you read books? Sure there are plenty of good reasons why you should read books: for fun, for concentration, to boost your brain power, to increase your intelligence, it can make you empathetic, to help you relax, and depending on the type of book, it can help push you into taking the next steps to reach your goals. But what is your reason? What kind of books do you like?

I've never liked to read because I used to think it was boring (sounds familiar?) until I was introduced to the book *"Rich Dad Poor Dad"* - *Robert Kiyosaki* by my mentor back in 2012 who had noticed that I wasn't managing my money well. I was always complaining that I didn't know how to spend my money for the right purpose. She gave me the book and told me, *"read this and apply it as much as you can, and your financial situation will improve."* I read it a few times, and it was a really good book, but I foolishly didn't apply anything from it. As you can guess, my financial situation didn't get any better.

A few months later, I caught myself in a devastating situation. It was a time when everything fell apart in my life. I remember it was December 2013, and for about 20 days, I didn't leave my dark and quiet room because I was sad, angry, depressed, full of negative thoughts and emotions. I didn't have a job (a month before I was fired from four different jobs over the course of 25-30 days). I had no money and was in huge debt. I hardly survived that time, but once the New Year came (January 5th, 2014), I decided to change my life. I was sick and tired of being broke, angry, and alone. But I didn't know how I was going to do this.

"You can attract anything in your life…"

That idea came into my mind! A few years earlier, I had watched the movie *"The Secret"* where for the first time I heard about something called the *"Law of attraction."* I admit that at the time I couldn't understand anything from that movie, but I did manage to remember one point that said *"you can attract anything in your life…"* so now with the terrible situation I was in, I decided to apply this principle. I decided to give myself a chance to change my life. A few days after that realization, I found a job in a local restaurant, and after my first paycheck, I went to the bookstore. There, I bought a book called *"Law of Attraction" by Esther & Jerry Hicks*. You can't imagine how happy and grateful I was when I bought it.

I was so excited that I couldn't wait to get home to start reading. I remember the look on my mom's face when she watched me rush into the house, quickly said *"hello"* and went straight into my room to read. After a few pages of reading, I knew that this book would help me change my life; and finally, there was hope in my heart saying it was possible for me to do just that. I discovered that the book provided concrete steps that were described so clearly that anyone could easily understand and put them into immediate action.

Some of the steps are:

- [ ] How to use your emotional guidance system
- [ ] How to increase your magnetic power
- [ ] How to use visualization as a tool to attract your dreams
- [ ] How to best utilize the law of attraction
- [ ] How to find what you really want
- [ ] How to deliberately create what you want
- [ ] How to allow your wishes to come into your life
- [ ] How to make a clear intention in every moment

☐ As you can see, there are so many steps that helped me to transform myself and change my life. I did absolutely everything that was said, and in the space of six months, I saw the results. I saw the difference in my thinking. I found a way to heal my relationships. I shifted my awareness. I even ended up moving to another city and country; a place that I desired to move to since I first began setting my goals after reading the book. I started a new life with better and much more positive thoughts; with a new belief system, new dreams, and with the hope and faith that I can be, do and have anything that I want.

During those six months of change, I read *"Law of Attraction"* more than 50 times, but that was just the beginning of my personal growth. I was attracted to other great books and I haven't stopped reading ever since. Every single day, I spend some time reading. Mainly, I read books on personal growth and business books because these books can take me to the next step towards my goals. Also, I'm always on the lookout for books that can help me achieve a specific goal. There are thousands of books that can help you in any area that you're interested in.

As you can see through my story, it's not only important to read but also to know why you are reading specific books. These were my reasons, and my hope is for you to find value in this life example and maybe become clearer about your reasons for reading.

Future: Nicely said. I have a question for you.

Serge: Go ahead.

Future: What if someone doesn't like to read? What will you suggest to that person?

Serge: There's always an alternative. You can listen to audiobooks. No excuses man. I'm sure that you know the benefits of audiobooks.

Future: I do, but I'll rather give it to you to talk about since you're doing so well.

Serge: I would never imagine that my *Future* will flatter me like that.

Future: You can't love another until you love yourself. Is that right?

Serge: True. All right then, let's move to the next subject.

The Power of Audiobooks

How many times have you heard someone say, *"I don't have enough time to read a book?"* Are you one of those people? Do you have excuses for not reading? Well, guess what? You can listen to audiobooks wherever you are. You can always find time to listen. Listen while you are driving to work, in the shower, when you are doing laundry, when you clean the house, while in the gym, during your walk, etc. The fantastic thing about listening to an audiobook rather than just reading a book is the power to multitask with the things you are already doing in your life!

So why would you do this? Let me tell you some of my reasons for listening to the audio content (I say content because I listen to audiobooks as well as motivational/inspirational speeches). As you read in the previous chapter, everything for me started with a book called *"Law of Attraction" by Esther & Jerry Hicks* and with the movie *"The Secret."* Both had a significant impact on my life.

Because of the huge impression this book left on me, I want to listen to it all the time. When I'm on the road to work, while I'm running or simply when I don't feel like reading but still want to listen. So I downloaded the audio version of the book, and when I listen, I discover that it feels like you are face to face with the authors. I felt like a child who is lying on the bed and listening to mom's bedtime story. The experience is different from just reading; it is like being spoken to. I also remember the time I was reading the book *"Conversation with God" from Neale Donald Walsch*, I wanted to find the audio version so I could be more involved in the story. If you like this book and you haven't listened to the audio version; I highly recommend you to do it, because you'll be amazed by the narration of the conversation that happened between the author and *God*. It feels so real, but it is also so calming, easy, and relaxing to listen to and so enjoyable. I have also listened to the audio version of almost all the books I have read up until now. This is because I want to be sure that I get a full message of each and every book.

Now, let me tell you my ***three very simple reasons*** why I started listening to audio materials:

1. *My desire and willingness to work full time on myself every single day*

2. *Because I wanted to learn English*

3. *I wanted to put some positive input in my mind every day*

As I said, my ***first reason*** was the willingness (and need) to learn every single day. At the time I started reading and listening, my state of being was bad. When I say bad, I mean sad, depressed, alone, negative, terrible attitude towards everyone and everything in life, etc. My financial situation was even worse than my well-being (several thousand indebted). My relationships failed miserably. My girlfriend left me. My friends gave up on me. Even my parents thought I was just a miserable guy who didn't know how to take care of himself. Everything required change. So I decided to start working on myself and every other area of my life that needed to be improved. I started with some amazing audio materials, and there are no words that can describe the impacts that these books have had on my life at that time. Some of these books are:

- *"The Power of Intention" by Dr. Wayne Dyer*
- *"Think and Grow Rich" by Napoleon Hill*
- *"The Magic of Thinking Big" by David J. Schwartz*
- *"The Power of Now" by Eckhart Tolle*
- *"Law of Attraction" by Esther & Jerry Hicks*

- *"Conversations with God" by Neale Donald Walsch*
- *"The Seven Spiritual Laws of Success" by Deepak Chopra*
- *"The Four Agreements" by Don Miguel Ruiz and many more…*

These were the books that I listened to every single day until I saw results in my thinking, my mindset, the way I behaved, treated others, and faced various events and circumstances, etc. I'm still listening to other great audiobooks to this day that help me develop my knowledge, awareness, consciousness, and focus on taking me to the next steps in my life.

The **second reason** why I began listening to audiobooks is to learn English. Now, this may not be the same for many of you, but, when I decided to change my life, one of the goals I had was to move to Canada. I wanted to start a new life from the beginning. One of the obstacles was my inability to speak English. When I came to Canada, I knew only a few words and could maybe put together one, maybe two sentences. Honestly, my English was pretty much at level zero! However, I decided to learn and told myself that I would find a fun way to do it.

Now, before I came here, I had already read about ten personal development books, and I had read them all more than ten times (some of them more than fifty times). To the extent that I knew all these books word for word in my native language. I found the audio versions and downloaded them to my cell phone to enable me to listen while I was working, exercising, or driving to work. I had also bought the same books in English so that I could follow along. In about two months, I saw my first results. I never had a fear of speaking, even if I didn't know the language. After all the listening, I caught myself speaking English in my dreams. I began thinking in English, and soon, I was able to speak it. Though not much, that was an encouraging sign, and it motivated me to continue to learn every single day. Up until now, I'm still learning because my English is not as good as I want it to be; but every day, I'm getting closer to my goal. Through this illustration, you can see the power of audiobooks!

Now let's move to perhaps, **the most important reason** for listening to audio materials. According to psychologists, humans think between fifty to sixty thousand thoughts in a single day; and more than 85% of those thoughts are negative! Can you imagine that? I heard a speech from *Les Brown* once where he pointed out that if someone tells you *"You can't do it,"* someone has to come and tell you *"You can do it!"* seventeen times, just to neutralize that single negative statement. Therefore, you have to find a way to put some positive thoughts in your mind.

Stop watching the negative news on TV, reading about it in newspapers, or listening on the radio. Read books that can inspire you to do something worthy. Watch various seminars that can help you with your goals. Listen to audio materials that will motivate you to keep on going when you find yourself down or losing hope. You have to find a way to put positive thoughts in your mind. I know it can be hard, but you have to do whatever you can to stay positive no matter what!

It is my pure desire for you to find value in audio materials that can help you in many ways, just as it has helped me in my life. As you can see through my experience, the benefits of listening to audiobooks are enormous. Permit yourself to learn. Permit yourself to grow. There's always a way to do it. I encourage you to start listening to motivational speeches when you exercise, business books when you are driving from home to work and back, inspirational books when you're at home and whenever you can. I can guarantee that if you use this strategy and hold the discipline to listen the audio material every single day, your life will improve in every area!

Future: I'm so proud of what you're becoming. You'll be a fantastic speaker, author, and teacher. I can see why we had a dream to teach everyone to become a better person.

Serge: Everyone and everything can be a teacher. They come in all forms and shapes in this world.

Future: Like?

Man in the mirror

> *"Smile in the mirror. Do that every morning, and you'll start to see a big difference in your life." – **Yoko Ono***

"When a student is ready, a teacher will appear."

Serge: Sometimes, we are not aware that there are *teachers* all around us, in different shapes and forms. Sometimes they come in the form of song that you've heard, a movsie you've watched, an event/situation that you've just witnessed, an interaction between animals, and even a passage in a book. This subject is about one *"teacher"* that came to me in the form of a song that I heard a long time ago. This song is *Michael Jackson's* **Man in the Mirror.**

"I'm gonna make a change for once in my life. It's gonna feel real good, gonna make a difference, gonna make it right…"

Now, I've heard this song dozens of times before, but it has been only a few months since I started to listen to the lyrics. It's something that we all do, and it is fun when you suddenly notice the true meaning coming to you. I had the idea to start a business for a while, and one day as I was going home from the gym, I was listening to the song and the words *"I'm gonna make a change for once in my life…"* literally triggered an inspiration within me to make a change. Coincidentally at that very moment, my heart had been telling me the time had come to do something that could make a difference not just in my own life, but in the lives of others; and BAM! The combination of heart and song just hit me.

"I'm starting with the man in the mirror…"

When I had the feeling that I wanted to make a change, my mind immediately started asking the question, *"How are you planning to do it?"* You have to know that the mind is designed to keep you safe and comfortable, it doesn't want you to take risks and get out from your comfort zone, and this is exactly what was happening to me at the time. However, you and I are bigger than our minds, and we have to listen to our hearts, as this is a real source of self-power. Getting back to the story, when my mind came up with the question, I immediately replied, *"I'm starting with changing myself!"*

When changing anything in your life, you have to start from ground zero - yourself. As I mentioned in the previous topics, you have to change your thinking, your words, and lastly your behavior. What do I mean by that? When you have a clear vision of what you want to do or who you want to be, and you start taking actions towards that vision, at some point, you'll face a challenge that can cause a temporary stop in doing what is necessary to achieve your goal. Sometimes, these challenges can even cause you to give up on your dream. This is because, if you jump into changing your life with the same mindset, you will deal with these challenges in ways you knew in the past. You can't overcome an obstacle if your mind is filled with fear. You have to change gears at this point and become solution oriented. You have to work on yourself!

Revert to some of the methods we have talked about in the past to keep you focused. Reading books that will help you grow your consciousness and develop your mind to think differently about the challenges, or listen to motivational audio books that will help you stay excited or the ones that can help you learn new techniques to become solution oriented. If you're eager, you can go to live seminars or communicate with the leaders you admire through Social Media so they can inspire you to be the best that you can be.

"If you wanna make the world a better place, take a look at yourself and then make a change..."

When I was a kid, I remember someone asking me what I wanted to do when I grew up. Even in my younger years, I replied that I want to make the world a better place for everyone who lives on the planet. I believe that this is something all kids want. I believe that =kindness is built into our DNA. We all inherently want to do something that will make a difference in the world; to leave a legacy or make some contributions that will be remembered for generations to come. I love what **Horace Mann** once said – *"We should be ashamed to die until we make a major contribution to humankind."* Ask yourself, what is your view of the world? What difference can you make? What contribution can you make to the world?

When you do something for yourself, you feel great. But when you do something for others, you feel terrific, fulfilled, valuable. When showing your kindness toward another, you can touch their heart and inspire them to do the same for another. Whenever you do something good, trust me, it will be noticed. Even the observers will feel the positive and good emotions in their hearts and will be inspired to do something similar for another. You're already making a difference; when you give a compliment; a silent blessing to someone who behaved poorly towards you; when you give those in need food to eat or money for a place to sleep; when you help someone realize how great they are, and when you help your friend to overcome the challenges they are facing among many others. These are all small examples of a bigger picture when it comes to helping others. I'm sure that when you help others find happiness by making a difference in their lives; you'll be able to find it in your life as well.

Remember, everything starts with you. One of my favorite quotes is, *"You don't get in life what you want; you get in life what you are!"* Meaning, whatever you are producing right now in your life is a reflection of you. Whatever relationships you have, they are a reflection of you. Whatever you may be doing, is a direct reflection of you. Your attitude about the world and its people is a reflection of your attitude about yourself. Therefore, whatever you want to do or be, you must realize that the first step for change starts with you. Only then can you change the rest of your life.

Do something that you've never done before. Go somewhere you've never been before. Pass your limits. I know you can do it. When you change yourself, you can inspire a change in other people, and you can change the world!

In conclusion to this topic, I leave you with some more lyrics from *"Man in the Mirror"* by the late *Michael Jackson*:

> *"I'm starting with the man in the mirror*
> *I'm asking him to change his ways*
> *And no message could have been any clearer*
> *If you want to make the world a better place*
> *Take a look at yourself and then make a change."*

Future: That's an amazing inspirational song.

Serge: It is one of my favorites. But when I think about all these people who want to make a change, there are always those (who I like to call *"Dream killers"*) who will give you all of the reasons why someone cannot change.

Future: Well, they will always be around us, but we have the power to choose if we are going to listen to them or not.

Serge: The problem is that most people don't believe they have that power. I want to talk more about this.

Future: Go ahead.

Serge: Let's go.

Dream killers

"Dad, can you teach me how to play the guitar? – Son, you're not talented
enough to play it. I want to open a business! – How are you going to do
that when you don't have money! You didn't finish college, and you don't have the
experience to do what you want to do. I want to travel the world and become a motivational speaker! – What? What about your friends and family? How are you going
to do it? You have never given a speech before, you're not good at communication, and
you're the kind of person who can't travel wherever he wants."

I can go on with thousands of examples of when you heard about someone
who has a dream, and when that person shares the dream; there's immediately a
dream killer who will tell you all the reasons why they shouldn't do that, or why
they can't do it or remind them that they don't have what it takes to do it, etc. I
could go on with thousands of examples where dream killers stopped a person
from following their dream. Are you one of many who have a dream or goal but
have heard so many times all of the reasons why you can't have it or achieve it?
Guess what? You are not alone! We all have these kinds of people around us. You
have to understand that the first people who will discourage you (sad to even
say this) will be your friends and your family. Some of them will do that mostly
unconsciously, and without any intention of putting you down; while others
will do it not because you can't, but because they don't believe that you can have
your dream that's not within the parameters of their belief system.

I believe that one of the reasons why dream killers want you to move away from your dream is fear. In other words, their consciousness is rooted in fear, and this is a nutshell for a frightened person. They don't want you to get ahead because if you do, you will become a mirror to them. All of a sudden, they have to look at you. They know that they are smart as you, they are educated as you, they've known you your whole life maybe and all of a sudden you become a mirror; and when they look in the mirror, they see themselves, except they're not where you are. And sometimes they can resent you because of that. It causes problems in friendships, in families, and that's all part of moving forward.

I remember a few years ago before I came to Canada, I got back to my hometown to be with my family before I leave, and I was going out with my friends to celebrate with them because I knew that a few years would pass before I would see them again. We were talking about life and things like that, and one of them asked me what I was planning to do in Canada and why I was going so far away in the first place. I explained to him what my dream was and what I wanted to do; I remember clearly; the moment I said what my dream was, he started to talk about all of the reasons why I couldn't have that dream. He was speaking on and on; but honestly, I didn't care what he said. I told him my reasons, motivations and I started to give him a list why I believe that I can have my dream, and that was the moment I realized something; although he knew me for 15 years, he realized in that moment that my way of thinking was something he hadn't heard before and because I had moved ahead, he was somehow cast down because he'll stay where he is. And that's part of life.

You'll lose some people along the way because you'll grow and expand and they may not. They will not understand what you are doing or where you're going. You may find that while you raise your level of awareness, other people that you hang around with are probably not. Now, you may ask, if you lose or remove all the people who are not supporting you or not wanting you to move on, is this a lonely journey? Well, think about your life; your 1st-grade friend is probably not your best friend now, and that's what happens in life. Certain things change. Relationships are changing. Don't worry about that, because when you're growing, you'll find new and more exciting people to hang out with.

The next reason you should move away from dream and passion killers is; **you don't want to sell your dream to somebody else's opinion or somebody else's dream**. I encourage you to surround yourself with people who want you to grow (we'll talk about **Circle around you** later in this book), to learn; people who have dreams, goals, who are excited and who want more from life. If you don't have those kinds of people in your environment right now, be patient. The right people will show up. You'll be attracted to those who have similar interests. When you find them, you'll see what a good relationship can do for you. You will also see how many people are out there just like you; who feel and think the same way.

To be clear, I'm not suggesting that you should move all the negative people from your life because there are some of them you've known for over ten years, but you can limit the time you spend with them. In my case, when I realized what I wanted to do and where I wanted to be, I decided to make a radical change. I removed all the negative people from my life, and now when I meet somebody, I always try to meet that person as much as I can. But once I notice that a person doesn't provide any value or is always complaining and don't have anything to live for, I'm moving away. It may sound harsh, but it works for me. We are all different, but I'm suggesting you; surround yourself with quality people who will accept you and encourage you to be who you are; people who will support you and be there whenever you need them.

If you want to protect your dream, you have to do that with everything you have. If that means moving away from some of your friends, so be it. Anything or anyone that is taking you further away from your dream has to go. Be aware of dream and passion killers. You should know that every person that is meant to be with you on this journey will choose a higher road with you. Yes, a tougher road, but also a much more rewarding one. You want your life to mean something. You want to be able to look back and say, *"Yeah, I made some tough decisions, but they were the right decisions!"* Don't let anyone steal your dreams!

Future: I think you should make a video on *"dream killers."*

Serge: Are you implying that I'll do it in the near future? Because I know that you know that was something we've been thinking about for a while.

Future: I'm not implying anything. Doing so would mean that I can predict a future which is not true since this whole conversation is going on in your *Imagination.*

Serge: I thought so.

Future: What else do you want to talk about?

Serge: Is there a blessing in a disappointment?

Future: For sure, every disappointment brings a hidden blessing with it.

Serge: Would you tell us a little more about it?

Future: It would be my pleasure.

The Blessings of Disappointments

"Men's best success comes after their disappointments."
— *Henry W. Beecher*

When I was your age, I used to ponder about life, and I discovered that... Sometimes, to succeed in life, you need **ENEMIES**... Yes!!!

You need people who will mock you so that you can run to God. You need people who will try to intimidate you so that you can be courageous. You need people who will say *"NO"* so that you can learn how to be independent... to stand on your feet.

You need people who will disappoint you so that you can put all your trust and faith in God alone. You need people who will work towards you losing that job so that you can start your own business.

You need people who will sell your *"Joseph"* so that *"you"* can get to Egypt and be a Prime Minister in a strange land of captivity. You need a cruel landlord so that you won't be too comfortable in someone else's house; then you can get your own home.

But sometimes, when we are disappointed, we feel very bad and we tend to remain in that condition; not knowing that the end point of disappointment is the *beginning of your accomplishments.*

Understand this – Every disappointment you have comes with a blessing! However, it is not everyone that partakes in this blessing.

You can't see a new OPEN door while you are still putting all your attention, time, and energy in trying to force the closed one to open. Again I say, *"No disappointment can ever come without an attached blessing!"*

When the disappointment comes, thank God for it and tell Him to open your eyes to see the new blessing that He has in store for you! *Disappointment is phase one, while accomplishment is phase two.* I doubt if one can bypass the phases. That is why it is called a **BREAKTHROUGH**. Something must **BREAK** so that you can go **THROUGH**!

Serge: I've read over and over again in *Napoleon Hill's* books that every adversity comes with a seed of an equivalent advantage; which means that in every disaster there's a hidden blessing and we have to open our minds to be able to see it. We need to train our mind to see the good in everything, and through practice, it will be able to recognize good in everything that we may consider as bad.

Future: When was the time you reach the next level in any area of your life till now?

Serge: After I had a temporary defeat or disappointment.

Future: You'll fail at some point in your life, but if you get back on your feet and keep your attitude positive, you'll experience a breakthrough.

Serge: I found this very true. My experience has taught me this.

Future: Why don't you tell us something about the experience?

Serge: What do you mean?

Future: Tell us about *"experience."* What does that word mean to you, and how do you look at it in total?

Serge: That's an interesting subject. Never thought about it but let's see what I can say about it.

Experience

"*Experience is the teacher of all things.*" ***Julius Caesar***

Sometimes we don't know what talents we have until we discover them, even accidentally. I never did any writing in my life, mainly because my teachers told me in high school that I was a terrible writer, and honestly, I never had any interest in writing. But when I decided to launch my website, part of it was writing blogs, and I remember thinking about how I was going to do it; since I've never done it before, and particularly not in English. My good friend told me, *"just start it and everything will develop by itself."* I started writing in the form of speeches that I would deliver one day, and the more I wrote, the more experience I gained, and the better I became. Now I'm writing only when I get inspired; I'm not trying to force anything. When I get an idea, I sit down, switch on my laptop, put some beautiful music on in the background, and start writing from inspiration precisely as I did with this book. Only a year ago was I doing it by forcing myself. Now I have the experience, and for that reason, I've learned that experiences teach you not just about writing (in this example), but how to live your life.

Experience is the teacher of all things

When I look at my life, I can see now that it was shaped in part through some unpleasant or rather bad experiences. One thing about those negative experiences is that they don't tell you that they are developing you. It doesn't seem like they are shaping you, but in fact, they are shaping you. Who you are today is the result of all the things that happened in your life in the past, whether they were good or bad.

I remember when I was about the age of eleven, I was playing with some kids in the backyard, and we were teasing and making fun of one another. But all of a sudden, a kid called me for no reason *"stinky boy."* I didn't care about it at first until the next day all the kids I knew started calling with that nickname. I was wondering what was going on; and a few days later, I believed it was the first time I began to experience Hell on Earth. At eleven years old, you can't understand many things, nor are you grown enough in your mind to realize that you have the power of choice about what you'll do or how you are going to feel about certain things. What happened is that for the next ten or eleven years of my life, I was experiencing hell in my mind because the bullying got out of control, and it seemed like a whole city was teasing me, calling me all kinds of different names; it was a terrible act of bullying that I couldn't get over at that time.

I had trouble finding real friends, and of course, you can guess that I had difficulties to find even a girlfriend because girls were terrified of my *"famous nickname"* and didn't want to risk being bullied like I was. It came to the point where I didn't want to go out, didn't want to talk to anyone. I was always hiding behind the corner whenever I saw kids that I knew would laugh at me or make some jokes about me. Since my parents didn't have time to ever sit down with me, I never told them what I was going through. Although I'm 29 years old now, I still believe that they have no idea what I've been through in my life. My point is that back then, I didn't know why I had to go through all of that. Now I believe I'm getting closer to understanding the reason for all of that.

I clearly remember the darkest moments of my life. It was the year 2013, where everything started to fall apart for me. Back then, I wasn't the person that I am today. I must confess now that, because of that experience (of losing my friends, family, clients, jobs), I was able to become who I intended to be. I was a liar, didn't care about the people in my business (only about the money). I was not a good friend nor a good boyfriend. I think I wasn't a good brother or son or grandson at all because all I cared about was my interest at the end of everything. I was so selfish that I didn't care about anybody or anything. Well, life is like a wheel. Today you have it all; tomorrow you can lose it all. That's exactly what happened to me. My girlfriend left me. My business was dwindling, and my friends gave up on me.

Even my parents gave up in a way. All of a sudden, I was broke. Several thousands of dollars indebted; my business was gone. My partners didn't want to have anything to do with me. My clients closed the door on me. I lost my friends, my family's trust, and I found myself in a devastating situation. I couldn't understand why it happened or what I had done to deserve all of that. I made so many wrong moves that led me to that devastation, and I thought that wasn't my fault (sounds familiar?). I was blaming everyone and everything for my new situation. I couldn't understand why I had to go through that process. Probably sometimes you too can't understand why you are going through all of that; that process where everything seems hopeless and meaningless.

There's a reason why we had to go through all we went through. There are certain things that you don't understand about 'that process' until you've endured it, suffered through it, cried through it, made mistakes in it, had setbacks in it, almost collapsed in it, and almost run from it. After you have experienced it, and you see that you did overcome all, you come to a point where you can see that it was necessary for you to become the person you are today.

Julius Caesar said that *experience is the teacher of all things.* If you knew the whole story and the transformation that took place in my life, you'd be convinced that if I could change, anyone can change.

Nothing takes the place of experience

You've already survived 100% of your worst days up until now. Isn't that a good proof that you are strong enough to go through anything? When you go through some rough times, you feel sorry for yourself. But after you've gone through it, that is; if you endured it, you would realize that it was good you were afflicted in that way.

In a more profound sense, everything that is happening to us is exactly what we need to do something or become someone that we want to be. Life can be hard. Life can be brutal. Life has a way of making you shut your mouth. Life will silence you, shut you down. I doubt there are people who don't experience the feeling of being overwhelmed by life itself. Sometimes you have ten issues, and they all hit you at the same time. And that can be crazy. Sometimes, you think that if your phone rings one more time or you get another email, another bill, face the same problem again or failed in doing something, you'd be destroyed internally. It can be challenging to stay strong when you're secretly worried to death about some things. But that's the time your experience will take place. *Experience will give you hope.* Because of all the past things you've been through, you'll know in your heart that you'll get through all that is happening to you right now.

Experience is patience

Not sure that I'm the right person who should tell you about patience since I'm still completely impatient about many things. However, sometimes God put you on hold so you can gain the necessary experience. You have to go through all of that. If you can fully accept this moment as it truly is, regardless of the state of being (good or bad), you'll have the experience to sail through that situation if it happens again. There's a quote that says, *"Patience is not about waiting, but the ability to keep a good attitude while waiting."* It means whatever you want is on its way to you. It is! I know because I've already experienced it!

Experience is your testimony

Now let me clarify what I mean by that. You've probably heard thousands of times when somebody tells you, *"I know that because I'm older than you. I've been your age, but you haven't been mine, and I've been through that"* or something similar. What they don't tell you is that the story they tell is their own experience, which doesn't mean you'll experience the same at all. Most people will share with you their testimony in a negative way because most people are negative. I hate to say that, but that's the truth. Just look around you, and you'll see what I'm talking about. When somebody asks me about something that I've been through, I always reply that I'll share my story, but I want that person to know that was my experience which means, it is not an indication that they will have the same experience. No matter how similar each situation may look like, the truth is that they are different because they occurred in different times, different places and with different people, in different circumstances, motives, events, etc. I always mention the kind of person I was at that moment, and the kind of mindset I had back then. For example, I can share how awfully I was dealing with bullying when I was a kid because I didn't know how to react and had nobody to teach me. But now I know, and I can help some kid learn how to face bullying. Even if you face something you've never faced before using your experience; try to do whatever you can to deal with it and always keep your mind and attitude positive because your experience is your testimony; and your testimony says that you've survived 100% of your worst days and you'll survive this situation too!

You don't know what you got until all hell breaks loose. You don't know what you can take until the pressure is applied to your life. You don't know what you can endure until people who you loved so much move away from you. You don't know how much courage you have until you've been under fire and struggle. You can't learn what's in you sitting on the bed and watching Netflix all day long. You don't know how strong you are until life hits you and puts you in your lowest point ever. You don't know how good you are until you experience how bad you can be. You don't know how kind you are until you experience how badly people can treat you. You don't know what's inside of you until your back is against the wall; that's when the 'real you' shows up. All the experiences you've accumulated till now you'll use instinctively at the moment you need them the most. When you don't know what to do, where to go… *Experience kills off the weaknesses.*

Experiences are important

Sometimes I wish I could live my life over again with the experience that I have right now. Do you know how much better I would sleep at night? If I can go back and tell my younger self who was sitting on the side of the bed crying about what somebody said, I would go to him and tell him *"Just go to bed and don't worry about it!"* Do you know how much better I would feel and how much better I would sleep? Do you have any idea how much better I would manage the level of energy I've invested in worries, doubts, fears, low confidence, anxiety, etc.? How many things I would do differently? I can bet that you think the same thing. By the time you were thinking if you'll able to have a wife and two kids and be able to do anything worthy in your life, you would go back and tell yourself *"Oh yes you can!"* You know what I'm talking about. So stop! Don't think about the past. Embrace your life as it is and use your experience to rewrite your future; to create it in a way you will enjoy every second of this delicious thing called life.

Experience is your resume!

You've been sick before – you made it. You've been broke before – you made it. You've been broken hearted before – you made it. You cried all night – but you made it. You've been lied on – but you made it. You've been rejected – but you made it. You've been betrayed – but you made it. You've been alone before – but you made it. You've been afraid before – but you made it. Do you see how much experience you have? Each one of us has the testimony that shows what we have been through. That's proof that you're stronger than you can imagine! *Experience is one of your greatest strengths!*

*"The only source of knowledge is experience." - **Albert Einstein***

Sometimes, I teach people things I've never done before which means you need to read a lot, do research, study to be able to help and encourage people, but nothing takes the place of experience. You find out through experience that some things are not as you thought they would be. When you were a teenager, you thought you knew everything. But when you had to put everything into practice, you found out that it wasn't as easy as you thought it was. What you learned in school will later become irrelevant when the real school (read: life after school) begins. *Everything will come down to your experience*. After reading all of this, I have a question for you:

What are you going to do with the time you have left and with the experience you have?

If you don't reposition yourself, you can miss the best time of your life. What I mean is that we have got to change the way we think, change the way we function, change the way we feel and the way we deal with issues. The reason we need to do this is that many times we are stuck between the lines of limited people, thinking, ideas and philosophies; and there's something creative inside of you that says *"I'm more than this! I know I can do more, be more, and have more!"* Of course, you'll have to gain the courage to stand out from the crowd and be who you are. You have to break through the barriers and limitations and get outside of the box because something good is about to happen in your life. So you have to take it (whatever that is) one day at a time and when you get to the end of the day you say, *"I'm not finished, but I've done everything that I'm supposed to do for this day, for this time, for this season."* With all my heart, I want you to see what's inside of you and start living the life that you desire. One day at a time. You still got something awesome inside of you.

Let me give you the words from not just my favorite speaker, but teacher as well - *TD Jakes* says: *"You haven't sung your greatest song. You haven't written your greatest book. You are yet to have your greatest victory. You haven't had the greatest moment. You haven't seen everything you need to see. You haven't had your greatest thought, written your greatest idea, and dreamt your best dream. You haven't laughed your best laugh, haven't experienced your best day yet; neither have you had your best experiences yet — it's somewhere inside of you! There are all kinds of things locked up inside of you that are about to come out for such a time as this! The time is right. The stage is set. The conditions are in order, and something awesome is about to happen in your life! Don't let anybody tell you that you're too young. Don't let anybody tell you that you're too old. Don't let anybody tell you what you should do with your life because your experience will help you along the way."*

Even if I don't know you, my experience will tell me this much about you:

> ***You're a MIRACLE looking for a place to happen!***
> ***You're a TRUTH looking for a place to be spoken!***
> ***You're a JOY searching for a place to brighten!***
> ***You're a TESTIMONY looking for a place to be delivered!***
> ***You're a LOVE waiting on a place to manifest!***
> ***Every day you wake up in the morning is a sign – The best is yet to come!***

And this is something that I know for sure!

Future: Boy, you are inspired!

Serge: I truly am!

Future: I thought you had never thought about this subject?

Serge: Hah, I didn't know I had this stuff in me! I'm surprised by all these words that came from my *Imagination.*

Future: I like *TD Jakes* words!

Serge: He had and still has a great influence on my way of thinking.

Future: The *Human mind* is so powerful. It looks like you had a breakthrough in your thinking thanks to him.

Serge: It seems so. I'm grateful I had a chance to hear him speaking, and also listening to his inspirational speeches every day.

Speaking of breakthrough, I wanted to ask you about that subject. How can you have a breakthrough in any area of your life?

Future: That seems like our next subject. Is that what you want to talk about?

Serge: Absolutely! That would be great!

Future: Let me share something with your readers.

How to make a quantum leap in your life

From a scientific point of view, a quantum leap is the abrupt change of a particle element from one state to another. In physics, a quantum leap or quantum jump is a change of an electron within the atom from one energy state to the next. Regarding day-to-day living, a quantum leap is a sudden highly significant advance; a ***breakthrough***. A breakthrough is breaking the barrier from something that you've struggled with for a long time. You say that you're going to change, you're going to stop smoking, lose weight, find that person that you desire, you're going to make a profit, but when the time comes you hold back; and then it finally happens. You have a breakthrough! *A Breakthrough is a moment in time when the impossible becomes possible!*

Quantum leap in personal growth

*Quantum leaps in personal growth require a **strong radical shift** from one mindset to another!* There may be some small steps leading to that shift, but at some point, there's a big change, and it happens instantly. A moment of clarity suddenly hits you, and you know what you have to do. The quantum leap occurs, and from that moment on, you're never the same again. Some of these leaps appear more gradual than others, but virtually all of them can be traced back to that moment of decision. Even before you manifest this change in your physical reality, you immediately know you're not the same anymore.

For me, this moment happened when I attended a personal development seminar at my old company back in 2012. I remember the speaker was someone who had already been in the company for a few years and had become one of the most successful in the field. I listened as he spoke about something that I had never heard of before (dreams, goals, etc.), and I remember saying to myself that one day I want to be at his level. However, I can say that the real breakthrough happened on the 5th of January, 2014, when I decided to change my life completely. It was a breakthrough for me because it created the quantum leap that would lead me to never stop reading, educating myself, and finding the knowledge that would grow my awareness and develop my consciousness.

A Quantum leap requires a large amount of consistent input and energy. Most of the time, when people pursue personal growth, they don't invest enough time and energy in a consistent direction to achieve that quantum leap. You need to exert some effort in that particular direction of where you want to grow, and you need to consistently sustain it until you achieve your quantum leap. If you stop short, you'll likely fall right back to where you started.

Quantum leap in business

Quantum leaping gives you the ability to compress time, to boost your efforts to the point that is so big you soar to your next best level. You seemingly go from point A to point Z in a single bound.

What stops you from quantum leaping in business? You're not sure why you're doing what you're doing. You see the opportunities only after they have passed. You can't see the bigger vision. You live from your old stories, allowing the past to dictate your present (and thus, your future). Your fear is bigger than your trust, your resistance stronger than your flow and your limits suffer because of the risk of the unknown.

One of my friends once told me, *"your business can grow only as fast as you do."* By growing yourself, you grow your business. The mystery that is in plain sight is that your growth opportunities reflect throughout all aspects of your life, including your business. What you see in your business as a challenge is a mirror of your life challenges; this includes your revenue.

When you struggle with limiting beliefs, distorted paradigms, and inner conflicts, they block the flow of success in your life and your business benefits. However, if you choose to express your unique motivations and messages in a focused way that promises and delivers value to people who are looking forward to improving their lives, your business is successful. When you're using your business to grow your life, you are successful.

You will always attract what you need to get in your next best level. The secret is in building the intensity to make it happen successfully, and that happens as a direct result of clarity. Therefore you have to know what you want to do with your business and where you want to go.

Quantum leap in relationships

Are you tired of being alone? Do you have conflicts in your life with other people, including the members of your family? Are you tired of continually struggling with relationships?

There is a way to make a breakthrough in relationships as well, and that is to use relationships for their intended purpose. But first, you must make a quantum leap in the relationship you have with yourself. I made my breakthrough when I applied what I had learned in the book *"Conversations with God" by Neale Donald Walsch*. In this book, relationships and their purpose are explained so clearly that anyone can understand. All of my beliefs and knowledge about relationships came from that book. Now let me ask you a few questions. How do you treat yourself? How do you talk to yourself? Do you love yourself?

If you can't love yourself, you really can't love another. Many people make the mistake of seeking love for themselves through the love of another. I remember times when I wondered why nobody loved me. I thought, if I loved others, they would love me and then I would be lovable enough that I could love myself. Of course, the truth was that I hated myself more because I felt that no one could love me.

You have to start to love yourself as who you indeed are and then you'll be open for the rest of the world to love you. Learn to honor, cherish, and love yourself. First, see yourself as worthy before you can start to see another as worthy. See yourself as blessed before you can see others as blessed.

When you finally start to love and appreciate who you are, then you'll be able to make a quantum leap in your relationships with others. ***Everything begins with you***. There will always be challenging moments in relationships, but don't try to avoid them. Instead, welcome them gratefully as an opportunity to decide and be who you are.

If you want to change anything in your life and make a quantum leap in any area of your life, you must first change your way of thinking; or to be more specific, to change the beliefs that you hold in your mind.

It's easy to take small steps to do a little more than what you're doing, but if you want to make a quantum leap, you have to stretch the beliefs that you hold. All the beliefs you have in your thoughts, you must keep nurturing! With small steps, you're not entirely changing your beliefs; you're just expanding them a little bit at a time. If you want a *Quantum leap*, you must release your old beliefs and adopt a new one. It requires exaggerated contrast, which will cause dramatic propulsion of your desire and will produce amazing results.

To conclude this topic, I want to leave you a definition that my *Present* invented of a quantum leap:

"A desire that becomes a burning obsession that moves you to an inspired action that can produce massive results in a short period, and that is called – Quantum leap!" - **Srdjan Bogicevic**

Serge: Again, you make me feel so good. Especially when I see the quotes that come from my mind; and by the way that's some good stuff! I think that people need to be more radical in their ways of changing their thoughts!

Future: You can say that. But what most people need to do to witness a breakthrough in anything is to get over a breaking point.

Serge: What do you mean by *"get over a breaking point"*?

Breaking point

F*uture:* There's a moment in your life when you say, *"I can't do this anymore. I can't take this anymore. I don't have the strength to continue. I'm not strong enough to keep going. This is too hard. I just want to quit. I don't know what to do."* All of us have been there and have experienced the same thing you're experiencing right now. In fact, we experience this every now and then. People reach their breaking point in different ways, and if you dig deep enough, you will discover how stress plays an essential role in getting us to a breaking point. Stress is a part of life, but it's not life.

Too much stress is bad for you but sometimes can lead you to a breaking point. A point where you either shatter internally or externally. You may have a business that has one million dollars in annual revenue, but you can't break past that. You can't make more money, and there is a reason for that. There's a reason why some marriages last thirty years while others last only three years and then fall apart ending in divorce. There's a reason why you're still not living the life that you desire, and you're not where you want to be. If you don't learn how to master the breaking point, you may have many ventures, but you might not have massive success in any of those areas; because you haven't mastered the breaking point. As a result, every time life runs you to a breaking point; you'll quit. You'll back away and run. You'll say *"This is too hard"*; *"This is too emotional"*; *"This is too stressful"*; and you'll back away.

Everything you've gone through in the past few months or years has prepared you for what is coming, and you're right on the verge if you can master the breaking point. What most of us do when we get to the breaking point is to go back to the default settings. We back away to the safety arena; to the comfort zone. Until you change your default, you'll always go back to being who you were because you never changed your mind. Every time you get to the breaking point, you'll need a new mind to break through.

I remember years ago when I was sure that my parents were going to get a divorce because they came to the point where they had to either change themselves or go on their separate ways. Somehow, with the help of God, they managed to stay together, and today they're happier than ever. They survived many breaking points. Years ago, I came to one of my biggest and hardest breaking points. I discovered at that moment something that I didn't know I possessed (at least not to that extent) and that was *courage*. To get up, change your country, leave everything behind, and go far away from the safety of your home. I had to start my life over in another country where I didn't speak the language, had no job, and was completely alone. I can see now how courageous a move that was and, as you can see, I managed to survive that breaking point.

*Jeremiah 29:11, "For I know the plans I have for you," declares **the Lord**, "plans to prosper you and not to harm you, plans to give you hope and a future."*

It does not matter where you start; it only matters where you finish. I believe if you know how to do something, God knows where you will do it, where you'll fit in. *The difference between the start and finish is how you handle the **breaking point**.* Every successful person in any area will tell you that he/she is there because they survived the hard times. They broke through their fears, challenges, obstacles, temporary defeats, and they survived the breaking points. In other words, God has a plan for you. There's a reason why you are going through different challenges. If you look a few years back, the person you are today is because your past has shaped you and if you look even deeper, you'll notice that you've already broken through many breaking points to come close to where you are today. So don't give up. Be strong because your work will be rewarded. Your life will be rewarded. The only thing you have to do is to defeat your enemy, and that is the enemy in your mind who tells you all of the reasons why you should quit, get depressed, isolate yourself, go back to default.

One thing that the *enemy* is determined to do when you are at the breaking point is to isolate you. If he can isolate you, he can terminate you. Every time you isolate yourself without knowing it, you terminate your dreams. We all know what men do when they are at the breaking point when they are pushed and can't take it anymore. We go back to work. And work. And work. And work. Why? Because it gives us a sense of responsibility. Yes, we get frustrated, we get depressed, we get angry, but because we have allowed our enemy to control us, we believe that more work will save us which is a false belief. Instead of changing our mind and gain more courage we back away and run. What we all need in those moments are people who can help us, who will lend us a hand, who will say *"Yes, you can! You'll break through!"* Who will touch you and say, *"I believe in you, I know you can make it!"*

Matthew 18:20, "For where two or more are gathered in my name, there I am with them."

Your dream cannot give birth by itself. You'll never get beyond the breaking point by yourself. That's why it is essential to have your board of friends, your mastermind, focus group, support system, call it whatever you want. When your hope is in the future, your support system will give you power in the present. But sometimes we believe that we are the only one who can do something, and no one else is capable of doing it. One of the reasons is that we are after profit. We don't see the purpose, and because we don't understand what our purpose is, our mind is not open to partner with somebody. We can see one example of this if we look at private businesses. Sometimes we see a hair salon in one building, a nail salon in another building, beauty shop in the third building, massage in the fourth. These businesses are all paying for rents, competing for similar markets of customers, taking on their business costs entirely on their own. If these businesses thought more about how they could work as a team, to share expenses, rent, and also customers, they would increase their profitability. They struggle to be profitable at times because instead of focusing on partnership and collaboration, they're focused on competition. As a consequence, meeting some of their goals becomes more difficult.

The only thing wrong with your dream is that you want to do it by yourself, and I had that problem too. I always thought that I could break through my breaking points alone and that all my dreams would come true by doing it all by myself. While I'm speaking about this chapter, my *Present* is looking for a partnership because he finally understands that he can't go where he wants alone. He truly understands his purpose. He knows what it is. Once you know your purpose, your mind can conceive the ability to partner. My *Present* is writing this fantastic book, but he'll not be able to publish it by himself. He'll need a group of people that will help him along the way to do that and also to achieve his goals.

Yes, he is at the breaking point. He has doubts. He's stuck. However, He also knows that if he perseveres and keeps going, eventually the idea will pop up into his mind that will help him break through. I know that. I believe that with all my heart. I believe that *with God all things are possible*, and if you have faith, everything will fall into place. ***Anything is possible to those who believe!***

Serge: Well, thank you for telling everyone that I have fears and doubts because it is true. But also I have faith that everything will be alright!

Future: Just because your circumstances don't reflect it right now, it doesn't mean you don't have it. Believe in yourself and do what you have to do. Don't let the current circumstances define you. Don't let life change your name. Don't give power to your breaking point that will hold you back and pull away from your dream. Say right now to yourself with power and conviction, *"I'm strong enough to go through this!"* and close your eyes and visualize with strong faith that you can do it!

YOU CANNOT BE A CHAMPION UNTIL YOU'VE SURVIVED A BREAK-ING POINT!

Serge: Wow I guess that a lot of this stuff you got from the legendary *Bishop TD Jakes*?

Future: You can say that he inspires your *Imagination*. And that's a good sign. You have to know that everything you know you picked up from somebody else and translates in your own words is an inspiration.

Serge: That's why sometimes, I wonder where are all these words come from. What you're saying is that some words or in this case my book is written partly thanks to somebody else's words?

Future: Absolutely.

Serge: But that means that I'm stealing somebody else's words? I don't think I like that.

Future: How many books have you read until now and realized that some of them are almost the same? Same subjects - only differently said. Do you think that other authors are writing only their own words? We've talked about the rapport between people. When you spend some time with somebody, be aware that you'll pick their words, thoughts or even behavior. When you're reading so many books, you are gathering a bunch of information, and when you talk about them, you'll notice that you're saying all of it in your unique way.

Your Imagination is limitless. It's an infinite field of all kinds of information that you don't even know it is there, that had been stored all your life. Also, you have the power to tap into the *Universal Imagination* and pick any information you need at any time! You go to a seminar and learn something new. When somebody asks you to tell them what you've learned, you explain them in a way that you've perceived it, and sometimes your words will come easier to somebody else's ear than if that person tells the same. Did you notice that sometimes you and your friend will say something (basically the same thing) to your third friend on a different way, and that third person will understand the version that you stated but not the version that other people have said?

Serge: That's true. I was always wondering why that is.

Future: Because you have the power to translate someone else's words in your unique way - some people will understand only when you say it, and somebody else may not. Trust me when I say that God was sending the same messages over and over again a thousand times across thousands of years with thousands of different sources, and He will continue to send it over and over again until all of humanity receive it. You'll have thousands of people that will share the same message in their unique way. So don't worry about the words that are coming from your *Imagination*. It is as it is supposed to be.

Serge: You've mentioned that when you spend some time with the people around you, you're picking their thoughts, words or even behavior. Are you talking about *Napoleon Hill's* principle called *"Mastermind"*?

Future: That's exactly what I mean.

Serge: I find that very accurate! It sometimes happens that I say something and immediately think, *"where did I get these words from?"* There were many situations that I had these thoughts and wondered where they all came from. Now when I think deeply about it, it is true that in a way we're the products of our environment.

Future: That's why you need to be careful with whom you're surrounded with. If you don't like the people around you, change them. Create a group of people that you'll enjoy spending time with. In your case, you have to create a group of people that will inspire you to become the best version of yourself, that will motivate you to break your limits, to be courageous and face the unknown. Those who will be real with you and tell the truth to your face and not speak behind your back. You need to create something that I like to call ***"Circle around you."***

Circle around you

How many times have you read the famous book by *Napoleon Hill* called *"Think and Grow Rich"*?

Serge: More than 20 times.

Future: Good. Then you've read about the experiment that *Napoleon Hill* did at one point in his life. For those of you that haven't read that book and don't know about the experiment I'm talking about, here's a small portion of it.

At one point in his life, Napoleon was going into his *Imagination* where he had "*meetings*" with the people that inspired him, the likes of *Thomas A. Edison, Henry Ford, Andrew Carnegie, Abraham Lincoln, Alexander Graham Bell, Ralph Waldo Emerson* and many more. Every night before he went to bed, he closed his eyes, and in his *Imagination*, he would call all the "*members*" of his group to talk about the questions or problems that were bothering him. Because Napoleon studied every member of his group all his life, he knew in his *Imagination* what kind of persons they were, and if he had a particular problem, he would ask in front of all these men and wait for a solution to come from them. He did that every night for a few months until he realized that his *Imagination* was so powerful that he was afraid that he'd lose sight of the present moment.

Serge: Just like me! It happened a few times, for example, while I was working on my daily job, I was thinking about what could I write, and I captured myself imagining these conversations with you. It was so powerful and scary at the same time because I was afraid that I'd lose awareness of the present moment, so I decided to do it only when I'm alone at home and have time to write this book.

Future: That's exactly what happened to Napoleon Hill. He realized how powerful *Imagination* could be because he had discovered many things that were so real at that moment that he didn't know if it was a reality or imagination. He noticed that he had adopted thoughts, words, and even behaviors from some men from that group.

> *"Imagination is everything. It is the preview of life's coming attractions."*
> **- Albert Einstein**

When he was doing some work, he noticed the words that were similar to Thomas Edison's sayings. He noticed the behavior that was typical of Abraham Lincoln. He was speaking in a way that was similar to Henry Ford. He had the thoughts that other members of his imaginary group had. His purpose for these imaginary meetings was to rebuild his character so that it would represent a composite of the characteristics of his imaginary members. He wanted to acquire the best possible qualities that every member of his group possessed, and by doing that through his *Imagination*, he adopted these qualities and applied them in reality! You can choose to believe it or not, but that story is one more proof of how powerful, and limitless human *Imagination* is.

I'm sure that Mr. Napoleon realized during his lifetime that he tapped into *the power of the Universe*! ***Imagination and the Universe are connected!*** *Everything you experience in your Imagination can become a reality!*

Serge: In this case, I'm having a conversation with "someone" who I want to become in the future?

Future: Exactly. You're putting yourself in a position where you can see yourself as someone successful, healthy, happy, and many more positive and beautiful qualities.

Serge: That's true. But I'm doing this with my eyes open.

Future: So what? Do you know that *true dreamers* are those who can dream while their eyes are open?

Serge: I guess I didn't know that, but I can believe it.

Future: Good. You're on the right track, so keep doing that. To get back on the subject, my point in telling this story about Napoleon Hill and his imaginary group of members is; even if you're not (at this moment) surrounded with people who will encourage the best out of you, you can still have your *Circle around you* in your *Imagination* just like Napoleon Hill had.

There are two types of relationships, one that is toxic and one that is uplifting. You want to move away from toxic and negative people who will bother you with all kinds of unimportant news; with all of the reasons why something can't work. Those who will not inspire you to grow, to become the best that you can be. You have to be honest and look at your closest circle of friends. Who are they? What are the subjects of their conversations? Do they have goals and dreams? Are they problem-oriented or solution-oriented? Do they inspire you to grow, or do they not want you to get ahead? Are they complaining about the weather, the economy, their job? Take your time and answer these questions honestly. If your answer is yes, is it now the right time to find some new and more exciting people that will bring out the best in you? Is it time to find people with whom you'll really enjoy spending time?

You don't want to be surrounded by people who compete with you, but surrounded by people who complete you!

I'll tell you this. One of the hardest things you'll ever do is to close the door to your long-time friends, to your family, to your colleagues and others. It can be harsh and scary because you're at risk to spend some time alone until you find more exciting and even better friends. Just ask my *Present*, he knows what I'm talking about.

Serge: It was one of the hardest things to do. I decided to be a radical person, which is not something that I'm suggesting anyone should do. That move comes with costs that some of you may not be able to handle. I've removed every person from my life except two friends because I realized that I don't want to have anything to do with them. They were toxic, negative, always complaining, didn't want to do anything to change their lives, jealous, envious. I knew that to improve my life, I had to remove some people from my circle. In my case, it wasn't that hard because I already knew that I'm moving to Canada and that I'll have to start all over again and find new friends. That decision helped me set the standards of whom I choose to be surrounded with in my future. My goal was always to be surrounded by people who want to grow, learn, expand. Those who seek more from life, who are positive and know what they want. Let me tell you one more thing that I did back in 2014.

First few months in Canada was Hell for me! I was working in a construction company where I used to strip skids (pallets) in pieces, and maybe you don't know what kind of job that was, trust me when I say that I would rather clean the toilets than to do that ever again! It was hard, painful, I had nightmares, but I couldn't quit because I didn't know anyone in Toronto and I had a huge debt that I had to repay. Also, my family in Serbia had financial problems back then, so I had to support them too. I'll not go into the details of the job, but trust me when I say that every day I was so tired, full of hate and resentment because of that work.

I had my problems and battles that I had to fight in my life and my mind. One thing I couldn't wait for was to call my family and talk with them so I can feel at least some sort of happiness. So every weekend, I used to call my family on Skype or Viber, and after two or three weeks, I realized that conversations with them felt unpleasant. The reason was that I never, literally never mentioned what I was going through, the problems that I was dealing with, the pain, the suffering, the tears, the blood, the unhappiness at that time. I didn't say a word about it! And there they were, waiting for me to call them so they could complain about their own lives.

Because I had faith that things would change and never lost sight of my vision to become a better and successful person, I decided to block them! Yes, I blocked them on Skype, Viber, Whatsapp, I removed them from my social media accounts and explained to them that I would not call them until they change the way they talk and think! In other words, I made them change their own life too! You may say that it was too cold from me but trust me, you must first take care of yourself and your wellbeing, and only then will you be able to help others. So I didn't call them for three or four months, and finally one day

I received a message from my sister, *"please call mom and dad, they said that they will never again complain about anything,"* and so I did. It has been a few years, and never again did they complain about anything. If they had a problem, they speak about it, and immediately, we're trying to figure out how to solve it.

I did the same thing with other people that I know or with my other friends too. It was radical, but it definitely worked for me.

Future: In this example of my *Present* you can see that it is essential to remove negative people from your environment or at least to limit your time with them. You can do it nicely, or you may do it radically as my *Present* did. Whatever method you choose, I promise you that there's something that you'll lose. You'll catch yourself in many lonely moments when you decide to go for a better life. As my *Present* likes to say, you're never alone! Especially when you have your *Imagination*! If right now, you don't have the people that you would like to be surrounded with, create them in your *Imagination*. Create your imaginary board of directors. Take people that you admire, that inspire you, that you would like one day to sit with and put them in your *Imagination* and talk with them. Talk with them like it is a reality. And you'll notice that after some time you'll see people that will come into your life and become your friends.

Serge: I have in my phone the pictures of people that I admire like Dr. Wayne Dyer, Tony Robbins, TD Jakes, Deepak Chopra, Bob Proctor, Jack Canfield, Jim Rohn, Neale Donald Walsch, Zig Ziglar, Les Brown and many more. I read their books, listen to their podcasts, imagine meetings with them, and when I'm in a situation, I ask myself something like *"what would Tony Robbins say now?"* or *"how will TD Jakes react in this situation?"* and somehow ideas pop up through the sixth sense. Every time I did this, I reacted and responded in a way that was beneficial for whoever was involved.

Future: That's an excellent way to approach the situation. If you're aware at that moment and you ask yourself something like "What would God do in this situation," trust me, you'll receive an answer immediately and mostly through a form of thought. If you don't believe me, try to remember some situations in your life where you demonstrated behavior that was similar or even the same as one of your friends and you were surprised that you reacted that way. When you spend a certain amount of time with somebody, you'll pick their thoughts, the way they speak or even behave. That's one more reason to be surrounded with people that will bring the best out of you, not the worst.

Serge: I believe to be accepted, we hang out with anyone not to feel alone. I also remember when I started to listen to metal & rock music; all of a sudden, I was surrounded by people who were listening to the same. They were wearing these metal t-shirts, had long hairs, drank beer, and did all kinds of things that I didn't like. Because they influenced me, I was behaving like them, and I didn't like it at all. I remember the decision I made to get out of that circle because I realized that's not who I wanted to be or the place I wanted to be. I'm not saying that everyone listening to metal & rock music is like I've described, but my circle of people was like that. It can be fun in the beginning, but later you'll see that it is not who you are.

Future: Exactly. We've been saying throughout the entire book that you have to decide who you want to be, where you want to go and what you want to do because that is the starting point of every change you would like to make in your life. If you're going to become a professional bodybuilder, will you be hanging out with some overweight people and do what they do or eat what they eat? Of course not! You'll get your butt up, go to the gym and find someone who is successful in something you want to become and be surrounded with those kind of people. If you want to become a successful businessman, you'll go and find people who did it before you and try to be in their environment as much as you can.

Serge: In my case, when I became interested in public speaking, I joined Toastmasters, and that was one of the best decisions ever! I didn't receive benefits just for public speaking, but being in a room with people who want to grow, learn, to expand and to be the best that they can be was indeed a remarkable discovery for me! I've realized how much I was enjoying being there, let alone having the opportunity to talk with these people and be empowered and inspired by them.

Future: In other words, you knew what you wanted, and the Universe helped you to find it. Once you know what you want, the Universe will give its best to fulfill your wish. The moment you became surrounded by uplifting types of people, you noticed that your life was improving in every area. I can't even express how important it is to create a circle of friends that will get the best out of you. It has been said that *"we are the products of our environment"* and that is a big truth.

Serge: Your suggestion is, if someone can't find these kind of people right now, they should use their *Imagination* to create an imaginary circle by putting themselves in that emotional state of feeling like it's a reality. The Universe will do its best to surround them with people they need at that moment. After a while, they'll notice new people coming to them and becoming their new friends or associates.

Future: Let me give you an idea. It has been said that to create the *mastermind*, you must have two brains that will connect on the subconscious level through the principle of harmony. But what most people don't understand is (you've discovered right now without knowing) that you can use your *Imagination* to create your *Mastermind* just like Napoleon Hill did. If you can create your circle of influence in your *Imagination*, you'll be unstoppable. You'll have access to the brains of people you imagine; provided you know their history and have studied them before. Remember: **Imagination is the key to unlock the Power of the Universe!**

Serge: If I understand, you want to tell me that I've tapped into the power of the Universe by using my *Imagination* to create this book and by using it consciously I've become happier and more grateful; and that this is why I've noticed a lot of positive changes in my life in the last few months?

Future: You are only one step away from completely transforming your life!

Serge: What do you mean?

Future: While writing this book, you're using the creative side of your *Imagination* consciously to the fullest. If you can use your *Imagination* knowingly throughout a day, you would live a different life; the kind of life that you're dreaming about right now.

Serge: But if I use it throughout a day, doesn't that mean losing sight of the reality and things going on at the moment?

Future: I don't mean using your *Imagination* every second of your daily life, but using it intentionally before some circumstances occur. You can have an impact on that moment even before it happens. In other words, if you can stop for a second before every interval of your daily life and close your eyes for a brief moment to imagine how you would like that moment to be, with enough daily practice, you'll become the true *Creator of your life.*

Serge: What do you mean by *"if you can stop for a second before every interval of your daily life?"*

Intentional moments

"*Make the NOW the primary focus of your life.*" - **Eckhart Tolle**

F*uture:* In reality, the only moment that exists is **NOW**. If you think deeply, you'll realize that past, present, and future exist at the same time. Whether you're thinking about your past or about the present or imagining your future, whatever you're doing is happening at this moment NOW!

Your creative power is in the now. Everything you're experiencing is happening now. You can experience the past in the NOW through your *Imagination*. Whatever you're doing right now, whether you're writing, drinking coffee, making love, watching a movie, or simply just lying in bed and thinking, you're doing everything NOW. If you imagine your future, you're doing it NOW. NOW is the moment that you can use to live the present happy life as well as to create the future of your dreams. There's something called *"intentional moments."*

Serge: That sounds familiar.

Future: It is something that you used a few years ago, and it's time to remember that and start using it again to live the **intentional life.**

Intentional moments are moments that you have throughout the day. And I don't mean literally as a moment that lasts only one second but rather the **interval from one moment to another.** To give you an example; you wake up in the morning - that's one interval. You get up from the bed and go to the washroom to brush your teeth - that's another interval. You come back to your room and start dressing and getting ready to go to work - another interval.

When you get out of your house and go to work - another interval and so on.

Serge: Oh, I see. So *every interval* from one moment to the other is what you call *"intentional moments."* I get what you mean.

Future: Good. I've said it earlier that you've been using your *Imagination* consciously and actively only when you were writing this book (because that was your Intention) and when you were visualizing your dreams before you go to sleep. What I'm suggesting to you and everyone who's reading this book is something that will change your life and your future!

N + I c/w I = F

Now + Intention combined with Imagination = Future

If there's one thing that you can use (from all the useful stuff in this book) to change your life, it would be this formula!

It means that the only moment that exists is *NOW*. If you use your *Imagination* and set up the *Intention* for this moment, *YOU'LL CREATE THE FUTURE YOU DESIRE!*

You'll do it by using this one strategy that will improve dramatically not just your daily life, but your future in advance if you become consistent in using it.

Let me tell you what you need to do. Firstly, you need to decide that you'll be aware of every moment of every day; that is not something that will happen overnight. Consistency is the key. By practicing every day to be aware of the present moment, you'll come to the point where it becomes your second nature, and by default, you'll be aware of what's going on every moment. In other words, you'll have the *power to take control of the moment* in a way that will allow you to have full control of your thoughts, words or actions at that moment.

Then, *you have to start NOW*. Whatever you're doing right now, stop it! If you're reading this book, STOP IT FOR A SECOND! Put this book on the side, close your eyes and say something like, *"My Intention for this moment is to get my thoughts together and focus on reading this amazing book, and while I'm reading, I want my subconscious to work for me to remember every piece of information that I can use in order to improve my life. I feel good while I'm reading and I'll give my best to be present as long as I read!"*

You did it? CONGRATULATIONS! You've started to learn how to live the intentional life by using this moment to enjoy the present and create your future. This is the essence of intentional moments. If you can stop for a brief second and close your eyes and set your *Intention* for what you want from that moment and if you can put your feelings into it, you'll have an impact on that moment, and you'll be surprised when you see that your *Intention* had an influence on what is about to come. For example, let's say your phone rings, and you take the phone, and on the screen, it says *"Mom,"* which means that mom is calling you. Since this is her action and she knows why she's calling you, it would be wise to answer the phone and say *"Hey mom, can you please wait a second?"* and then you close your eyes and set up the Intention for that moment. You may decide to say *"I love when my mom is calling me. I want to enjoy our conversation, to have a laugh, to empower her with some encouraging and uplifting words and tell her how much I appreciate her,"* and then you take your phone, and you're ready for that moment. You'll notice that the conversation will feel pleasant and somehow different. You'll see the magic of setting the Intention for that moment.

If you're about to get into the building of your company I would recommend you to stop for a few seconds and close your eyes, set a clear intention of what you want to experience that day. You may say, *"I'm grateful for this job. It is a place where we have so many geniuses who wants to express themselves in their unique way. I want to be of service. I intend to be as productive as I can; to do my work in the best way I can, to help others if I'm in a situation to help and to make it a better day for at least one person from my company by saying some motivational or empowering words. I want to feel good, and when I'm done, I want to be full of energy and be happy."*

Of course, you can say something in your own words, but you get the essence. If you can do that for every *intentional moment* of your day, you'll be the *Creator* of your day, and the day will become a month, a month will become a year and one day you'll look back and see that you were the *Creator of your life!*

The best way to predict your future is to create it! Create your future by setting the *Intention* for every moment, and every day. Practice a daily visualization of your goals and dreams.

Serge: Do we need to stop before every moment or can we set the Intention for that day? For example, when we wake up, we can say, "*My Intention for today is to feel good. I want to enjoy my work. I want to uplift others, to laugh and smile as much as I can. I want to learn one new thing and to grow by having the experience of this day. I'm grateful to be alive, and I want to live this day to the fullest.*"

Future: Is that your *Intention* when you wake up?

Serge: Well, I used to say every morning when I wake up "*My intention for today is to feel good no matter what!*"

Future: Did it work?

Serge: Not always.

Future: You can set the *Intention* for that day, but it is possible that you'll not be aware of the moments that will happen throughout the day, and that's why you think this will not work. Setting the *Intention* before every moment is invaluable. I can't even express how much this will change your life for the better!

Serge: But what if somebody starts today to set the intentions before every moment and still don't create the desired effect and feel disappointed? That person can say that this technique is not working.

Future: It is possible that in the beginning, when you start using this technique, you still will not experience that moment as you desire because of your past thoughts and beliefs. In other words, if a person who was going to a job that he doesn't like and for months had thoughts like, "*Oh, I have to go to work and engage with these same boring people*" and all of a sudden starts to set a new *Intention*, in the beginning, he may not see the desired results because he has not fully convinced himself of new intention, but through practice and over time - by changing his thoughts and altering his beliefs, he will wake up one day and realize that he actually wants to go to that job. He might begin to notice that somebody whom he didn't like before started to treat him differently, and he starts to enjoy conversations with people. By setting the Intention for every moment over and over again, you'll see the impact of your Intention, and you'll be amazed by what your *Imagination* can do.

Also, for the majority of people who are stuck in their lives and want to make a change, sometimes it's hard for them to see the bigger picture. You were (let's say) lucky enough to see the bigger picture by having that vision when you were at rock bottom, but not everyone will have that privilege. So if they can't see it, it will be easier for them to do something right now that will improve their current situation which can be done by setting the intentions for every next interval; imagining the small things, doing it and becoming a master at creating them. Eventually, they end up with a bigger vision that will be believable for them because they learned how to take control of those things.

It takes time to change your thoughts and beliefs as we've mentioned in other parts of the book. This formula that I've shared with you will always work, no exceptions, no matter what. Like in everything in life, every new thing that you learn takes practice until you master it.

For example, I know for a fact that before you sit and open your laptop to write this book, your subconscious mind was working in your favor by setting a clear *Intention* to write because your mind knows this is something you like to do; this is your passion. If you can use that to your advantage and start setting *Intention* for every moment in your life on a daily basis, soon, you'll realize what it means to be the *Creator of your life.*

You have the power to choose the thoughts, words, and actions at this moment. Choose wisely. Also, you have to know that to affect the real positive change in your daily experience; you must disregard how things look, as well as how others see you. Give more of your attention to the way you prefer things to be by setting the Intention before every moment, and you'll see how life will unfold to you most beautifully and blissfully.

*"Follow your bliss, and the Universe will open doors for you where there were only walls." - **Joseph Campbell***

*The key to unlocking the power of the Universe is your **Imagination**.* However, if you set up the ***Intention*** for every moment of your daily life through ***the***

power of Imagination, you'll create the future you want and live the life that you consciously created.

Remember these words because they are yours, and you'll use them to teach others how to tap into this high power.

Serge: Again, you inspired me!

Future: So many people are looking outwardly for inspiration, but the best and most powerful inspiration comes from within.

Serge: I agree. I don't need anything from the outside to be inspired. I use my *Imagination* for that. By the way, I have the next subject that I believe we need to talk about.

Future: And that is?

Serge: It's something that just popped into my mind, and in a way, I'm sad that the majority of people who are living in this world don't know the power of emotions and how to use them to their advantage. You've said that if we mix our feelings with *Imagination* to set up the *Intention*, we're on the verge of attracting anything we want in a specific moment as well in life. Is that correct?

Future: That is correct.

Serge: That's interesting because now I know that we are threefold being, which includes the body, mind, and spirit. Some people call it conscious, subconscious, and superconscious. I know that whatever we want to do or be, we need to learn how to put all three of these to work through our emotions. I also know that our *Spirit* is already working for our benefit at all times. So can you please explain how we can teach our mind and body to use emotions to create what we want or how to use them in applying your formula for creating the future?

Future: You picked a very crucial subject to talk about. Without further ado, let's move to the topic of emotions.

Emotions and the Original thought

What you must know is that you're much more than you see in your physical body. While you exist in this *dimension*, there's another part of you, your ***Soul*** that exists in another dimension. It's a sum of all of the past life experiences you had.

Serge: Wow, that sounds deep. Is the *Soul* the only name that it has, or is there any other label for it? It's not that I care, but it sounds familiar.

Future: It doesn't matter how you label it; the truth is that you exist simultaneously in two dimensions. I prefer to call it your ***Soul***, and your *Soul* knows everything about you. Your *Soul* knows who you are and who you always have been. It knows all the experience that you've been through from the beginning of your existence. I'll not go deeper into that topic because it may be incomprehensible for somebody who's reading. Maybe we'll write another book someday that will talk more about your *Soul* and its purpose. For now, let's stick to this important part.

"Your emotion is the bridge that connects you with your Soul."

In other words, if you're focused on one subject, and you have your own opinion about it, your *Soul* is also focused on the same subject and has its personal opinion about it. Whatever emotion you're feeling in that moment is an indication of the match or mismatch of those opinions.

For example, you're in a conversation with someone, and you're in the middle of some argument, and that person says to you, *"You don't know anything about that. You're dreaming about something that is not real. Don't think about that nonsense; life sucks! You can become rich only if you're lucky enough or you rob a bank."* You were talking to that person about your dreams, and that person can't see what you can see and maybe that person doesn't even like you and said those things just to hurt you. Immediately you may say, *"You are right. I'm dreaming about the impossible. I don't have what it takes to become successful. I'm not good enough and not lucky enough to become successful."*

Now, if you're not strong enough mentally and you still don't know who you are, you may feel a *negative emotion*. This negative emotion is a sign from your *Soul* who knows who you are and knows that what you want and what you feel are not in alignment. In other words, you want success, but you still don't believe you can have it. And your Soul is giving you a sign in the form of negative emotion so you can alter your beliefs and start thinking differently.

Let's say that you're in the market to buy some groceries and while waiting for your turn to pay, the lady before you forgot her wallet, and doesn't have money to pay for what she has bought. Your instinct jumps in, and you pay her bills. She turns to give you the most beautiful smile and says, *"Thank you so much sir for this act of kindness. I hope that I'll see you again so I can repay you. Have a beautiful day."* What do you think? How would you feel at that moment? You'll feel a *positive emotion*. In this case, that's also a sign from your *Soul* because your thoughts and beliefs are in alignment with what you feel and who you are.

There are several kinds of emotions that people speak about; whether you call them anger, joy, resentment, fear, peace, love and so on, but in truth, there are only two emotions - the **emotion of love** and the **emotion of fear**. Only one can exist at a time. You have no alternative about these emotions, but you have the *option* of which one to select. **Yes, you can choose how you want to feel at any moment of your life.**

By knowing that you have the power to choose of which emotion you want to feel, by selecting the emotion of love, you can use it to your advantage at any point in time to create what you want. Your feelings are coming from your thoughts, and every thought has a frequency. You are living in an era where you can measure a thought. The thoughts of a higher frequency are thoughts that will make you happy, blessed, fulfilled, and peaceful. The thoughts of a low frequency will have you in a sad, angry, depressed mode. What you don't realize is that every emotion you feel is coming with a frequency that causes a like frequency to be attracted to you. Whatever feelings you choose in a certain moment will have a level of frequency that will send the vibration to the Universe, and you'll get what you feel. That's why so many people become confused because they believe that if they think positive they will attract positive things, and it is not like that. You always get what you feel. It is possible for you to try to think positive, but if you're not feeling good about these thoughts and not set up in the vibration, you'll not get what you think about. Because what you want and what you feel are not in alignment. Your *Soul* sends you a message through a negative emotion so you can change it.

Serge: But how can someone raise the level of their vibration? If somebody feels sad at the moment, how can that person change their state of being?

Future: Emotion is *energy in motion!* You can change your state of being by changing the physiology of your body through principles that we've already talked about in the chapter of "*How to put yourself in a positive mood.*"

Serge: I get it. If you're not feeling well, you can change it through action. I guess that's a good enough point for someone to go back to that chapter and reread it.

Future: Exactly! By changing your state of being through some form of physical activity, you'll put yourself in the higher state of being with higher thought frequency and emotional vibration. The more you understand that you are in charge of what you feel and that feelings are vibrations, the more you will realize that nothing happens or can happen in your physical reality that you did not authorize by way of your feelings. And the physical reality is the energy at unique vibration.

Serge: Let's see, did I get it right; It's not what we think about that causes the feeling; it's how we think about a thing that combines emotion with that thing. The thought together with the emotion creates the feeling. The feeling then creates a unique frequency. The repetition and sustainability of that feeling along with the depth of the emotional charge determine how dominant that frequency will be; the more dominant the frequency, the quicker the manifestation of that frequency. In other words, the faster you will attract other *"things"* that have an equivalent frequency into your life.

Future: You've stated it correctly. The positive emotion is a signal from your *Soul* that you're in alignment with what you want. It's the same with the negative emotion. If you say *"I want a promotion in my job,"* and you imagine yourself having that promotion, you're putting yourself in alignment with what you want, and you are feeling a positive emotion. But, if you think like, *"but I don't think I can have it, because I'm not good enough, and Brian is the next one anyway..."* you're pulling yourself to where you were before you had the thought that you want the promotion. And now you're feeling a negative emotion because you don't believe in yourself, and even if your *Soul* knows that you can have it, as long as you don't change your beliefs, you'll not be at the higher frequency of getting what you want.

Serge: What is your suggestion about using our emotions to our advantage? How can we use them to serve us well?

Future: By deciding that you'll use them as your guidance system. Your emotions will guide you to the path of choosing only what you want. If you're going to do that, *you have to be aware of the signals that your Soul is sending you through your feelings.*

Whenever you're feeling a negative emotion, stop whatever you're doing at that moment at all costs! It's not in alignment with your highest thought; it's not in alignment with who you are or what you want. What you must do, and I'll repeat it, what you *must do* is to immediately shift your focus to something that will make you change your thoughts then and there or do something that will shift your emotions. You can't afford to feel the negative emotion!

Serge: I know from personal experience that when you're in the middle of deep negative emotions, it can (usually is) be hard to shift your thoughts and feelings from negative to a positive; no matter what you do. Sometimes, no matter how bad you want to, there's a thought behind the thought that don't allow us to shift our focus.

Future: Okay, first we'll have to move to another important subject because

I want everyone to understand something, and later I'll come back to your question.

Original thought

What you have to understand is that there's always a thought behind the thought which you may call the **Original thought**. It is the prime force. That means that behind every thought that you have, there's an original thought that is your actual thought. In other words, if you want something and you speak about it, even put your intention to it, your original thought will remind you that you don't have it yet at the moment; that what you want is missing from your life.

Serge: I don't think I'm following.

Future: Every thought and every emotion you have is based on love or fear. We've already said that in essence, there are only two emotions, either the emotion of love or the emotion of fear. Every action you take is based on one of these two emotions. You have no choice with it because there's nothing else to choose, but you have the choice of which one to select.

Now let me tell you what I mean by *"there's always a thought behind the thought."* Let's say you're dating this beautiful girl. For a while, your relationship is going well, and you're enjoying it a lot, and after a few months, you realize that you're feeling something that is called *love*. Now you're in love with that girl. You decide that you'll tell her how you feel about her. You go out in the middle of the night, thinking the moment has arrived; the moment when you want to say to her that you love her. At that moment, you'll experience a thought behind the thought. At the moment where you pledge your highest love, you welcome your greatest fear. At that moment, the first thing you worry about after saying, *"I love you,"* is whether you'll hear it back. If you hear it back, then you begin immediately to fear that the love you just found, you might lose. And so the action becomes a reaction, a defense against loss.

Serge: This is not real.

Future: What do you mean?

Serge: I can't believe it. I can't f***ing believe it!

Future: Wow, I don't think that your readers will like the language that you've just used, but can you tell me what happened?

Serge: I'm not concerned about the language because I can't believe what you just said. It all makes sense now. I've never, and I mean never realized why it happened. I finally understand after so many years.

Future: I'm confused now. What are you talking about?

Serge: I can remember that night when I decided to tell my ex-girlfriend that I loved her. I didn't plan when I was going to do it; it just happened. And I'll never forget the fear that I had at the same moment when I spoke the words, *"I love you."* That fear lasts for only two or three seconds in reality, but in my world, those 2-3 seconds were like a century! I was so frightened whether I was going to hear *"I love you"* in return or she'll say something that might end our relationship. Oh my God, I can't believe it.

Future: I remember that, but please keep going. I have a feeling that you'll realize what I'm talking about.

Serge: I know exactly what you are talking about. Trust me, I swear! The moment she replied, *"I love you too,"* I began to fear how long it would last. That same night when I was in my bed, I couldn't sleep because I was worried about how long it was going to last. Since that was the first time that I've felt *"true love,"* I had these overwhelming thoughts that the love that I've just found, I might lose! I felt horrible! The emotions were so negative that I couldn't stop feeling them! So from that day, all my actions became reactions because everything I was doing was motivated by fear, and I made so many mistakes. It's no surprise that I lost that girl. ***It was thought behind the thought!*** It was the ***Original thought*** that you spoke about, and now, when I reflect upon that, I realize something that really shocked me. And that is, my original thought was that I was not worthy of being loved, that I didn't deserve this girl and a happy relationship; that if I lose her, I'll never again find somebody who would love me, etc. I didn't understand back then, but now everything makes sense!

Future: Now, you understand. If you knew then who you are, you would not have those thoughts about yourself. ***If you knew that you're the most*** *magnificent being God has ever created, you would've never experienced thoughts of unworthiness.*

The reason why you had these thoughts is that you were taught that way from an early age. It all started when your parents, relatives, teachers, and many others taught you that love is conditional. You have forgotten what it was like to be loved without condition. You've learned that if you don't obey what your parents want you to do, you'll be punished. Your religious leaders have taught you that if you don't obey God, you'll end up in Hell as a sinful being. Your teachers have taught you that if you don't listen or don't learn something, you'll be punished in the form of bad marks. You can see how your thoughts of fear were planted in your mind from an early age. Although your parents, teachers and other people in your life didn't have any harmful ideas or thoughts behind their words or actions when they were telling you all these things; the truth is that they unconsciously planted seeds of fear in your mind. But you can't judge them for that, because it was the same way they were raised by their parents, their teachers, and religious leaders.

Serge: So to *"protect"* me, they were doing a lot more damage than good?

Future: It may seem harsh, but that might be the right way to say it. They had the best intentions, but clearly, they missed something. Obviously, something that they didn't know and still don't know, but you now know; and with this knowledge, you can change the *original thought.*

Serge: How can anyone change their thoughts and beliefs – beliefs that are a result of ten, twenty or even more years of accumulating false thoughts and beliefs from all kinds of different sources?

Future: I understand your frustration but trust me when I say it is possible.

Serge: I have no doubt that is possible, but I can't help it! It just came to my mind right now. So many situations are just popping into my brain. All these words that I have been listening to were nothing but big lies!

Future: That is true. You've been told that love is limited and conditional; that you can't even depend on God's love. They said to you that you're not good enough, you don't have what it takes, it's not in your DNA to be who you want to be, or you'll never be rich if you were born in a poor family and many more lies. You've learned that your reality is a fear-based reality. To go even further, it's not just that you've been told that love is conditional, but you've seen yourself conditionally giving love. And even while you withhold, retreat and set your conditions, a part of you knows this is not what love is.

To change that, you'll need to do something that I believe will help you to change not just the original thought but all these false thoughts and beliefs.

Serge: And that is?

You must act before you think!

*"Act before you think. Your instincts are more honest than your thoughts." - **Sanford Meisner***

Future: You must take action before your mind kills the idea that you're holding. You need to act before you think.

Serge: What do you mean?

Future: Let's say that you've just come home from work. You woke up early, you've worked 10 hours that day, and you're feeling tired. You know that you have to go to the gym because you have that goal, that vision of how you want your body to look like. So you're in your bedroom, putting your workout clothes in the bag and just when you're about to get out of your bedroom, the thought *"arrives"* - *"Hey man, you're so tired that you can't even move. You're sleepy. Let's go to the gym tomorrow. Now is a good time to go for a nap."* Then you say to yourself; *"No way, I have to go to the gym. I don't want to be inconsistent anymore; this is something that I need to do no matter how tired I am."* The thought comes again; *"You're not listening to me. You're sick and tired of your work. If you go to the gym, you'll come back even more tired. You'll not have enough time to sleep, and you have to wake up early again to go to work! Take a break today and go eat something, read the news and go to bed!"*

And now you're in a situation where you need to decide quickly what you are going to do. But if you take too much time to think, your mind will kill every desire you had before your *original thought* came and soon you'll decide that you should take a break and rest and not go to the gym because *"it's just one day."* Now you're lying in bed and another thought sprouts again; *"Man, what the Hell are you doing? You should've gone to the gym already! Come on, for real?"* But it's too late now because you've already allowed your original thought to control your behavior.

Serge: I read something from **Mel Robbins**. In her book *"The 5-second rule,"* she explained that you have exactly 5 seconds to decide before your mind kills the idea. If you don't decide in these five seconds, you'll face one of the biggest human enemies, and that is *procrastination.* Is that what you're talking about?

Future: Yes, it is. Although you'll probably have less than 5 seconds to decide. If you've decided to act before your original thought jumps in, you would reverse the situation and destroy the possibility of your Original thought to have any effect on your decision. If you've acted after your first thought that said, *"you're tired, sleepy and you have to take a rest,"* by taking that bag and leaving the apartment, you would be on the way to altering your beliefs.

The only thought that can replace the Original thought is a thought of faith! You must have faith that the Universe will give you anything you want even before you ask. We already talk about developing faith where it doesn't exist, so there's no need to repeat it here.

When you ask God or the Universe for something, believe that it's already on the way to manifest in your life. Then and only then, whatever you want is becoming a statement of *gratitude.*

To get back to your question about how somebody can shift their focus in the middle of a negative situation or circumstance, you must have faith that you can do it. You have to try as hard as you can to shift your thoughts and do something that will change your state of being. You've heard so many times, and you probably hear this every day that so many people are saying, *"I'm too old to change, I was like this all my life, and you can't change Me,"* and they're right. You can't change anyone by forcing them to do it. Age is not a problem. The problem is that they don't see how they can do it. What they say is, *"I don't have faith that anything good can happen in my life and I don't believe that if I change myself, my life will change. Factually, it may get worse because I don't know what others will think of me and maybe I don't even have enough time to change it now, who knows how long I will live anyway and to be completely honest, what's the point anyway?"*

And so it is. They will stay like that for the rest of their lives. Sadly, most people don't realize they can change their life by just deciding to do it. So they are never *"awake."*

Another way to change your thoughts and beliefs is through **gratitude**. Gratitude can shift your emotions from negative to positive in an instant. Be grateful for every moment, every day you have to live. Be thankful for everything that you have right now in your life. For everything that you'll have, even if it's not there yet! But you must know that it's on the way to manifest in your life! You must have faith that whatever you want will be manifested and the best way to attract it faster is to be grateful in advance. When you wake up in the morning say, *"Thank you; I'm happy and grateful for one more amazing day of my life."*

Throughout the day, be grateful for everything that happens that day. Appreciate the air, the water, the food you eat, the people with whom you interact, the problems you have because they're shaping your character, the unfortunate situations you had that day because through them you're growing. Be grateful for all the good things as well as bad. Be grateful for grace, mercy, understanding, kindness, peace, prosperity, your parents, wisdom, growth, hard times, lessons, and your body. Don't take anything for granted. I can't even express how powerful this is. Be grateful for all you've been through till now because it has made you whom you are today.

Serge: I find this so true. When I look at my life, I didn't understand in real-time why I went through a lot of things a few years ago, but now I know. And I've said so many times that I'm grateful for all of them because if that didn't happen, I'm not sure I'll be who I am today.

Future: Every happy and successful person will tell you that they are grateful for every temporary defeat they had because it made them who they are today! In a more profound sense, everything that happens to you and that will happen is for your own good! One day you'll realize this.

Serge: As I've said, I know now some things that I didn't know a few years ago. But you've mentioned something like, **'there's no such thing as failure.'** You said there are only temporary defeats. What do you mean by that?

There's no such thing as Failure

Future: *You were not created to fail!* And you can't fail.

Serge: What do you mean?

Future: Exactly that. You can't fail. There's no such thing as a failure except in the human mind. What is *a failure* by your definition?

Serge: I would say when you don't achieve or accomplish what you intend to. For instance, you have a goal to open a restaurant. After some time you open it; work for a while, and then close it after a while because it didn't work as you wanted, making you lose money at the end. You lose some relationships and further get into debt, and I assume that somebody will look at that as a failure or that you didn't achieve what you wanted. In other people's eyes, that will look like a failure.

Future: You see, you've said it correctly; *"in other people's eyes."* That's the key. Who cares how it looks in other people's eyes? Nothing is a failure until it is accepted as a fact by your own choice.

Serge: By my own choice?

Future: Yes, by your own choice; although, you may not be aware of that choice because it is often made subconsciously. I'll repeat it; there's no such thing as failure. It only depends on how you perceive it in your mind. In truth, there are only lessons and temporary defeats, and they all have their purpose in life.

You can't be successful until you have been unsuccessful - until you experience a temporary defeat which is by the way necessary for you to grow, to know what doesn't work so you can change it or reorganize it into something that will work. You've heard so many stories about people who experienced temporary defeats; dozens, hundreds and even thousands of times!

Serge: Like *Thomas Edison*, who had about ten thousand experiments before he perfected the incandescent electric light bulb? When you said, *"even thousands of times,"* this example popped into my mind immediately.

Future: That's perhaps one of the most famous stories about experiencing a temporary defeat. You see, in other people's view it may look like Thomas Edison failed ten thousand times, but the truth is that he didn't fail even once! He invented the incandescent electric light bulb after ten thousand trials. It was just a ten thousand steps process. He tried over and over again until he reached his goal.

If he, after few experiments or even few hundreds gave up and accepted in his mind that he'll not accomplish what he intended to, that would be a failure. Note again, only in his mind. What you see as a failure when something doesn't work as planned somebody else might see as a lesson. Sometimes you just need to change the plan to succeed. Occasionally you have to make a mistake to see what's not working because only through mistakes can you see what will work. That's one reason I agree with you about the school system failing by punishing kids for making mistakes instead of encouraging them to make mistakes and learn from them in a positive way. What you see as a failure can be just a mistake that needs to be corrected to work.

You can see through the examples of athletes. If you're a sprinter on a hundred-meter race, and you want to become a world champion in that discipline, and that goal is your burning obsession, what will you do if you end up 6th in the first race? Will you give up and say, *"I can never be a champion,"* or go back to train even harder so next time you can win? But then you may say, *"What if he doesn't win next time?"* He'll come again and again until he succeeds. The crowd may see that as a failure, but the athlete will see it as a temporary defeat. Next time he wins, people will always see who's on top, but they will fail to realize what it took to get there.

What you see in all successful people you can think about, is only the tip of the iceberg. You don't see the tears, doubts, disappointments, defeats, so many nights without sleep, fears, obstacles, work ethic, learning, reading, studying behind that success. You don't see how many times that person has faced adversities and defeats and yet, they never gave up. That person has never accepted a defeat as a failure. The defeat was used as a fuel to succeed. These people embraced defeat and used it as their greatest strength. They didn't allow life to smack them down. Every time they fell, they stood up. That's what makes them winners. They knew that as long as you can stand up after every adversity, you can do it.

People face disappointment in love; they give up. They say, *"I don't want to go out and date somebody because I'll fall in love and get hurt again."* People face an obstacle in business, and they give up and say, *"Well, this doesn't work, everybody was right. I can't do this,"* so they don't even try again to start something new because, *"What's the point anyway, sooner or later, I'll fail."* People face defeats in life overall, and they say, *"Well, I guess it's not meant for me to live this life abundantly."* So, they give up on life and let life do with them whatever it wants.

You can't let life shut you down. You have to stand up and fight. If you want to be successful, you have to be prepared for some disappointments, defeats, obstacles, but that's what makes life interesting. That's what makes life so beautiful because ***every temporary defeat is another chance to learn, to grow, to expand, to see what's not working so you can discover what will work to be successful.***

Serge: I think I know the answer to why people are accepting temporary defeats as failures.

Future: Let's hear it.

Fear of criticism

Serge: I believe that most people accept temporary defeats as failures because when they face a disappointment, there's always somebody who will tell them that they *"knew"* it will not work. There's still someone who will remind them of all of the reasons why it didn't work and why they should give up.

Future: In other words, even if they want to try again - because they are so afraid that they will fail again and afraid of what others will say, they don't try again. And we know that fear of criticism is one of the most influential fears that exist and you still have it; although you came to a point where you're close to losing that fear but again, you have it.

Serge: Are you going to expose me now?

Future: I'm your *Imagination*; my job is to shake you a little bit. Maybe these words will wake you up a little bit. Not just you, but everyone that is reading.

Serge: Me: I guess it's better to be shaken by my *Imagination* than by somebody else. Go ahead; tell me what you know about my fear.

Future: It's not only yours. More than 95% of people have this fear. It is the fear of what others will say if you fail.

Serge: But I don't care what others will say!

Future: That may be true when it comes to your personality, but when it comes to doing something that requires courage and to step out of your comfort zone, and I'm talking about your dream and your passion like writing this book, you still have these thoughts about what others will think about you. Although, I must confess that you're closing that gap and soon you'll be free of this fear, but you must start to make changes now!

The irony is that most of you care too much about what somebody (that you even don't like) will think or say about you. You're scared that if you fail, you'll become a loser and you'll have to listen to all these people that already knew you'd fail. But the worst thing you're scared of is the voice from your mind that will haunt you if you let it. You're living in a world of social media where everyone wants to show only the positive side of their lives. You see all these beautiful photos of all kinds of different places, parties, barbeques, vacations, etc. You see all these people having a good time with their friends, and it seems that everybody is living a happy and fulfilled life except you. So to be "accepted" on social media and validate yourself in the form of *"likes"* and *"comments,"* you're posting only good stuff like everybody else because it will make you look good and cool in the eyes of others. But the real reason why you are not posting something that you may like to post is that you'll not receive enough likes and comments, and that will determine your value in your own eyes.

You're living in a world where people will grab their phone and take a picture or a video of you falling on the street rather than help you get up on your feet. No wonder the fear of criticism is more present in the minds of most people now than it ever was. Every step you take may end up being criticized. How you will dress for tonight's party will depend on what you think others will think about you. What you'll say in tomorrow's meeting will depend on how you think others will look at you. Fear of criticism is present in every moment of your daily life.

Serge: How can we change that?

Future: First thing you have to do is t**o *look where the critics are coming from.*** Are you scared of what your girlfriend, parents, relatives, or friends will say? Or are you afraid of what others who don't like you and who you don't like either, will think or say about you? When you figure that out, then you must ask yourself, *"Why am I afraid of their opinions at all?"* Why does it matter to you what anyone will say if you face a defeat? Do you know that ***anything worth doing will always be criticized?***

If you look carefully, you'll realize that you have never been criticized by the people who are on a higher level of consciousness than you are. You have always been criticized by those who are a level below you or maybe at the close level. The reason why these people will still do that is; when you fail, it will make them feel better about themselves. If you keep rising to the levels they know they will never be able to reach, they will criticize you because they're envious and jealous of you. They don't want you to move ahead because they'll have to look at you as a mirror except they aren't where you are.

When you decide that there are some people whose opinions matter to you, **seek improvement, not approval.** In other words, some people will give you constructive criticism with the best intentions behind it. You can take these critics to improve whatever you're doing. There will be people who will have the intention to hurt you with their criticism, but there will be those who want you to succeed, and they will intend to help you.

> *"There's only one way to avoid criticism: do nothing, say nothing and be nothing." -* **Aristotle**

Of course, there's always a way not to be criticized at all, and that's to do nothing worthwhile.

Serge: There's no fun in that.

Future: There isn't. But you must be prepared that anything worth doing at all will be criticized. To go back to social media for a moment, you have to teach your kids that they are the most amazing human beings with all kinds of different talents, abilities, skills, and beauty inside of them. Do not allow them to value themselves through social media likes, followers, and comments because the worst critics you'll have to face is from your mind. If they don't have enough followers or likes, they will think that nobody likes them and that they are not *"in"* or *"cool"* and that's not true.

Teach them to believe in themselves and to put the content they believe in and there's one thing that will never get old, and that's the *"truth."* Posting what you love will always be disliked by somebody. It is easier to critique a thing than to create a thing. And teach your kids not to allow anyone or anything to make them feel worthless. There's a bunch of other things that I can say about social media, but I'll save that for some other time. My point is that whatever you do; don't let the critics stop you from going after your goal or dream.

Serge: I think that everyone who wants to do something worthwhile will sooner or later decide to not care about criticism. Eventually, they will lose the fear of it.

Future: Are you implying that you're about to lose it?

Serge: Absolutely! I believe I've already lost that fear in almost every area of my life.

Future: So you still have it for something, right?

Serge: I do. I have it about this book, sincerely. Because I believe this is the first time in my life that I've put my whole self into something. I've never done anything before with passion, focus, and discipline that I have right now. Sometimes it's not easy to write and use the *Imagination* as I wanted, but I'm improving, I'm giving my best. One thing that is bothering me is that I'm writing about the power of *Imagination* and while I'm writing these words, I've noticed that sometimes I have a hard time to set up the clear intention for the moment and to use my *Imagination* to my advantage. Here I am writing what others should do to change their lives, and I can't do it sometimes.

Future: You're afraid that what you're writing about is not something that you'll master by the time you publish this book, and it will look like a lie to you?

Serge: Something like that. I don't want to write something that I'm not practicing because it will not just look like a lie to others but for me as well.

Future: Do you know that one of your favourite speakers *Les Brown* has given speeches where he was saying to people that they can have their dream, that they can live the life they desire, but at that time, he was dealing with financial problems, divorce was knocking on his door and many more issues? Life is not black and white. There will be a time where you'll have to talk or teach about something that you've never done before, and that's okay! It is! ***You're in the process of mastering The Art of Imagination! Be patient.*** You're learning. You've just tapped into that process. The more you know and apply; it doesn't get easier, but harder. It's because the Universe is testing you on how badly you want it. How badly you want to learn and master it and teach others to do the same. That's why it may look and worked easier yesterday, and it becomes harder and doesn't work today. It's a test. Like everything in life; life will test you to see the truth of your desire; to see how bad you want what you desire.

Serge: I have that thought in my mind that it is a test. I remember when I started meditating and visualizing; it was so easy for me to focus and do it. And my very good friend told me after I've said to him that these things are easy to do, that it will get harder because the Universe will test you on another level. In other words, I've passed the beginners stage, and after that level, the Universe will give you a test for the next level, and the next, until you fully master it and it becomes second nature; a part of you forever.

Future: In this case your friend is right. To fully understand and master something you have to go through different levels of the process where all your senses, your willpower, your burning desire, your faith will be tested over and over again until you fully master it and it will become a part of you. Once you master it, you'll do it subconsciously without even realizing it.

Serge: That makes sense. So even if I'm in the process of learning and mastering *The Art of Imagination*, I don't need to feel guilty that I'm writing about this even if I haven't fully mastered it?

Future: Correct. As we said, you'll face critics on this. You'll be criticized like every great teacher writing something you don't fully understand. Now you can see that you still have some fears and that's okay. It shows you that there are still some things you have to work on. But like I've said, soon you'll lose that fear. And then whatever others say or think about you will not matter to you at all. I'm sure that you're aware that not everybody you know will buy this book. Neither will they like that you've published it. Some of them will be shocked and have opinions like *"What can he write about it? He doesn't look like a smart person or someone who knows how to write at all."* Some will laugh at you. Some will call you all kinds of different names.

You'll be judged and criticized. Those who don't like you will observe you daily to find a fault in something you'll say or do and use your words from this book against you. Some that don't know who you are now, but still have a screenshot picture of you from before will use this book against you; knowing who you were but have no idea who you are now. They don't know that *your history is not your destiny*. And so on. Are you prepared for all of that?

Serge: I'll be sincere, I'm not. But not because I don't want to be prepared, it's simply because I'm not sure that I'll care about all that stuff. Because I know the power of *Imagination*, I'll use it to focus on those who need my help, on those who want more from life, who want me to be around them, on those who will have the highest possible benefit from my service. I truly believe that.

Future: Now, you're talking! I like what I'm hearing. That's an excellent approach to the fear of criticism.

Serge: Honestly, even if I face a defeat, why should I care what anyone will tell me or think of me? Nobody will pay my bills; rent, food, clothes, etc. Nobody will have to fight my battles except me. So it will not matter at all what others will say. But failing is not an option. Not anymore. I'm way too prepared to work as hard as I can to make my dreams become a reality.

Hard work

> *"Hard work beats talent when talent doesn't work hard." -* **Tim Notke**

Future: What does *"hard work"* mean to you? How do you look at it?

Serge: I used to hate it. I thought it was pointless. I saw so many people that worked hard all their lives and still end up broke, alone and with nothing to show for it.

Future: You mean with regard to material things?

Serge: Not just in regards to material things, but in their spirit too. Deep down inside they're broken because they see that what they worked for wasn't what they hoped for when they were younger. I've seen my parents working so hard only to make ends meet. I've seen so many struggles that I didn't understand why it is that people who worked so hard end up with nothing when they get older. But now, I know. The reason is that they didn't have dreams. They worked for something they thought was right. They worked so hard but ended up broke because they didn't know why they were working in the first place. And that makes me sad. It motivates me to work harder; to teach so many people how to work smart and live the life they will love.

Every time I have tried something before, I never put my whole self into anything. No wonder I didn't want to work hard. And to be honest, I guess I didn't work hard because there was nothing I truly believed in.

Future: You work hard for something that you believe in. You work hard when you're passionate about something; when you have a goal that is so important to you that even after you're tired of working hard, you'll go the extra mile to achieve it. You wouldn't mind doing one more rep on that machine, taking that shot, using that opportunity, making that call and closing that deal.

Serge: Exactly! Whenever I hear this *"calling"* from *Hard work*, I try to run away from it. When I knew that it was coming, I used to hide from it. When *hard work* was influencing others to talk to me, I quickly made excuses to get away from it.

Future: And why was that?

Serge: I was afraid of the pain because I didn't want to get hurt; afraid to fail, so I didn't even try. I was scared of what I've seen hard work do to others. Every time I take two steps forward, it always seemed that life knocks me three steps back. I had a belief that hard work can't pay off, making me so afraid that I thought hard work was a shadow behind me who will always fail me.

Future: Are you still afraid?

Serge: Hell, no! I'm embracing it now! It made me who I am today. Because of hard work I've developed never giving up attitude. When somebody tells me to quit, I keep going. When most people sleep, I'm awake, ready to work. Now I'm a dream chaser, and I can defeat hard work by using it to my advantage. Now I know and believe that hard work does pay off, and because of that, I love it. You should like it. My advice to all of you reading these words is, don't hide from hard work - wait for it! You need it. You need to trust in it. If you're passionate about what you're doing or what you want to do, embrace hard work. It will pay off to those who don't give up. I'm sure my *Future* knows this.

Future: You work hard because you care. You're not working just for yourself. You're working hard because of your family; because of your community and because of all these souls that are counting on you. It's bigger than you. You work hard because of those who still don't believe that it will pay off because when it pays off, they will look at you as an inspiration; that what was possible for you will be possible for them. *Life rewards those who work hard*.

Hard work alone will not lead you to success. Consistency will. These small things that you're doing daily no matter how hard they are, or how tired you are, they are what will lead you to success. I have never seen or heard that someone successful did it without working hard. Michael Jordan took more than 500 shots each day from only one spot on the court until his arms were completely fatigue and almost broken from the pain. *Jack Canfield* was rejected from 144 publishers before one publishing house gave him a chance and today his book *"Chicken Soup for the Soul"* has been sold in more than 500 million copies! There are thousands of examples that we can talk about, but you must know that hard work comes from the will! It comes from the heart!

It's not about your physical strength; although, you'll need it too along the way. It's not even about your mental toughness. It's about will! When you're tired physically, exhausted mentally, your willpower will help you to keep moving. Your heart will never fail you. You must know this; **the harder you work, the harder it is to give up!**

Because you've invested so much into it, it becomes harder to surrender, and that's good! This book is all about using your *Imagination*. I dare you. I dare you to use your *Imagination* while you are working hard! *Imagination* will take you far beyond your wildest dreams. The more you use it, the harder you work and the closer you're getting to your goals. One day you'll be grateful and proud of all these days you have to work hard because you'll be at the top and you'll appreciate the way you had to climb that mountain to get to the top.

Serge: That's why it has been said that the toughest climbs always lead to the best views. And right now while I'm writing this chapter, I'm watching the US Open Finals between Novak Djokovic and Juan Martin Del Potro. It's September 9th (2018), and Djokovic just won the 14th Grand Slam title. Only a year ago, he was the only player who held all 4 Grand Slam titles in a calendar year, and he's considered maybe the best player of all time. Soon after that, he had an elbow injury that required surgery, and he couldn't play for nine months. He came back and started losing in the first and the second round of the tournaments. Everybody thought that he'd never be like he was before the injury, that he'd never be able to win a grand slam again. But he came back stronger and won a Wimbledon and the US Open. He's another good example that faith and hard work do pay off. Coming back from an injury, fighting in your mind if you will be able to win again and putting the hardest possible work than you have ever put before has just paid off! You can see it through his eyes full of tears of joy and knowing that the hard work he put in has paid off.

I'll give you one more example. I started going to the gym in 2014, and since then I was going for two months, and then two months break. Then four or five months in and then again a few months off and so on. I was inconsistent. And believe it or not, I was frustrated because the results didn't show at all! I thought I had a good workout and that I was eating healthy, but not a single muscle showed up! And so I stopped again a year ago. Then I remember another instance on July 2nd, 2017. I was in the washroom, and I didn't look at the mirror for months, like didn't even notice my body in the mirror, but for whatever reason, I looked at it that day, and I saw the big fat belly! I couldn't believe it! I ran to find a scale and to measure myself. I found it and measured myself; I was shocked. I was 210 pounds! It may not sound shocking to you, but I'm 5'11, and I've never in my entire life weighed more than 183 pounds; and all of a sudden, I was on 210 pounds. The worst thing was that everything went into my waist. I was disgusted, angry, and mad at myself because I allowed that to happen. Immediately, I reached a decision that I was going to the gym that day to lose every possible percentage of fat.

I went to the gym with a decision to lose weight, and I've decided that every day, I'm going to run 5km. I got to the gym after a few months of not going at all and started running on a treadmill. I was on the first mile, and I was dead! I couldn't breathe, couldn't even move from how tired I was. Only one mile! I went home. I came back the next day. I said, *"Today I'm gonna run 5km no matter what!"* I went on the treadmill, started running, the first mile again, and I was exhausted! I went home and came back the next day. I repeated the same thing that I was going to run 5km no matter what; I got to the gym, started running, this time even harder. I reached that first mile, and I was dead again! The fourth day in a row, I'm going to the gym, but this time I've said, *"You piece of s*it! You've never given your all. Today you're going to run that 5km, and you'll not stop until every muscle in your body break even if that means you're going to die! You're going to do it, no matter what!"* I was seriously dead. I mean it. You can't imagine my determination. I said I was going to do it or I was going to die on the treadmill. I started running.

I clearly remember, just when I was about to reach that first mile, my body began sending me all kinds of signals to give up. That area in your stomach where it hurts you because you're not in a comfortable condition was such a pain. My mind was telling me to give up. My legs were starting to hurt. Every muscle in my body was telling me to stop and go home. But no! This time I was determined to do it, and I've started to talk to myself to talk to my mind and my body. Now we're talking about a higher power. It was about willpower. About my heart! I knew that I had to do it to break the current limits. Only by breaking your limits will your hard work make any sense!

I went through pain, through all kinds of thoughts of doubts, but eventually, I made it! I ran 5km. Immediately, I sat down, and it took me several minutes to catch my breath! But man it was worth it! I felt great! I felt relieved! I felt so good because I knew that when I almost gave up my spirit stepped in, and I made it. I went home so tired, but I said I was coming back the next day again to run 5km and so I did. And I came the next day again. It was the 7th day since I made that decision that I was going to lose that weight. After three weeks, I'd dropped 17 pounds of fat! On September 3rd, it was the first time I ran 10km! It took me only two months to come to the point of running 10km.

Then I set a new goal. I have this picture of the type of body I would love to have. Initially, everything I was doing didn't work out; so this time, I decided to ask for help. My very good friend who is also a personal trainer talked with me, and after showing him the picture of how I want to look, he sat down with me and designed a 2-year workout plan and program to achieve it. But then he told me that this would require a great deal of self-discipline and consistency, not just in working out but in my nutrition as well. So I had a workout plan, but now I needed help with my nutrition because, although I know a lot about it, I didn't have time to prepare the meals for myself and to be honest I didn't know how to make anything except two or three things. So I've decided to find help and see how I could make it work.

Maybe a month later after I started this new workout program, I saw on Instagram page of one of the other personal trainers who I knew from the gym, and he was selling prepared meals that can last five or six days. Every week he had a different food menu, and you can pick as many meals as you want for a very affordable price. I texted him and told him what I wanted to achieve, and from then, he makes my meals. Of course, he has a lot of customers, but my point is that I've found a way to put everything together. Here I am, finally having both workout and nutrition plan, what's next?

Next is ***discipline*** and ***hard work***! Nobody can do it for me except me. What I did this time was that I was and still am so focused and determined to have that body just like I was determined that day when I said that I'd run 5km or die trying. And for the first time in my life, the results are starting to show! I can see that all early mornings are starting to pay off! Thet hard work that I'm putting into it is starting to pay off! That's one more proof for me to believe in hard work and to embrace it!

Future: These are perfect examples that hard work always beats talent. You can find why others are better, faster, smarter than you but you can't find an excuse for not working hard. I love the fact that you're giving a lot of personal examples in this book about almost every subject.

Serge: Like I said many times, I love to teach about what I've been through. That's how people can relate to the story. There's one more example that I want to put into a whole new chapter.

Future: And that is?

Serge: It's an example of how hard work beats talent but also a lesson on how I believe that life should be lived. I'll use a Serbian folklore dance as an analogy to explain how I see life through the eyes of a dancer and how all the hard work I put in to beat the talent I didn't have for something that I love so much.

Dance through life

I always like to say that my first love is a *dance*. In Serbia, where I come from, we have a national dance that we call *folklore* (Serbian folklore dance). My second love was a handball. And my third love is the love I feel for my family. But let me tell you a little bit about my first love and how I see life through the eyes of a dancer.

"Dance is a hidden language of the soul." – **Martha Graham**

Years ago, when I started learning how to dance, I didn't begin with the hardest possible steps. I started with a few elementary steps that can give me the feeling that I can do it. When you were a baby, you didn't immediately begin to walk. Your parents helped you with small steps. And you practiced step by step. How many times have you fallen? You're right. Several times you fell, but you never gave up and said, *"That's it! I can't do it; I'm not meant to be a walker!"* No baby does that. You get up and keep going, and one day you catch yourself walking! It's the same in folklore. Step by step, and soon, you'll learn how to dance a simple dance.

After you learn a few basic steps and simple choreography, you're ready to go to the next level, which is a little bit more complicated with different steps and moves. I'm quite a slow learner, and I'm not ashamed to admit that. I remember in my group, almost everyone had always learned new steps before me, and I remember when I was about 14 years old, at that time my teacher told me that I was not good enough and that this was not for me. I continued to dance for a while, but eventually, I quit after a few months when I heard that. I was aware that I didn't have talent, but I loved it so much that I made one of those decisions that you can only regret and at that time, I didn't have anybody who could give me a word of encouragement not to give up. That's precisely what happens in life. You want to do something that you love, and then someone comes and tell you all the reasons why you are not good enough for that, and if you're mentally weak, you'll accept that as your truth, and you'll give up on your dream.

"Someone's opinion of you does not have to become your reality!" – **Les Brown**

If you love something, and you have a passion for doing it, you feel the joy while you do it; don't give up on what you want to do. Don't give up on your dream. People who can't see themselves doing something that they would love to do will not see that you can do it because they believe if they can't, nobody can. You have to be brave and keep going. Hold that dream with your whole being and never let anyone take it away from you.

A few years later, I decided to go back to dance. Only this time, surprisingly, I had the support of my parents and closest friends. These were the same people who told me a few years earlier that I had *"two left feet"* (which means that I don't know how to walk, let alone dance).

I came back and immediately I faced the challenges. I was a few years and several choreographies behind all the members of that group. But I didn't care. I put myself into work, and I was dancing every single day. We had only two practices per week, but I took the videos of all the dances that I didn't know, and I was learning them at home. In only two months, I learned everything and got back in the group (until then, I was dancing on the side because I didn't know the steps).

In life, when we face challenges, sometimes it may seem that there's no way out. But we don't have to accept that as something terrible but as an opportunity to stretch ourselves, grow and learn new things; things that will shift our thoughts and help us overcome whatever problems we face along the way to achieving our dreams. You always have a choice. You can turn around and regret because you didn't dare to do something or you can give it a try. I did exactly that.

Every year at the end of December, we have a yearly performance. After months of practice and hustle, the moment of truth came. I remember how nervous I was especially because I hadn't danced for years in front of hundreds or thousands of people. I was scared. My legs were shaking. Suddenly I forgot the dancing steps before we got on stage. I won't tell you the details, but in the very first dance I made some huge and visible mistakes, and during the whole performance I made a lot of mistakes and wrong steps. You can guess all the thoughts that I had after I finished that concert and all the words that came to my mind that I wasn't good enough and dancing was not for me etc.

> *"Every adversity, every failure, every heartache carries with it the seed of an equal or greater benefit."*
> *– Napoleon Hill*

Life will test you. When you want something badly, life will send you many different tests to see how badly you want it; to see how strong you are, and you have to know that every time you find yourself defeated, always remember that nobody accomplished anything without experiencing temporary defeats. What is your job when that happens? ***To get up on your feet and do it again!*** What will keep you or motivate you to do it? ***Your reasons!***

My reasons were my passion and the love I felt for dancing. Those moments were one of the most precious moments that I've experienced in my life. And because everyone told me that I couldn't do it, I decided to come back and do it again. I was working even harder not just on my steps or moves, but I imagined the stage, music, dances and even envisioned myself performing without mistakes.

I returned the following year with one of the best performances of my life. ***Hard work paid off.*** That moment when I was dancing together with my sister on stage, the proud look in my parent's eyes, the feeling of joy and happiness that I felt, the big applause that we received from the audience was something that words could not describe. You have to experience it! I want you to know that the greatest moment wasn't the moment when I was performing (although that was my dream and it was absolutely magnificent moment), but the moment when *I decided to do it!* The best time was the time I spent in the process of becoming a person who is capable of overcoming obstacles and doing what is necessary to achieve that goal. What I want to say is, it's imperative to enjoy the process.

In 2011, I decided to quit something that I was so passionate about because I thought it was time to do something else in my life. And I remember the feeling that I had at that moment. It was hard, and somehow, I felt that I didn't give it all that I had. And it's funny how life can play with you sometimes. You never can tell what life can deliver to you. Life will bring you precisely the right people, events, and resources at the right time; I genuinely believe that. Like I said, when I thought that I was finished with folklore, two years later, I came to Canada. I found out that there was a *Serbian Culture Association Oplenac in Toronto*, and that was the best way for me to socialize and meet new people and find new friends.

When I got there, I was accepted by the group immediately, and I found a feeling that I never had before. The love that I was feeling for folklore became greater than before. I couldn't wait to come to practice. That passion… That's how life is meant to be! ***You need to have a passion for life! You have to know why you are waking up every morning.*** What gives you that passion and energy that you can't wait to get up in the morning and do something that you really love? ***Life is a gift!*** And our job is to find what we are passionate about so we can spend every moment, every hour of every day in that state of love and passion. My passion is talking; I love to talk to people. To teach them, share my experience with them and help them to realize how beautiful they are and to find their feeling of belonging on this planet. That is something that drives me every day, that feeling of improving not just my life, but the lives of others too.

It was the beginning of May 2016; we went to Vancouver to stage a performance. Although I had dozens of concerts around the world, I must say; that night was the most special in my whole career as a dancer! I will never forget the moment of pure joy when we received an applause more than ten minutes long. In the end, the emotion I felt in my heart and tears of happiness that I had in my eyes. I remember saying to myself that now I'm ready to say goodbye to folklore. The moment when you get there is always exciting, but as I said, your greatest moment was the moment when you decide! I remembered the moment when I decided to come back, and ten years later, I saw it was the greatest decision about dancing that I've made!

Now, I'm delighted and grateful for everything I've experienced with folklore, and I'm still dancing. I'm doing it for my soul. I've achieved my goals in folklore, and now I'm just enjoying and having fun. That's how life should be; pure joy, happiness, and fun. When I dance, and in the middle of choreography I make a mistake, I don't just stop and go on the side to cry and feel sorry for myself about that mistake. No! I even put a bigger smile on my face and keep dancing! In life, when we fail, make a mistake, we become frightened. But that's the moment you have to stand with your head up and put a smile on with full faith; knowing that you'll solve that problem, that you'll overcome that adversity and that you'll find a way to start your dream job. That's the moment where you need to continue to dance! Because in the end, it will be worth all the efforts, all the tears, all the hard work that you put into that goal. The most beautiful moments weren't those times when I finished choreography, but the moments I experienced during the choreography; which means, *enjoy the process!*

Life is beautiful! It really is. Whenever you face a challenge, always remember that you need to continue to dance with a smile on your face, because if you persevere and don't give up, soon, you'll live your dream!

Future: That's a beautiful story. And in that one story, there are so many lessons about life that anyone can learn from. Did you ever talk about it with a teacher who told you to give up?

Serge: Never about that, but the funny thing is that after my comeback he actually hired me to work with the kids because I knew every single step correctly and I knew the style of the dances because we have so many choreographies from different parts of the country, and every part have their unique style of dancing. I believe that I did it because he told me that I couldn't, and I've never blamed him. Maybe I didn't know then, but I know now that he didn't realize that hard work beats talent and then he underestimated my will to do it. I've never taken it personally. As a matter of fact, from this perspective, I'm grateful for that because it has shaped my life in a way because that was a massive proof that I'm able to do many more things if I put hard work and passion into it.

Future: I believe that's a good formula for success:

Hard Work + Passion + Determination = Success

Serge: There are so many formulas out there, so that's one more for someone that is looking for a *"secret"* formula.

Future: There's one thing that you've mentioned that I believe we should talk about.

Serge: What is it?

Future: You've said that you didn't take it personally when your teacher told you that you were not good enough. So let's expand on that so your readers can gain some valuable information that will help them to change the way they look at some things.

Don't take anything personally

This is a sensitive topic to talk about because most people, and I mean about 95% of people take everything personally. Whenever someone tells them something, they take personal irrespective of its nature, good or bad.

Serge: Especially if it's bad.

Future: Correct. Someone says to you, *"Hey you look so fat,"* you take it personally and start feeling the emotional poison that you need to fight back and say something (probably not appropriate) in return or you may try to defend your beliefs about your body. What you must know is, just because that person told you that you're fat does not say anything about you; it just makes them someone who needs to put a label on others. They are dealing with their feelings. Whatever they say is not personal, although it may look like it is.

Serge: Well, I'm not sure that you've used the right example since sometimes people can tell others that they're fat simply to motivate them to lose weight and get healthier. They tell them because of their own good.

Future: They might tell you for your own good, but you still take it personal no matter the intention behind it; especially if you're dealing with your own emotions about (in this example) your body. But to explain my point, let's use a different example. Let's say that somebody tells you, *"You're so stupid."* What will you do in that case?

Serge: Break their legs?

Future: That's funny but seriously, what will you do?

Serge: Right now, I would not care because I learned about this principle a few years ago. But if you ask me about who I used to be, I would probably take it personally. I know for sure that I would have these overwhelming thoughts like, "*Why did he say that?*" or "*Everybody tells me that I'm stupid, I guess I am!*" and many more.

Future: Then you would be thinking all night about it, and you wouldn't sleep because of it.

Serge: Probably.

Future: You see? That's what I wanted to talk about and help each one of you reading this. Using this example, somebody can tell you something without even knowing you. Maybe that person said it just to hurt you, and in a way, it did hurt you. It beats you because you take it personally. You agree with whatever was said, and as soon as you bring it close to your heart, the emotional poison is going through you, and now you're stuck in your mind where you're experiencing the hell of destructive thoughts.

What you must understand is that nothing others do is because of you. They have their own opinions and beliefs that are coming from their world. How they see life may be different from your perception of how you see it. What they say about you is none of your business. It doesn't matter.

Serge: But some people are so close to us that we care about what they say.

Future: You shouldn't care about what anyone has to say about you. The only reason why you care too much is that you don't know who you are. If you know who you are, you'll listen to what others say about you, but you'll hear nothing because you wouldn't care. You'll understand that everything others say is a reflection of who they are. Everything others are doing to you is a reflection of who they are.

Serge: In other words, all the bullying that I've been through for eleven years was nothing but a reflection of who the bullies were. To feel better about themselves, they were doing all those inappropriate things to me because they wanted to hide the negative feelings they had about themselves?

Future: You must know that you'll never be bullied by someone who is on a higher level of awareness than you are. A successful person will never laugh at you when you fail because they understand the process you're going through. And yes, to feel better about themselves and to hide their imperfections, all these people intimidated you because of that. Can you remember a time when the bullying would happen? And who was the person that was bullying you?

Serge: Hmmmm I can remember so many situations, but now you make me think a little bit deeper about it. I remember when I was in high school, for instance, during lunch break when all the boys were talking, if someone teased another person, and it was getting personal, the person who was being teased will say something like *"Don't tell me these things, I'm not like stinky boy,"* and he was referring to me for no reason. This happened in my class several times, and I always wondered why they needed to refer to me. But I must admit that I really had this thought, *"Maybe because they were afraid that one day they would be bullied,"* and that was the reason why they did that.

Future: Now, you understand even better than before. That happened because, in that situation to avoid further teasing or joking and to feel better about himself, that kid was turning the story towards you. But as you can see, it wasn't because of you; it was because of him. He knew that he was insecure; he had imperfections and he, like many others who were doing all that stuff to you, deep down inside of him was afraid that one day, he would be intimidated as well.

Serge: If only I knew this before, I would never have to go through all those nightmares and suffering for eleven years.

Future: You're wrong. You have to go through all of that to learn what you now know, so you can teach others about this and help them avoid taking things personally. That was a path that your *Soul* led you to become who you are today. So be grateful for it.

Serge: Of course, I am grateful. I know what you're saying, but still, it was a pain in the ass.

Future: You'll be judged by your words here but don't take it personally.

Serge: Ha-ha, of course, I will not. So if somebody stops worrying about other people's opinions; if they stopped taking things personally; if they stopped being hurt by what others are doing to them, they'd put themselves in a position to never be wounded again?

Future: Exactly. If you stop taking things personally, the words and actions of others can no longer hurt you. You have immunity towards them. You have a shield that will always protect you.

How others see you has nothing to do with who you are. If they see you as who you truly are, they would never say or do anything bad or wrong to you. If they were in alignment with who they indeed are, they would see you as a perfect manifestation of your Source, and they would show you nothing but love. Also, there's one more thing. We were talking about not taking anything personal when it comes to negative things.

Serge: Let me guess, you want to point out that we should not take anything personally even when somebody tells us something positive?

Future: Exactly that. Even when somebody tells you, *"I like you, you're a really good man,"* they may think that today, but tomorrow they might change their opinion about you. There are so many people who are nice to people they need for personal use. If you want to know someone, look at how they treat people they don't need in their life. Today, someone will tell you, *"You're so nice,"* and tomorrow you may hear from the same person, *"You're such an idiot!"* So don't take it to heart, even if it's a positive thing.

Serge: May I ask you something?

Future: You don't need to ask me that. Just ask.

Serge: I believe I understand this principle of not taking things personally, but it may be misused in a way that people will take words literally, and they may become impervious to everything, to the point that even constructive criticism or positive suggestions roll off them like water off a duck's back. How do we avoid not going too far with this principle?

Future: That's a good question, and you have a point. Not taking things personally doesn't mean rejecting everything you hear, it does mean that you're still open to listening to other people and listening to them honestly; taking their feelings and opinions into account. It means staying open to constructive criticism and honest disagreement in the hope that others can help you grow through expressing how they see you, through showing you your reflection in the mirror of life. That's a healthy perspective of this principle.

Serge: Make sense! What is your suggestion for practicing this?

Future: As with everything, you have to acknowledge it and be aware of it. It starts with awareness. You're aware of the moment, and you understand that you have the power to control your thoughts and feelings. Whatever somebody tells you, use your emotions to realize how you are feeling and if you feel a negative emotion, ask yourself why you're feeling the negative emotion; and as soon as you answer it, you'll feel a positive emotion and you'll be free in your mind and will not take it personally.

Or if somebody tells you something negative, reply, *"What you say about me is none of my business. I don't care about it."* and don't give a second thought. Just let it go then and there. The exciting thing about any principle known to the human mind is that people in most cases, want to learn how to use it for the short term benefits instead of looking at the bigger picture. ***Everything new you try to learn or apply requires practice.*** And not just practice, but a lot of practice! And practice again and all over again; because in the process of learning, mastering you'll make mistakes. You'll be tested, and you'll fail to use the principles when you need them the most. And that's okay. It's a part of the growth process. That's a path to mastering anything in your life. When I speak of being aware of the moment, that's not something that will happen all of a sudden; it takes time.

Serge: That's so true. So many times I've been in situations where I didn't react as I was hoping I would and after the moment has passed, I felt so angry and so mad at myself because I knew I should have responded better or acted better than I did. And I remember my thoughts were like, *"I can't believe that you've reacted like that. I thought you had learned this. Damn! Now you have to learn it all over again."* and I think about it all day long, but now, I don't think like that anymore. I make a mistake knowing that it is inevitable sometimes, and that's okay. Because, it still means that there is something to learn, something to remember, and that's the beauty of this learning process; the same with not taking anything personally. Even now sometimes, I take something personally, but this time it's easier to shift my focus because I'm more aware of the moment than I used to be. And yes, it didn't happen overnight, I've noticed recently that I'm becoming aware of every moment of every passing day. But this happened after years of not being aware of anything, let alone of the present moment.

Future: It's a constant conscious reminder to yourself daily to be aware of this moment right now. You have to talk to yourself. Through time you'll become aware of every moment, and only then will you discover your real power and ability to create a life that you want. This is my advice to you and your readers:

No matter how hard it is right now, be patient. You're in the process of learning, gaining wisdom and remembering who you are. With faith, you'll soon discover the power you have within you.

Serge: Huh.

Future: Yes.

Serge: I think we've covered so many subjects that will make an immediate impact on others. I'm going to need some time to absorb all this information.

Future: But you still have some topics that you want to talk about.

Serge: Indeed, I do. Can we talk about relationships? I know that we have mentioned something about it in the previous topics, but can we expand on it? For example, I understand that relationships are consistently challenging, but how can we be happy in all our relationships, no matter how rough they can sometimes be?

Relationships

F*uture:* By using them for their right purpose.

Serge: And what is that purpose?

Future: That's up to you to decide. As we have mentioned in the topic **"Quantum Leap in Relationships,"** you have to use them for the intended purpose. They are constantly challenging. They require you to grow, express, adapt, and experience the magnificent versions of yourself. Every relationship you've experienced with other people, places, and events, you must use to decide who you really are. You can only do that through relationships. Through every relationship that has to happen and will happen in your life is the perfect opportunity for you to choose who you are in that moment. You can choose to be someone who will let the relationship shape you or you can shape yourself by using that relationship as a tool to improve yourself and be the best version of yourself at that moment.

The reason why relationships are so great, and some of you may even call them sacred is because they provide you with an opportunity to create and produce the experience of your highest conceptualization of self.

Serge: But why then so many relationships fail?

Future: You've been told that in relationships, one is supposed to worry only about another, and when you worry about the other, your focus upon the other is what causes relationships to fail. But in the extreme sense of it, relationships never fail. It just means that the reason you wanted to use them didn't work or better still, you've entered into a relationship for the *"wrong"* reason. In a more profound sense, relationships never fail. They will always be the experience of whom you were at that moment and who you are in this moment.

Serge: You've said that relationships are an opportunity to create the highest conceptualization of self. What do you mean by that?

Future: This may sound radical, but you must be Self-centered.

Serge: What do you mean by that?

Future: You have to love yourself first, and then to love someone else. Most people think that if they love others, others will love them and then they will be lovable so they can love themselves. But the truth is, that most people don't love themselves because they feel that nobody loves them, and that is not true. Other people do love them, but that doesn't matter because it's not enough.

Serge: You mean those people don't believe that somebody can love them?

Future: Correct. They believe that if you show them your love, it means that you want something from them. Then they will try to figure out what you want. When they accept that you might love them, they will want you to prove that you love them. This may require you to alter your behavior. If they finally come to a point where they start to believe that you actually do love them, they immediately get worried about how long it will last. And now the action is becoming a reaction, and to keep your love, they start to alter their behaviors.

Serge: Like we spoke on a topic about the *Original thought* in the example of my experience with my ex-girlfriend; when I began to alter my behavior to keep her as long as I could. And because of that, I lost myself in that relationship.

Future: Not just that you lost yourself in that relationship, but she lost herself too. Both of you entered into a relationship hoping that you'll find yourselves, only to find out that you've lost yourself instead. This might sound harsh, but it is true for every similar relationship as well as yours. The moment you start losing yourself in a relationship, you're becoming lesser than you've been when you were single; less attractive, less capable, less exciting, less happy and less joyful. You've given up who you are so you could stay in that relationship.

Serge: I agree on this. I've experienced everything you've said right now.

And I believe that because of this experience I've learned how beneficial it is to spend some time alone, or to be single for some time so you can remember who you are because when you do remember, you'll be ready to get into any relationship without worrying what others will think, speak or do.

Future: That is true. If you've spent some time alone researching your mind and your life, you'll not have to go through all that trouble you've been into. That's why a ***relationship with yourself is the most crucial element in this process***. Therefore your first and most important relationship has to be with yourself.

Serge: That's why it has been said that you can't see others as worthy if you don't see yourself as worthy first. You can't see others as light before you acknowledge yourself as someone who radiates light. You can't love others if you don't love yourself first.

Future: Exactly! Secondly, make sure that you're getting into relationships for the higher purpose; for the right reasons. Do not enter into a relationship because you're feeling lonely or to end your depression, solve your ego, just for sex, or because you're bored. None of these reasons will work in the long term. Although it is possible that things will change along the way, that's less possible if you enter for the wrong reasons.

Serge: I came to a point where I realized that there's no point in short-term relationships; that all of the reasons you mentioned will not work. I know so many people who are getting into relationships just to forget the previous one, for example. And I always say to them to stop and take some time to think about what was wrong with the previous relationship before they jump into a new one. The need for the wait is because there's a huge possibility that they will end up with the same person just with a different name.

Future: That's a good point. If you just got out from a relationship and you immediately jump into another, nothing will change. You're still the same person you were in the previous one, and your level of vibration will dictate the kind of person you will attract in the next one. Because you didn't take some time to change your level of vibration and your state of being, you will enter into a new relationship with the same thoughts, belief systems, patterns, and with the same behavior that you had in the previous relationship. You'll be with the same person as the previous one just with a different name. Maybe not in the beginning, but sooner or later, you'll notice the same words and behavior of another one that you'll ask yourself a question: *"How is it possible that she's the same as my ex?"* and you'll not know the exact reason why that is.

If you are reading this right now and you're the type that jumps from one relationship to another, I recommend you to go back to the subject *"Singleness as a Gift"* and reread it because it will help you to avoid the mistakes you made in previous relationships.

Serge: Thank you for promoting my topics like that.

Future: You're welcome. I have to promote myself as much as I can right?

Serge: Ha-ha true! So to my understanding, long-term relationships are the best opportunities for mutual growth and mutual fulfillment.

Future: True. If you and your special one agree on a conscious level that you'll enter into a relationship for the right purpose of creating an opportunity for growth; fulfillment;, for living your lives joyously at all times; to complement each other; to learn how to communicate, to understand that there will be challenging, and difficult times; that would be a great beginning of something special that is about to come. It will be comfortable when everything is going right. But when things don't go as you planned, and you face the challenges, don't try to avoid them; welcome them because they are the perfect opportunity for the growth of the relationship itself as well as your individual growth.

Don't worry about what others are thinking, doing, working, or speaking. Remember, no matter how selfish it may look like, *be self-centered!* Love yourself first, and then you'll be able to give your love to another because you can't give somebody something that you don't have for yourself. Understand that there will be a need for both of you to tolerate each other, to be patient, to persevere through some rough times, and to compromise.

Serge: When you say *"to compromise"* you mean that relationships are about giving, not just taking?

Future: That's why I've said most people enter into a relationship for not so good reasons. If you think of what you can get from it rather than what you can give to it, the other person may resent you because of how much they give you and how little they receive back from you. The both of you must agree on a conscious level that you'll invest as much as you can into that relationship and give something rather than take away.

Serge: To summarize this, you are saying, to have a happy and successful long-term relationship it would be wise to talk with one another about the purpose of the relationship, the goals that we can set for it, and that we'll develop our relationship through constant communication?

Future: Yes, that would be wise to do. Maybe not in the beginning but after spending some time together, it would be wise to talk about these things you've just mentioned. Most relationships don't last because people are afraid to ask questions. And you'll have to ask them to improve a relationship, to grow, or maybe to solve some misunderstanding that you don't even know that exists. You must be open to communication. If two people can't find a way to openly and honestly communicate their needs and feelings to each other, the relationship doesn't stand much of a chance in the long term. Now, don't get me wrong, this doesn't mean waiting for an argument to tell your significant other how much they bother you with throwing their clothes on the floor instead of the hamper. It means telling them when you feel the need to, and doing so in a manner that is respectful but assertive.

Serge: I totally agree with this. Communication is essential not just in a romantic relationship but in every human relationship; whether it is about friendships, business, or whatever. I think the one *tool* that will be helpful to keep the relationship healthy is to ask the question, *"Rate our relationship from 1 to 10?"* I heard this at a seminar where *Jack Canfield* was a guest, and I found it so compelling because when you ask this question for the first time, people will look at you with a funny expression on their face. And when you repeat the question and ask them honestly, they will actually pause for a moment and tell you what they think. If they, for example, say, *"I think it's about 7,"* I would immediately reply, *"What would it take to be 10?"* and then you wait for a response. As long as it's not a 10, you can continuously change something to improve it. Perhaps you need to make lunch once in a while or clean the laundry instead of your partner, but this question can be an excellent tool for improving a relationship.

Future: That's an excellent question to ask, but people are afraid to ask. Meanwhile, it is the only way to know where you are and how your relationship can improve or get out of trouble; by asking the right questions.

Serge: I think we have covered a lot of things about this subject, but I have one more question. Although I know this may be different from one relationship to another, but what are your thoughts on how can we keep our relationships exciting and not get bored?

Future: That's an interesting question. Do you remember your first kiss, your first girl that you really liked?

Serge: Of course I do like it was yesterday!

Future: That's what you have to do to keep your relationships exciting all the time. Always do what you did on your first date in the first six months of your relationship. The truth is, you will not marry the person you date the first night. Everybody will make themselves look the best they can on a first date to give a good impression. But after some time, maybe after a few months or perhaps years, couples start to get used to each other, and lose the effort to keep things exciting; and after some time they get bored so to speak.

If you can maintain that *first date spirit*, I can guarantee that your relationship will be exciting all your life. With time you'll meet your partner better and better, and the more you know about her, the more creative you can be to do some things that you did in the first six months. Call her by her favorite name. Buy her a flower that she loves now and then and go on dates once in a while as if it's the first date. Do something every day that will make you both happy. After your work, run home and jump into her arms! Kiss her like it is the first time! Be passionate! Find out what you love doing together; swimming, traveling, hiking, watching movies, playing tennis, whatever it is, do it as long as you enjoy doing it. There's one thing that you must realize; when you fell in love with your mate.

You didn't fall in love on the first date nor was it the second. They didn't fall in love with you on that specific day. She fell in love with you because when you get out of bed and go to the kitchen to take your juice, you bring her a glass of her favorite juice as well. She fell in love with you because when she comes after a very stressful day at work and although you had a great day, you will not tell her after her complaints, *"Yeah, yeah, but let me tell you about my day."* No! You will sit down and listen to her and say not a word. No specifically known moment made her fall in love with you. The reason she fell in love with you is because of the accumulation of all of these little things; she wakes up one day and realizes that she loves you.

Small things on a consistent daily basis are what make the difference. That's what will make a happy and exciting relationship every day. When you ask your girl how her day was, and you care to hear it. If you make her a coffee while she's talking and you're engaged in a conversation; that's what will keep your relationship less boring. There are so many ways that you can try to help keep your relationship exciting, but you must discover them on your own.

Serge: I am so happy to know this now because I'm sure that I can have the best relationships thanks to this knowledge. Thank you for these words.

Future: I appreciate your gratitude, and I'm happy knowing what kind of person you're becoming. You're on the right path, but you don't need to thank me because these words are all yours. Just remember, every relationship is a perfect opportunity to see and decide who you are.

Serge: I understand that.

Future: Do you want to move on to the next subject?

Serge: Yes I do. I actually want to talk about giving. You've said that when we get into a relationship as a complete person, we should look at what we can give instead of what we can take from it.

Future: And you want to talk about giving?

Serge: But not about giving something to a relationship, but giving in life overall.

Future: I understand, let's move to that

Learn how to give

*"Since you get more joy out of giving joy to others, you should put a good deal of thought into the happiness that you can give." - **Eleanor Roosevelt***

Firstly, let's stick with relationships a little more. When you're a complete person, and you love yourself, you understand that you have more than enough love for yourself and you can give it to others as well. And by giving your love to others, you'll notice that love is coming back to you from different sources. Learn how to give everything to your relationships. Give a compliment. Be kind. Say something sweet every day and do something for your loved ones that will help them change their moods. Be of service and do it without the expectation that you'll receive something in return; do it with all your heart and mind. Only true giving from the heart without expectations is something that will provide you with joy; or better yet, ***the intention behind the giving*** should always be to create happiness for both the receiver and you. And you must know that return is directly proportional to the giving when it is unconditional and from the heart.

Kids know how to give! Just look at them. Whatever you give to them they will look for somebody to give it to. They offer a smile; they give love and joy. They give from their pure heart and without a single expectation to receive something in return. And that continues until they start to grow up and learn from their parents, teachers, and the environment overall that love is conditional; that there's not enough of it and not just that, but that there's not enough money, food, joy, peace, which is not true! They become so influenced by these thoughts and words from others that they start to believe it too and little by little, they stop giving unconditionally. If you want to learn how to give, you must wake up that innocent child in you and practice giving without the expectation that you'll receive something in return.

I'll tell you this, no matter what you believe or what others have told you, **the truth is; there is more than enough love, happiness, money, joy, peace, people, water, food, you name it!** This planet has an abundance of everything you can think of! It's an unlimited source of everything you want! You just need to remember how to love and give unconditionally!

Serge: I remember my thoughts about giving a few years ago. I thought that foremost, I have to receive something to give in return. In other words, if I saw a homeless person in the street, I would always think that I don't have enough for me, let alone to give to him. Also, because of not loving myself, I know that I didn't give anything to others. I'm not afraid to admit this, but I was a terrible friend, son, brother, boyfriend, co-worker, teammate, all because of my expectations to first receive something to give.

Future: I'm glad that you're brave enough to talk about these things from your own life openly. It takes courage to talk about these things. It takes courage to face the past and learn from it. You may have been like that before, that's not important anymore. The question is, who are you now? What kind of son, brother, boyfriend, co-worker, friend are you now? That's important. What is the intention behind your giving now?

Serge: Now I'm a different person. I realized that I started giving thoughts, words, or appreciation more than I ever offered before. I'm also giving money without expectations. I'm giving everything without expecting to have something in return.

Future: And how does that feel?

Serge: It feels great! I've noticed in the past few months that the more I give, the more I receive happiness. And even if I don't receive it at the moment, I don't care. I'm giving my love to everyone. Even if somebody doesn't like me, I'm sending to that person a silent prayer through my thoughts and wish them all the best.

Future: That's good to hear. I'll come to that just a little later. First of all, I want to clarify something that you all have to realize. *If you're going to receive anything in your life, the easiest way to do it is to give exactly that which you want!* In other words, if you want more joy in your life - give joy to others; if you want more money - help others to earn more; if you want more love - give your love unconditionally to others; if you want more happiness - make others feel happy when they're around you. If you want to be great in any area of your life - help other people feel great, in the best way you can.

To come back to your words, when you said, *"I'm sending to that person a silent prayer."* That's a perfect way to change your state of being, and then to impact that person too. Sending your silent thoughts of appreciation to others - even to those that do not like you will affect them in a positive way (that they'll not know what happened).

Serge: That's true. I was once on a bus, and I saw this lady, who was obviously sad, and for no reason, I smiled at her, she looked at me, and somehow she smiled in return. Immediately, I silently sent her my thoughts of happiness; *"Whatever you're going through right now, endure it because you're strong enough to survive it. I wish you the most amazing day and to be happy as soon as you can."* I can't remember the exact words, but I remember when I got out of the bus, she was looking at me with a bigger smile and somehow, I knew that my thoughts had impacted her positively.

Future: Indeed. Your thoughts are so powerful that they can make an impact like that. The best way to receive anything you want is to make a decision that anytime you want something; you'll give that exact thing to someone from the bottom of your heart. It doesn't matter if it's a compliment or a flower or a smile; give something whenever you get in contact with anyone. *The more you give, the more you'll receive!*

Serge: It is so simple that we often misunderstand a lot of these things.

Future: It is! It is so simple if you learn how to give anything without expectations!

Serge: Is *"giving and receiving"* related to the principle of *"Cause and Effect"*?

Cause and effect

Future: It is. Basically, with your unconditional giving, *you're causing the effect* of it. You give love (that's a cause), and you'll receive love (that's the effect of your action).

Serge: In other words, every action will result in a specific reaction or every cause will result in an effect of that cause.

Future: Precisely. Every thought you have, every word you speak and every action you take is a ***cause***; with that, you'll create a future that will be the ***effect*** of it.

Most of you are not the cause of your life, but the effect of your life. That means that you're allowing life to happen to you. Whatever happens, you accept as it is. If you lose a job, you'll probably think that you're *"unlucky"* and that negative things are always happening only to you and you don't even know why they are happening. You don't understand that you always get what you create, and you're always creating with your thoughts, words, and actions. For every thought, word and deed is a cause that sets off like a wave of energy throughout the Universe, which in turn creates a desirable or undesirable effect.

For example, if you insult me, I may feel offended as a result, and by insulting me, you're sending your negative energy into the field of the Universe that will affect in such a form that somebody else will offend you sooner or later. That's why it is essential that you be a witness to your thoughts, words, and actions.

Serge: Me: I understood this law a few years ago when I found myself broke and without any relationship in my life. It was the result of all my selfish thoughts, words, and actions that I had back then. To be more specific, when I was working as a health coach, at one moment, I've had about 55 clients. And I didn't care about a single one! The only thing I cared about was how to sell them the products and take their money. As a result, they left me and of course didn't want to buy from me, and I'm sure they sensed that I didn't care about them; and not just that, it happened that later I couldn't find a single client! It's like whatever I was doing didn't work at all. And I believe that the reason was that I still had these thoughts that I just wanted money.

Future: That's a perfect example of *"what you sow is what you reap."* You were planting the seed of taking whatever you can without giving anything in return. There's no such thing as *"something for nothing."* It doesn't work that way.

Serge: I know. That's why I ended up with nothing. I lost my friends and all my relationships with my clients and other people in my life. But I'm happy that I went through that. I'm really grateful because of that experience. I've learned how to appreciate and value all the people that I get in touch with. Thanks to that experience, I learned how to manage money properly, how to develop myself, how to be kind, and how to give! Also, I learned that I want to be the cause of my experience, not the effect of it.

Future: That's good. It has been said that, **"Cause and Effect" is God's law.** It is the law of all laws. And that's one more proof that every adversity brings with it the seed of an equivalent success. In your case, because of everything you went through back then, you became who you are today. And yes, you've learned how to give. And that's the best gift you can give to others. Give them something. Just a single smile or a kind word may change the whole day of that one person and believe it or not; it can change their lives!

Now let me tell you something that you've noticed so many times in your daily life. People are always blaming their circumstances for who they are. They blame all the events that happen to them and think that there are coincidences in this world. There are no coincidences in this world! Everything you've experienced is the effect of your thoughts, words, and deeds. ***You become what you think about all day long.***

If you don't have a goal and you have no idea where you are going, you'll probably let life throw anything at you; and you'll feel powerless to do anything. As a result, your life will become a frustration, and your mind will be filled with thoughts of fear, anxiety, and worry. That's because you've planted all these negative seeds in your mind. To reverse that, you have to begin planting the seeds of love, happiness, joy, grace, peace, kindness, compassion.

Nothing happens by accident. Everything is connected. You may not understand why this negative event happened to you. But if you look deeply in your mind, in your heart, you'll see that for an extended period you had thoughts of losing your job. That you'll not have enough money to pay the bills, that you'll end up alone, that you'll not do anything worthy in your life, and later when these adverse events become a reality of your life, you wonder *"how is this happening to me?"* Because for a long time you were planting the seeds of negative thought patterns and beliefs and the Universe had no choice but to respond to your thoughts and feelings and manifest what you were thinking and feeling about. The *Law of Cause and Effect* always works. No exception. It doesn't matter whether you are planting the seeds of positive or negative thoughts; it will respond according to your feelings. That's why the *Law of Attraction* works. The law of attraction is tied with the law of cause and the effect.

Maybe you're feeling unhealthy and fat. That's the effect, or you may say the result of the actions you were taking over time. Your diet was poor, you didn't exercise for years, and as a result of these unhealthy habits, one day you look at yourself in the mirror and get disgusted with how you look. You may end up hating yourself because of that.

Serge: Unbelievably true! I told you about my story of being fat a year ago. I was wondering how that happened, but when I was looking in the mirror, I was brutally honest. I knew that my diet wasn't, and I didn't work out for months, and as a result, I ended up being fat. Now that I'm fit and healthy, I'm trying to explain to others that this is the effect of my change. In other words, I decided to be the cause of my experience and took the matter in my own hands. I put all my thoughts, words, actions, feelings, and energy in alignment with who I want to be and the effect of this cause have started showing up in every sphere of my life!

Future: That's amazing. That's my biggest advice for all of you reading this - *be the cause of your experience.* Don't let life just happen, and then wonder why it is happening to you. Because if you ask those who are happy, prosperous and joyful, how they got all of that, they will tell you everything you've read here; they were planting those positive seeds. Only those who don't understand how to control their thoughts, words, actions, and emotions will think that everything that is happening in the world is caused by some *"chance"* or *"luck."*

Those who do understand this law will know that they're the creators of their reality. To put this law into work, you will need to start planting the seeds of hope, love, joy, success, and peace in your daily life! Some trees in this world need five years to grow out of the ground! Imagine! Five years! If you planted a seed and you start watering and cultivating, and if at any moment during those five years you stopped watering it, the tree would die in the ground. But if you continue cultivating and watering all the time, the tree that has been deep in the ground for five years will in six weeks grow 90ft tall! And the question is, did the tree grow in the six weeks or five years? The answer is obvious. In those five years, the tree was busy growing.

Be patient with your life. You have the seed inside of you that is about to show up. But you have to cultivate it. You have to put every thought, word, and deed into that seed. And what is the seed inside of you? It is your future! Right now, you have all kinds of things locked up deep down inside of you that are about to show up and manifest in your life if you continue cultivating it!

Serge: You mean, if we continue to *cause* it?

Future: Exactly. You want to look fit and be healthy? Find a good workout plan that you believe will work for you. Ask someone to teach you how to eat properly. Apply that in your daily life, and soon you'll see the effect. Do you want more success in other areas of your life? Good. Ask somebody to show you the way on how to be successful in business and apply that. Be relentless. Be consistent. Cultivate that seed that you have planted. It may sound a little harsh, but it will take time to achieve whatever you want. And that's the hardest thing to do; to wait! Whenever you feel like you want to give up, remember the story about the tree. Don't let the current circumstances define you. Don't just let life happen to you. Take control of your life starting today by planting the seeds of success in all areas of your life! Do something today that your future self will thank you for!

Serge: I'm doing exactly that.

Future: I know it. And I'm glad you're doing it; because a more fabulous life is waiting for you just around the corner. Be aware of the *Law of Cause and Effect* at all times and trust me, it will never fail you if you persevere and use it for the best possible benefits, not just for yourself but others as well.

Go the extra mile

Don't just go - go further! Go the extra mile. When you plant the seeds of success, sometimes you'll need to go the extra mile to be successful.

Serge: Nice. That's also something that I wanted to talk about, **"Going the extra mile."** I know for a fact that if you're doing something; let's say your job is to do something specifically, and you finish it, it feels good, you know. Your manager will be satisfied because you did what you were supposed to do, but if you do that and do something that may not be your job, it can be extremely satisfying. I know from personal experience that doing so can be your ticket for a promotion. And if your boss doesn't recognize the extra effort you're putting into that work; you should know that somebody will notice you and take you to work for them. You may end up opening your own business, or even if nothing like that happens, the Universe will repay unexpectedly, especially if you do the extra mile without expectation.

To give you an example: I used to work in a restaurant as a waiter, and I enjoyed working there! The reason was straightforward; you're serving others, and you can meet all kinds of interesting people and have some of the most pleasant conversations ever. So when I got there, and I knew what my area was, I made sure that every person that sat in my area was happy, satisfied and left the restaurant in a better mood than they were when they came in. That was my goal. I greeted them with the greatest smile. I asked them how they're feeling, engaged them in conversation and always tried to give them some nice compliments or words of encouragement; or even a short motivational speech. I was treating them like they were the most important people in the world. And 99% of the time, I had the biggest tip of all my colleagues, and it made me happy when they were leaving the restaurant with a huge smile. Their coming back and even asking our owner for me to be their server again, was the good proof that I was doing not just *"my job,"* but I was also going that extra mile.

Future: Extra mile is a term for those who want more from life. It means that you don't just do what you're supposed to do but do more. Do something extra today that will benefit you tomorrow, and you'll be successful. Your example is a good one. Going the extra mile can and will benefit you more than you think. I love when you said that maybe nobody will notice you in your job, but the Universe sees everything. *The Universe notices everything you do!* Your manager will not notice, the Universe will and it will give you back when you expect the least. It may reward you with unexpected opportunity in the form of a new job offer or in the way of someone who wants to collaborate with you in a new business.

As we said, most people have a tendency to do just as much as they need to; but if you noticed all these people that are trying to find a way through without doing anything productive, always finding a way to skip the work, they are not doing anything meaningful in their life. They're often unhappy, frustrated, they hate their work, and they always do just enough not to get fired. You must know that if you want more, you have to do more.

Your mind will develop according to the work you put into developing, and you'll notice there's always something to work on so you can grow in your mind and expand your awareness. When you're doing more than you're paid for or supposed to do, you're adding more value to your whole being, and that's what will separate you from others, and it will result in more opportunities for your services. But there's the tricky part. Some of you may start doing the extra work, and after a few days, you go back to your old habits. That will not work, my friend. If you adopt this habit of doing more as your life philosophy, soon the door for new opportunities will be opened for you and others will envy you thinking they also deserve more without knowing how much extra work you've put into everything you do. It is easy to say that nobody will appreciate your extra work, but that's just an excuse for not working harder. Going the extra mile intentionally will always be worth it sooner or later.

Serge: I believe this! I truly do! At this moment while I'm writing this book, I still have a full-time job at a construction company. The owner is a very good guy, but he doesn't know how to appreciate his workers, especially those who work very hard. My job is to load and offload the trailers, organize the workers in terms of what they need to do, and that depends on the orders from our customers and to make sure that everything is going as supposed. I didn't like that at all. I used to wake up with dread and hate and didn't want to go on with that work at all. But something has changed in the last few months.

I'm going to move away from this subject so that I can tell you my point and also to clarify what kind of change happened. About two months ago (I believe that it was at the end of July 2018), I don't remember the exact day or moment that this happened, but all of a sudden, I said to myself *"I'm happy!"* Literally, nothing remarkable happened. I didn't receive any great offer from some other company, I hadn't met the love of my life, I didn't have any breakthrough idea, I didn't receive any money or win a lottery, and I can't explain how this happened or why, but just for no reason, I realized that I was happy.

From that day until now, I started to look at all things in my life differently. To be specific because this is a subject that we're talking about right now, I noticed that my attitude about the job has changed as a consequence of that inner change. In other words, I do not love my job. I want to make that clear. But I started appreciating my job and being grateful for it because I understand that's the place that God put me in so I can learn how to manage conflicts, pressure and all other things on that level and be ready for the next level that God is about to put me! I'm supposed to be there. There's a reason for that. And I decided to go to that workplace and give my absolute best. As long as I am there and go the extra mile, I know that the Universe will give back in one way or the other, knowing that my boss might not appreciate my hard work, knowing that he won't even see what I'm doing and how hard I'm working. But intentionally I've put myself in that position of learning to become a leader who will know the way, show the way and most importantly lead the way!

I've started doing some things that are not part of my job that some other workers are supposed to do. I even started organizing and managing the orders from customers that my boss is supposed to do. I've started doing things as if I'm the owner, and I'm doing it with a maximum concentration, not to the point that I'll completely overwhelm and exhaust myself, but I'm giving my absolute best because I know that the Universe is watching and I even learned how to do it and be happy and satisfied. I am grateful for everything I'm going through; understanding that it's a part of the process and that I'm on my way to a greater life.

Future: First, I want to tell you that your pure and honest desire for happiness over the long period has led you to the *"waking up"* moment. And it's only a matter of choice how long you will stay in that state, but I urge you to make a conscious choice to be happy for the rest of your life! When people say, *"I don't like my job"* or *"I hate my job,"* and you ask them, *"then why are you still there?",* they will look for an excuse like they need to pay the bills; buy food; they're hoping that something better will happen one day; they can't find anything better; and many other excuses. Although paying bills and providing for yourself and your family food and shelter is important, but that should be used as motivation to go out and find something that you can at least enjoy a little bit. *Working hard at something you don't like is called* **stress.** *Working hard at something you love is called* **passion**. The reality is that most people are stressed because they work so hard on something they hate. And because they hate and don't believe that there's something good in their job, they are not willing to go the extra mile and improve their situation.

Serge: I can't blame them. It's understandable. It's tough to be willing to do extra work at the workplace you don't like; especially if you know that nobody will appreciate it or it will be unnoticed and without any reward.

Future: Then, why did you start doing it?

Serge: As I mentioned, I have a major goal, and my current job is one of my motivations to work harder on my dreams to move away from it as soon as I can.

Future: So we're going back to a definite purpose in your life, to what it is that you want to do in your life. At the end of this book, we'll talk about the fundamentals, or you may call them principles of life; but for now, let's stick with this. There's nothing more that I can say about the importance of going the extra mile. I understand what you're talking about when you say that it is hard to be motivated or inspired to do something that at first may not be rewarded. That's why you need to push yourself a little and have faith that it will be rewarded sooner or later in one way or the other. One of the reasons why people don't want to go the extra mile, or to change their current situation not just in their jobs, but their life, is because they're too comfortable with where they are.

Comfort zone

Serge: You mean they got so used to it that even if they know there's no happiness and progress where they are, they feel they have *"security"* there, and are so comfortable that they become scared of making any change, because change would put them into the unknown, outside of their comfort zone?

Future: You are creatures of habit. When you get used to doing what you always do, and you know how to do it, you become a master at doing it, no matter how much you like or don't like it. For most people, it would be hard to change the way they do something which they did for years in a certain way or to change their workplace or profession. If your work is the leading cause of your stress, but you're so afraid to drop it because of the bills, there's little or no chance that you'll do the extra work except if it is required from your managers and there's almost a zero chance that you'll try to go after something else. Even if you decide to go after something else, you'll always end up where you were before because your mind has stayed the same! ***To change anything in your life, you have to change your mind!***

Serge: You made this point before. I know that. I've gotten comfortable where I am right now, but I know that is not something that I'll do for long. I have the belief that I will get to the point of letting go of something to get what I want. In other words, I've put myself purposely in a position of discomfort to grow and learn and to move on; to demand more from life.

Future: What exactly did you do to put yourself outside your comfort zone?

Serge: Well, I did many things. Let us start with my workout plan, for example. I've learned in the past few months (because I studied every day) that to build the body I want; I need to work harder and allow my muscles to *fail!* For muscles to grow, they need to fail at first! I believe that is true in life as well; *sometimes we need to hit rock bottom and experience a temporary defeat to succeed.* We already said this, but it's always good to repeat sometimes and remind ourselves of this statement. Before I was lifting weights to the point, I felt comfortable. Whenever I started to feel the pain and discomfort, I stopped. I didn't go beyond that. That's why my muscles didn't show and grew no matter how good my nutrition was.

Another example is that I started waking up early, to be exact at 4:30 am every morning except Sunday morning. All these days I sleep on average for about five hours at the most, only on Sundays I allow myself to sleep eight or nine hours to recover and have a full rest because rest is a huge part of developing my body and mind. By waking up early, I put myself in discomfort, and I've brought back some morning rituals like meditation, writing my intentions for that day and been grateful for everything that I have and will have. I don't snooze the alarm no matter how tired or sleepy I am; because to do something I've never done, I have to be someone I've never been. I knew that to write this book; I'll have to find a time to write no matter what. So I devised a plan to put my life together; it's meant to be hard and outside my comfort.

I wake up at 4:30 am. I'm always in the gym at 5:05 am for my workout. I understood that to **win the day; I have to win the morning first.** Meditation, setting intentions, gratitude, and working out are the part of my morning rituals. After that, I go to work, and I work around 8.5h or 9h per day. After work, I get home and immediately I go to do a quick cardio training. After that, I shower, I sit to write until I feel sleepy. Now, this may not look like anything special to you, but for me, this is a way to be uncomfortable in a way that I have never been. Because you have to find time for your friends, family, other activities and unexpected events; if I wanted to do all of these things I love and enjoy doing, I would have to put myself in discomfort.

Before, I would only write when I got inspired. Now I write even if I don't feel like I want to; because my dreams and goals are dictating my time of waking up and going to bed, and I love it. I love this self-discipline. I love the discomfort. It feels great. In the beginning, I thought the discomfort was my enemy, but now I've embraced it, and I enjoy it. I love to be in the unknown. To do something I've never done. I genuinely believe that the *comfort zone is our biggest enemy* besides our very own negative voice.

Future: Anytime you do something that you've never done before, it will be uncomfortable in the beginning. And I agree with you; your comfort zone is your enemy. One of the biggest ironies is when you are trying to live your life staying comfortable; life will send you more and more discomfort. Life will throw rocks at you, and you'll keep struggling. You'll have more problems, issues, resistance, and pain because you're more concerned about being comfortable than to learn how to grow and stretch yourself. You're not here on this beautiful planet Earth to just be there, live your life and die! You're here to learn or better to say to remember who you are! To grow! To reach the heights that you thought you could never reach! To do the impossible! To break the limits! And if you will not put yourself in uncomfortable situations, life will make sure to give you plenty of reasons to push yourself out of your comfort zone.

That's what I like about your story and putting yourself intentionally in discomfort because you have two choices in life. Either you commit yourself to constant growth and expanding your knowledge and awareness and put yourself outside of your comfort zone, or you try your best to stay comfortable and face the struggles and issues of life that accompanies it. We spoke about this in the section *Cause and Effect.* You will either commit yourself to be the *cause of your life* or to be *the effect of it.* You either commit yourself to constant growth, or you commit to being in the same place all your life where there are issues and struggles of life.

You must know that the reason why most people like to be comfortable is that your brain is designed to keep you safe. Have you noticed that every time you come close to the edge of some really high rock in the mountain or even in your balcony, and you see how high it is, you start to have this feeling in your gut that you might fall down. And you're starting to feel the fear and your brain says, *"move back because you might fall and end up hurt or even dead."* Every time you face something new and challenging your mind will give you a signal to back down. It's designed to do that. When you back down from the challenges of life; from trying new things, doing something you've never done before, your body which is your subconscious mind gets used to it.

Every time you want to do something new, your brain and your body will resist and tell you, *"Come on; you've never done this before; you haven't tried it for the last 20 years what makes you think you can do it now? It's not safe; it's uncomfortable! Back down."* and because your willpower is not strong enough in this moment, you'll give up on that opportunity; you'll not apply for that job; you'll not start that relationship; you'll not go to that dream place. In your heart, you know that you're more than this, and you want to go after it, but the body is stronger than your mind, and that's the biggest challenge. I think I mentioned in previous chapters that one of the hardest things to do to change your habits and do what you like is to **teach your body how your life will look like ahead of the actual experience.** And that's when your Imagination goes in!

If you can close your eyes ahead of the upcoming moment and simply set the intention of what you want from it, you'll have an impact on that moment. But not just at that moment, but your future moments as well. That's how you can teach your body what the next moment will look like before it happens; also, the next one and the next one. And when you do that over and over again, you'll have the momentum that will help you to break old habits and do what you like to do. Another way to break patterns and train your body not to resist your mind is by applying the principle of reversing the cycle of *"think before you act"* and actually *"act before you think."* That's how you'll get out of your comfort zone.

Every successful person will tell you that there's no pleasure in being comfortable. That's not a place where you want to be. Especially not all your life. Look at athletes, for example, the greatest ones amongst them like Michael Jordan, Muhammad Ali, Wayne Gretzky, Usain Bolt, Novak Djokovic, Serena Williams, Michael Phelps, and many others; they all had an insane work ethic that pushed them outside of their comfort zone every single day. They say that Michael Phelps is crazy, that training on how to swim twice a day is madness; that the human body can't endure it and that he'll collapse. What did he do? He was relentless, didn't care what others were saying; he was pushing himself outside of the comfort zone, breaking his limits and limitations that other people put on him, and what happened in the World Championships or the Olympic games? He won every gold medal in every discipline that he was competing! Can you imagine that? Do you think he paved his way to success staying comfortable?

Serge: No, I don't think that he achieved everything by being comfortable.

Future: Then, to all of you that are reading this, it's time to stop procrastinating things that you know in your heart have to be done. Get out of your comfort zone and do what you have to do.

Serge: From personal experience, being outside of your comfort zone means that you'll have to go alone for a while to get where you want to be. And people are afraid to be alone. But let me share you one more story from my personal experience of getting outside of comfort zone.

Back in 2014, when I decided to come to Canada, I bought a ticket, and everything was ready. My parents asked me why I didn't want to go somewhere in Europe since we have some relatives in other countries and I'll be closer to them in case something happens; and If I decide to come back, it will be easy for them to come to pick me up. I believe that what I said to them was shocking because they couldn't understand it, but they accepted my decision anyway. My response was pretty much surprising to myself as well. I told them that the reason I was going that far, across the ocean was that I wanted to put myself in a situation where I'll not have anyone to rely on, where I would have to find a way to survive and do something for my life all by myself. If I was in Europe, I'm sure that I would be comfortable knowing that if anything went wrong, I could go back. In Canada, there's no going back. My parents didn't have a visa to visit me, so I was alone doing whatever I could to make a living and do something with my life. Even back then, I knew subconsciously that to move; I had to put myself in the unknown, somewhere I'll feel uncomfortable. And yes, it was lonely in the beginning. That's why I believe that people are scared to go into the unknown.

Future: We already spoke about this, so no need to repeat that. But it doesn't matter if you have to walk alone for a while. It's better to walk alone for a while chasing your dream and going in the right direction than follow your friends who don't aim for anything and go in the wrong direction. Trust me *you would rather aim for the stars and not hit them, than not aim at all. You would rather go outside of your comfort zone and fail than not go after that dream at all. You don't want to live with the idea of what would have happened if you had done more with your life.*

Serge: That sounds a little scary.

Future: It's meant to sound scary. Sometimes you need to scare people a little to try to wake them up.

Serge: When you mentioned this now, there's only one fear that I have, or I had until now since I don't know for sure if I have lost it or not.

Don't die with your dreams still inside you

Futer: And that is? Speak freely.

> *Serge:* I've heard this before, not sure the source of these words and they are not mine, but they had been memorized so deeply that I've promised myself that I'll do everything I can to never come to the point where I'll speak them loudly:

> **"By the time I figured out what life was all about, it was time for me to go."**

This is my greatest fear and my most powerful motivation to hustle every single day, so I'll not come to the end of my life to realize in my last moments what life was all about. Even now, while I'm writing these words, I have goosebumps. I'm not afraid of losing everything, of not achieving my goals, or to even die, but I am scared of going through life just to come to the end and realize that I didn't even live.

Future: You're right, that is scary. Most people go through life trying to make a living without living life. They're going unconsciously without knowing who they are nor where they're going. But in the moment of your death, in your last moments of this life experience, you come to realize who you are. That's when most people realize that they didn't live at all and that's a moment when they will speak about all their regrets. And that my friend, is one of the saddest moments that you can witness; seeing your loved ones going to another dimension and knowing that they didn't even live.

Serge: That's so... I don't know man. So many times when I think about the fact that I'm not yet where I want to be, I have this thought that there's no way I'm going to come to the end of my life only to realize that I didn't even live. That's my promise to myself! I will give everything I've got to be fully awake in this lifetime and to live by my own rules or at least die trying.

Future: That's a right attitude to have. You see, you have used those words as motivation, but you must know that not everybody will react as you did. Many are afraid of even trying because they've experienced way too many defeats that they don't believe they can do anything meaningful now. But my point is that *you must!*

You must try one more time to go after that dream again. To take at least that first step no matter how small or big it is. Give it a try! There are so many of you who have that book inside of you waiting to be published and read by millions whose lives will be impacted by it. Who has that amazing song waiting to come out and be performed and sung with millions of those who will listen to it. Maybe you have a project that will improve the environment in your community. Perhaps your dream is to provide water in the most critical places where it is non-existent. Or you want to become the next best basketball player of your generation. Listen to me and read these words carefully; ***you must go after your dreams and don't let them die inside of you!*** The only emotion you want to avoid is the emotion of regret!

Serge: So true. The thought of having regret is one of the worst you can have. To illustrate this through a silly example, you see a girl, and even if she smiles at you, you're too scared to go to her, and when you don't, you feel regret because you didn't dare to go to her. I don't want to even mention the much bigger things in life than this one. I'll not go deeper into this since we've already spoken about it in the section of *"Dream Killers,"* but it can be terrifying just thinking about these things.

Future: What do you suggest your readers do to find that spark of motivation of going after their dreams and not coming to the end with lots of regrets?

Serge: I believe that we all have to have something written down, that when we read it, it makes us think about our goals and in a way forces us to work on our dreams.

Future: You mean like your text, *"By the time I figured out what life was all about, it was time for me to go?"*

Serge: Exactly. If we put that into our subconscious mind and decide that no matter what, we'll do whatever we can for those words not to manifest. In other words, we should have a definite goal or a major purpose that we're striving for; but also I believe that besides our dream, we should allow our biggest fear to reminds us that if we don't give our best in accomplishing that dream, our fear will become a reality. Maybe it sounds a little too harsh, but that's just my perspective.

Future: I can agree on that; sounds very reasonable to me. I'm deeply touched by your desire to give to the world a full expression of yourself and make the world a better place.

Provide the best possible service

"I have learned to imagine an invisible sign around each person's neck that says - Make me feel important!" - **Mary Kay Ash**

S*erge:* I wasn't always like this. But yes, I indeed want to be of service. I noticed in the past few months that I've loved people more than I have ever loved before; even those who don't like me. Every single person on this planet is worth loving. Every person can be the change they want to see in the world. And to be honest, it may sound selfish in a certain way, but helping others and providing them with the best possible service will also help me in achieving my dreams and goals. By helping enough people and giving them what they want, the Universe will provide me with what I want. But, don't be fooled by this; we have to ensure we give unconditionally. Also, we must give with the intention of truly helping others from our heart and not just for our benefits.

The best way to live your purpose is to be of service. Whether you're working in a restaurant, selling ice cream on the street, teaching kids in school, making your environment cleaner, or providing the food for those who don't have any; whatever you do, do it with the clearest possible intention. Do with the attitude that you'll give the best possible quality and fullest possible quantity of service. I'll use the company with which I was involved with some few years back as an example. It's a health company that has some fantastic products that can help one achieve specific goals such as losing excess weight, maintaining weight, or gaining muscle, among other goals. I personally know some very successful people from that field that are providing excellent services that make people stay loyal to them no matter what.

However, what I've discovered is that previously, all those successful people were the best clients to themselves. This means they were really taking care of themselves by using these products. They were also disciplined and good leaders because they were leading by example by doing what is required of them. Because of the way they treated themselves, they were able to replicate the same treatment to their customers and distributors. They were always providing honest and best possible service. They listened carefully to their clients' needs and were able to make available nutrition plans and programs to best achieve their goals.

In most cases, most people will stop here. They will do what they're *"supposed to do,"* and that's it. But not these leaders; they were always going the extra mile. They organized the group cardio and weight training plans that would help their clients achieve their desirable goals faster. They were always doing a proper follow-up with clients, staying in contact, and be there for them. They even became friends because of the long-term relationship that was built on trust and honesty. The reason why they were successful was that they wholeheartedly provided the service their clients needed.

Future: Your example is a good illustration of what we talked earlier about leadership, success, and going the extra mile. All of that is necessary to provide the best possible quality of service. It's not just enough to have a right product. People are not buying the products; they are buying your emotion. You can listen to your favorite speaker *TD Jakes* at home every day or on your phone, and you're doing it, but the reason you want to go and listen to him live is the emotion that he awakes inside of you.

Serge: Thank you for disclosing my favorite speaker.

Future: You're welcome! The reason you're listening to him is that he provides the kind of service you need at this particular moment. Also, the reason you're listening to him every day in the last year or so, is because of the quality of content he provides, am I right?

Serge: Yes, you are. Another example of good service is this: in the past two or three months I've been subscribed to a meal plan from a company based in Toronto. I buy healthy and balanced meals from them because I don't have time to make the food. Also, I don't know how to make anything other than a few things. This company makes food every week, different meals that taste insanely good! And I remember giving them some suggestions on how to improve and personally I've asked them a few times to make some adjustment according to my needs like adding more protein, less carbs and also removing some veggies that I really can't eat. And they were doing all of that, and because of their commitment to having me as their client in the first place, I've been and will always be loyal to them because of the quality of service.

Future: There are so many good examples of providing the best service, but the essence is that you'll have to learn how to do it. Like anything in life, it takes hard work, consistency, and willingness to make mistakes because mistakes will show you what works and what doesn't. That is something that you too, my dear *Present*, will have to face when you publish this book and create programs that will transform other people's lives.

Serge: What do you mean?

Future: When you become a published author, you will be taking responsibility for the words that are in this book. There will be a lot who will accept your words as truth and start living their lives through the principles described here. And that's where you'll have to jump in when they ask you for help. By leading with your example, that may be enough for some, but for others, you'll have to learn how to teach them personally how to apply some or all of these principles that we're talking about now. ***Your job is not to sell the books, but to help those who will be buying the book. That's when the real work starts.***

You'll have to do a follow-up, to be there for them, to answer millions of questions, create seminars that will be transformative and effectively be of service. You'll have to use every social platform to be in touch with your clients; millions of them. This is because the moment every single one of them buys your book, they have automatically become your clients! With some of them, you'll make mistakes. Some of them will be disappointed. Some will even be more successful than they have imagined. Some will seek your guidance to show them step by step what they need to do. It will be a lot of pressure because you'll enter into a new season of your life. But will you be able to handle it? Will you be ready to deal with all the good things that will come with this book and also the bad? Choose your thoughts carefully and wisely because they will create your reality of which I'm sure you know everything about.

Serge: You make me want to rethink publishing this book. It sounds scary when you talk about it.

Future: You are the one thinking about it. You know this in your subconscious mind. The reason I'm talking about this is that you're thinking about it right now, and you know exactly what is coming and what you will need to do to jump to the next phase. You know everything I've mentioned, and you're ready to provide the best possible quality and possible quantity of service as an author and inspirational speaker, leader, and ambassador of transformation.

You also have to know that people will experience the wisdom of your transformation. You are the cells through which your message must pass. You are in the energy business; the truth is that you're always selling yourself! Your vibrational message is more important than any word that comes out of your mouth.

Serge: Trust me, I know that I'll have to work extra hard to be of service. And that's what I want. I genuinely want that with all my heart; to be of service. To give people something to believe in, and to live their lives as they desire. I believe that providing my best service will improve their lives and also skyrocket their success. To me, there will be no greater reward than looking at someone who has changed their life give thanks to me.

Future: Can I safely assume that you're ready for the next level?

Serge: What will be the point of writing all these words and using my *Imagination* to put myself in a state of readiness if I'm not ready for the next level? Of course, I am! I can't wait to jump into another adventure, to the next season of my life.

Future: Nothing makes me happier than knowing that you're ready for the next level. We've come a long way to get to this point. You've already written a lot of things that will be helpful to your readers, but is there something else you need to talk about before we move on to the final chapters in this book?

Serge: There are a few more things that are on my mind that I want to include here before we conclude.

Future: No problem. What would you like to talk about?

Popularity based identity

> *"I don't live my life seeking validation from people on social media." - **Ricki Lee Courter***

Serge: I know that we've touched a little bit about today's social media platforms, but I would like to expand more in detail. Specifically, I would like to talk about something I call, ***"popularity based identity."***

Future: What do you mean by that?

Serge: Well we're living in a world where everyone (not just kids) want to be popular on social media. If they don't have enough *followers* or *likes,* they think they're not cool. They try to identify themselves based on the popularity they can attract on social media, and in the process, they lose themselves very early. And this is catastrophic in a sense that the whole generation can be lost in a wave of trying to find who they are based on their online presence.

Future: We've already talked about that, but I understand your need to expand more on it. I believe you want to say that if someone else has enough followers and likes than *"He/she is."* Let's say that you're the one craving to be popular based on social media rules. If enough people like you and you have enough followers than *"you are."* You're trying to identify your identity based on what others think and speak about you. We've said many times in this book that you don't want to create a false image of yourself to please others. And unfortunately, that's what most young people are doing today. They're accused of being entitled so to speak, self-interested, unfocused, lazy; you name it. They all want this *"popularity"* on social media, and by having that, they think they will be happy and fulfilled. But in the real sense, they're getting more and more unhappy and depressed; and that's a scary thing.

Young kids are so impatient today because of the world we live in. They want everything now! They order food to come straight to the door because they are too lazy to go out and buy the ingredients to make their own food. They're too lazy to take a 150m walk to go to the closest market, so they take a car instead. If they don't receive 50-likes today; they feel depressed. That's madness. They're watching all these reality TV stars and using them as their role models. They see all these celebrities on Instagram, Facebook, and Twitter, and they try to copy them to be just like them even if that means they have to lose their own identity. So many kids take hundreds of selfies in a day to find one *perfect* picture. And they still have to take time to filter and edit it for posting.

And afterward, all they look for is how many likes and comments will appear in the notification bar. Some of them even go as far as dressing as if they are going for a party; holding a glass of wine in their hand, taking pictures of their leg with nice shoes, then posting the pictures on Instagram with a caption *"Enjoying the night with a special person."* But the truth is that they are at home alone feeling sorry for themselves. But to keep these likes and followers updated, they post fake pictures because they believe the pictures they post on social media are representations of who they are. That's crazy. It's a modern addiction. More dangerous than any other you can name. And this is not even limited to social media but also the smartphone. Social media is designed to be addictive! You have to understand that.

I cannot express how sad I am when I see all these kids becoming so attached to their smartphones that they can't even have a single moment without their phone.

Serge: It is sad. It's frustrating when you're sitting in the restaurant with five, six or more people and almost all of them are looking at their phones. We are so close but so far away from each other. It happened to me many times that I was just looking at people around me and wondered how it is possible that they are all on their phones, and if we stay for an hour, the conversations will last maybe 15 minutes, the other 15 minutes we will eat and other 30 minutes staring at the phones. If you go with friends and families for a BBQ somewhere outside of town where you are surrounded by beautiful nature such as mountains on one side and a river on the other; it's a perfect time to connect with nature and enjoy the beauty of it, but most of them are always looking at their phones missing all these simple and beautiful things around them.

No wonder today's kids are such terrible communicators. They didn't learn how to talk in person. They're sitting in the same classroom and chatting on their phones. I mean, that's absurd. They're showing each other the pictures from others and trying to imitate them and be *cool* like them. All of this makes me crazy. Just thinking about it gets on my nerves.

Future: Slow down, buddy. I understand your frustration, but it will not do you any good when you are frustrated. You have to set a good example to inspire others with your change through your personality and behavior. That's the world today's kids are growing up in. They would rather spend the whole night watching Netflix than to read ten pages of some personal growth book that will improve their life. They will spend ten hours on their phone without trying to speak two sentences with their friends. Trading temporary pleasures for long-term happiness is something most kids do these days. Impatience is their second name literally. They would rather spend most of their days on the computer and smartphone than go outside and have fun. The time when old generations were spending outside playing creative games and enjoying beautiful evening nights; risking being punished by their parents for coming home too late is gone.

Serge: I believe that my generation and maybe two or three years younger are the last ones who know what it means to be outside all the time and not even spend a single minute on the phone. One of the reasons is that we had cell phones, but they were not as good as the smartphones available today. We could only message and call each other. I remember the time my parents couldn't drag me into the house because I wanted to stay outside all day long. And now, I see all these kids that their parents find it difficult to drag them out because they want to stay inside all day long!

Being at home all day long, and doing nothing is what caused kids to become lazy and procrastinate. That's why I said that the change has to start at home with the parents and also with the school system which has their faults too.

Future: Relax a little bit. What you need to do is to find people who will teach your kids to have ***purpose over popularity***. And that will not be an easy task. Instead of looking for approval, today's kids have to learn at an early age how to find their purpose in life. That's the solution to your problem.

Serge: So we're coming back to discover what our vision is, and what we want to do or become.

Future: I can see more frustration here.

Serge: Yes, I am a bit frustrated, and can't hide it. It's much easier to help adults than to help kids, especially if you don't work with them. Only if you're working with them, you can hope to have some positive influence on them, and help them discover their purpose in life.

Future: My dear friend, it's not your job in this life to fix the planet, and all the problems that exist in it. In a more profound sense, everything is perfect as it is. Imagine if you fix all of the issues that exist, what will be the purpose of others? Imagine if you help all the kids in the world to discover their purpose, what will others do; parents, teachers, coaches, religious instructors? I love and respect your desire to serve. But I'm sure you know that everything is happening for a good reason. Who knows what the future will look like? You may have your predictions based on what you see in the world, but can you be sure that it will always be like this? Or that the world will be in the shape as it is right now? Or that your ecology is dying and the planet will destroy itself? Or that some great disaster will happen as it is perfectly and eloquently described in your best-selling movies? I'll tell you this - only our *Creator* knows what will happen. And that's okay. Leave that to Him because He alone knows what He's doing.

Serge: That's easier said than done.

Future: I know it is, so I want you to hear me now. You have to do whatever you can to help not just the kids but everyone that you get in touch with. Help them realize who they are and who they want to be. If that's your purpose, you can do whatever you can with the help of others that will eventually join you on this journey. And together you will accomplish far more than you can ever do by yourself. It's noble of you that you want to help others at all; to serve them and to be there for them. It's amazing that you have that project about teaching kids the basic principles of life through all kinds of activities.

I'm telling you to go for it with all your heart. Understandably, you want to do it right now, but first, you must help yourself with publishing this book so the world can read your message. And guess what? Who knows how many parents will read this book and feel your pain (that you have shown in some parts of our interview) and decide to change the way they speak and act. Who knows how many parents, coaches, and teachers will read this and realize that their job is much more than just doing what they're supposed to do?

I'm not sure that you know, at least not yet, how significant impact this book can and will have. You're talking in a way that allows people to physically go right now to make a change, but you forget that just by writing and publishing this material will take you to certain places and heights where you can make a much greater impact that you could ever imagine.

Serge: What if my ego gets on the way in the course of trying to enjoy that *"popularity"* and I lose my sense of purpose?

Future: I'm glad you've asked that. You see, it's not just the kids that want to be famous. Adults too want to be accepted and loved by everyone. It's a natural thing. But guess what? It will never happen. You'll never be loved and appreciated by everyone. You have to accept that, and that's okay. To go back to you; do you think that if all of a sudden you got all this attention and you become popular, it would change you?

Serge: To be honest, I don't think so. I've walked alone long enough to realize that I don't need anyone to be happy. The only thing that I believe I'll do if it comes to that is, I'll use all that attention to my advantage to make an even greater impact on other people's lives. It will get me closer to the people of influence that can help me achieve my goals.

Future: That's what your current state of consciousness says. You will have the challenges when that day comes. You'll have to learn how to deal with success because success has to be managed. You'll have to deal with your ego, with chances of becoming lazy because finances will not be a problem anymore. The procrastination, phone ringing more often than not, receiving thousands of emails and many more things. It will not be easy, but I'm positive that you'll handle it all.

Serge: I don't want to talk about something that didn't even come to fruition yet. I'm a little scared because of all these things you mentioned. I have all these questions, doubts, and fears, but also I'm way more excited about what is coming than being scared. And that's what drives me. Faith that God knows what He's doing and everything I'm going through is exactly how it is supposed to be.

Future: Faith is the starting point of all achievements. To close this chapter, I'll say just one more thing; use your authority and position to empower your kids to have purpose over popularity. Popularity can last for so long, and it can pass like it was nothing. Purpose stays forever.

Now, is there anything else that you would like to ask before we go to the final chapter?

Serge: You want to tell me that we're close to finishing?

Future: Of course. You didn't notice because it has developed so fast and you were inspired while writing the book.

Serge: Damn, you're right. And somehow I don't want to stop. This is so much fun. I know it may sound crazy, but I'm enjoying having these conversations or interviews with you or my *Imagination* that I want them to last as long as they can.

Future: I know you do. But first, you have to absorb all this information, because I'm sure that you'll read and reread your book hundreds of times.

Serge: I'm already doing it.

Future: That's good. You've just started. This is not the only book that you'll write, and I know that by developing this method of using your *Imagination* and tapping into its power at will, you will write many more that will be of great value as this one, or maybe even greater. And not just that, only by using your *Imagination* to do this, you've already learned to use it for other things in your life too; like your relationships, job, finances, and other areas of your life.

Serge: That sounds exciting. But honestly, for whatever reason, I don't want to stop this, because I found myself enjoying this process so much. Just by tapping into this power while I'm writing makes me so excited that I can't wait to utilize it in other areas of my life fully. I can see now how powerful this is, but it's also scary knowing that it can be used for the wrong purpose.

Future: Believe it or not, *Imagination* has been used for the wrong purposes so many times that you're not even aware of it. But that's not something you should worry about. You need to focus on how to teach others to use it for their greater good. Where your focus goes, there will your energy flow. Focus on the positive side of everything, including people, events, relationships, circumstances, etc.

Serge: I know. I will do it. Okay. So, before we end this book which is sad but inevitable, can we speak about two more things? How can we manage our time the best, and what are the obstacles to connect our mind with the universal power through our *Imagination* from your perspective?

Time management

F*uture:* What do you want to talk about first?

Serge: Let's talk about *time management,* and then we'll talk about the obstacles that I've mentioned.

Future: Time has been a subject from the beginning of your world and will always be. In reality, ***the only time that exists is now***. If you believe that past, present, and future exist at the same time, you're right. When you say, *"now it is 5:45 pm,"* that's because people needed to find some method to put the time into a measurable form or it would be more understandable if I say that time is usually defined by its measurement - what your clock says; that's it! I will not try to go deeper into this because it will require that we delve into quantum physics which I don't intend to do; but for now, it would be the best to understand that the only time that truly exists is now.

We have said it several times throughout this book, but it's never a bad thing to remind yourself of this notion. To talk specifically about your topic, we'll have to speak in relative terms to explain how to make the most practical use of your daily time.

What you call *time management* can be described as a way to decide how to utilize your daily time best to achieve short-term or long-term goals. You can put it in the form of how to use your time to do everything you want, or need to do in a day like; going to work, seeing your friends, being with your family, working out, reading a book and many more activities that require a great deal of your time and energy. Also, time management can be one of your most exceptional skills to develop.

First of all, you must plan your days. You can do it the night before, which would be the optimal thing to do, or you can do it as soon as you wake up. Once you do it, you set your priorities for that day. For instance, you want to have a productive workout so it would be wise to set your plan for how long it will last, what exercises you will do, how many sets and reps, etc. If you have a critical meeting in your company, you should plan precisely on what you would like to talk about and try to hold it within the time you prepared for. *Productivity in anything starts with the clear intention of knowing what you want from that specific thing that you want to do. In other words, to do more in less time.*

Every successful person in this world knows the value of managing their time correctly. We all have the same amount of time in one day (when I say this I mean in your relative world because in other dimensions there is no time and even space; which I will not talk about right now because it's not the subject of this book). How you manage the time you have in a day determines the level of success you will achieve. Therefore, you must know how to manage time properly and not lose balance in your life. Most people think about time management as part of their work but not as a part of their life overall. They think that's important to manage their time wisely only in their work, but they forget how to manage their life.

Serge: In other words, they become so overwhelmed that they forget to set the balance in their lives.

Future: Exactly! *Balance is the key.* One of the biggest problems that most entrepreneurs have isn't just about how they can get enough done, but also how they maintain some semblance of balance without feeling too overworked. This isn't just about achieving and going after goals around the clock. This is also about quality of life. Are you working too hard at your job but not on your relationship with your wife or kids? If you lack balance in your life, you're going to feel stressed out. Even if you're able to effectively juggle your responsibilities without proper balance, you're going to reach your breaking point eventually, and for those who didn't understand what it means to come to the *Breaking point*, I highly suggest you go back and reread that chapter.

It's essential to not only follow a system that will help you get things done, but also one who prioritizes personal and family time. What is it that you like to do every day? Is it spending time alone so you can meditate? Maybe you like going out with your dog and enjoy the walk, be with your spouse or spending time with your kids, reading or being with your friends; whatever it is, you have to find a balance between all these areas which can be hard at times depending on what your priorities are.

Serge: That is true. I found this very important; to do all the things that make me feel happy and fulfilled. I'm sorry for interrupting here but may I speak about the recent change that I made? I believe it will illustrate the example of using time wisely to be more effective and productive.

Future: This is your book, and I've said this many times, you don't have to apologize for anything, especially when you can contribute to the point with your personal example. Go ahead and tell us what you have to say.

Serge: I know, but still I hate to interrupt you when you're at the peak of your creativity and giving your best to provide the best possible value.

As we spoke throughout the book, it is so hard to do some small things that will improve our lives dramatically just because we want to do them only when we *feel like it*. So I realized that for a few years, I wanted to go back to meditation and visualization and a few more things like writing the intentions for the day. I learned that if I win my first one or two hours of the day, I can win the whole day. The first change that I made, was to wake up early, around 5:00 am and go to the gym at 5:30 am. Then I'll workout till 6:30 am – 7:00 am and then go to work. After work, I'll have enough time to do some other activities, like cardio or playing handball or basketball, or going to folklore, be with my friends, my girlfriend, and other things. But I still knew that something was missing. For the first time, I was happy that I started waking up earlier not because I wanted to, but because I had to. Then *that day came*; I didn't know what hit me, and I discovered that I was happy for no reason. Immediately, I decided to wake up even earlier because I knew I wanted to get back to my morning routine to have every day as productive and effective as possible. That includes meditation, writing intentions for that day, reading my affirmations, listening to motivational speeches, and having moments of gratitude. Of course, working out in the gym is a must.

So I decided to wake up every morning at 4:14 am (there's no particular reason why I set the alarm at that time except that I love both numbers 4 and 14) and do the things that I knew would improve my life dramatically and make me happier throughout the day as well as more productive and effective. And not just at my work but in everything that I have to do that day.

Every morning when the alarm rings at 4:14 am, I get up from the bed, put the headphones in my ears and turn on a motivational speech because I want my mind to be filled with the positive things from the first few seconds of waking up. While I'm doing my stuff in the bathroom like brushing my teeth and washing my face with cold water, I'm listening to a motivational speech and having a short talk with the mirror where I recognize myself as perfect as I am right now. Once I'm done, I get back to bed and turn off the headphones because it's really early - around 4:30 am, and it's so quiet, then I use that time for a 10-minute meditation (I set the alarm for ten minutes). After that, I take the book that I have on my table in my bedroom and start writing the intentions for that day. After that, I take the affirmations that I keep in my wallet and read them loud and clear. After all of that, I take a few moments to express my feelings of gratitude. All of these last around 30 minutes. Because my bag for the gym with my gym clothes and my meals for that day is ready the night before, around 4:55 am, I'm off to the gym, and I'm there at 5:05 am. Since I intend to be productive and I have a workout plan for the next few months, I'm not wasting any time in the gym. I'm focused, determined, and because I have the goal of how I want my body to look, I'm giving my best to it, no holding back. Usually I'm done by 6:30 am, and that's the moment I take 10 - 15 minutes to do a quick visualization process because I found that after gym is the time I'm most open for imagining my goals as they are already achieved probably because that's the time when I'm really happy and open to visualize it. When finish working out, I take a protein shake, and I'm ready for the day.

Technically every morning I have around two and a half hours just for myself; it's *"me time."* From the moment I started doing this up until now, I've never had a single bad day in my life. Yeah, there were some challenges, difficult situations but because of my morning routines and my ability to put myself in the highest possible state of mind before work, I was able to handle things with ease. Not did I find myself more productive and effective at work, but I found myself happier, and almost zero stress. Because of my waking up early, I have more than enough time to write this book, to go out and do other things I love. Being with my friends, spending time with my girlfriend, doing other activities that I enjoy and many more things. Yes, there is less sleep, but I believe that meditation helps a lot in place of sleep.

Also, and this is huge, I don't look at my phone for the first few hours. I mean, I don't read emails, social media posts, or news. Of course, I'm using my phone to set up the music while I'm working out, but the first 3 or 4 hours I don't check messages, emails, social media or news. Nothing! Because I know that doing these things in the morning when my mind is most open to information can negatively affect my day and life. As a result of all I've mentioned, I became a happier person than I ever was and I found myself to be way more organized and productive; that's one of the keys to having good *time management skills.*

Future: That's a perfect example of how good organization of your daily life can lead you to a more balanced, successful, and fulfilled life. Knowing what you want and what you have to do to achieve all of that is and always will be the first step. So I'll sum up what it takes to develop this *time management* skill to do more in less time and put an end to laziness and procrastination. Maybe I'll repeat some things that you've mentioned, but that will be to get the point. The first thing you have to do to manage your time wisely is:

Plan your day the night before

This means that you'll know what you have to do tomorrow and when you know it, it becomes easier to manage your time properly. Of course, there always will be exceptions when something unexpected happens. That's okay; if you plan your day, you can always adjust to new situations that occur. Sometimes your day will not go as planned, so yes, you'll have to make some adjustments. When you learn how to plan your day, it will become easier to plan your week and even the whole month.

Set your priorities for the day

Setting your priorities will let you know what it is that you must do for that day. Having a conversation with your neighbor about last night's game may not be that important to you as going to the gym is because you have a specific goal to achieve. Or going for a coffee with that friend may not be necessary as having a meeting with your boss about raising your salary. As you mentioned in your example, you set most of your priorities when most people were sleeping, and that's good. Because you have so many interests and you want to do a lot of things throughout the day, the way you're managing your time is good as long as you do not get too overwhelmed or overworked.

Adopt good habits and let go of the bad ones

Like *Serge* said, winning the morning may be one of your best accomplishments. It is accurate, and every successful person in this world knows that when you win your morning, you will win your day. Doing little things like giving thanks, setting your intentions, reading your affirmations, reading some good books, setting goals, meditate in the first thirty minutes of waking up, will place you in the best possible state of being.

The first thirty minutes of your waking up are the most important; that's the moment where your mind is the most creative and open for information. Most of you take your phones immediately after you open your eyes and you're looking at emails you've received, comments or pictures that you're tagged in on social media or reading the negative news; it's no wonder why so many are feeling negative throughout the day. Looking at your phone first thing in the morning immediately after waking up without saying *"good morning"* to your husband or your wife is a sign of addiction. It's a bad habit. You want to adopt the good habits that will improve your life through time.

By setting your priorities, you'll know what's important to you and what's not. Then you can decide what habits you can add to be happier, productive, and fulfilled. For *Serge,* having his two to two and a half hours first thing in the morning is what will lead him to a happier and healthier lifestyle. Also, he didn't mention, but I know this; before every night he has a habit of reading at least a few pages of some good books. First and last 30 minutes of your day is the most important. I urge you to use them just for yourself.

If you know that you have to make ten phone calls today to sell that one product, do not waste your time going out with your friends for a coffee just because they don't have anything to do. I'm not saying that you're not supposed to have time for your friends, but you must know when you can go out with them, and when it's time for your other priorities. If you don't value your time, nobody will.

Self - awareness

This is one of the easiest skills to develop because it requires only a little of your attention and effort. It allows you to do all things throughout the day in a way that best suits you by reducing your resistance. Time management is really about how we manage ourselves. It's about how we focus, how we discipline ourselves, and how we stick to habits that we know work. If you observe one of your days, you'll quickly figure out if you are aware of what you're doing or not. Taking the pen and paper and writing can help develop self-awareness.

Do your most creative work at the peak energy of your time of the day

Huge one! Are you a morning person or afternoon or maybe a late night person? For *Serge*, his best time for creative work is either early in the morning or late evening. He likes to have his own time every morning, but the moment he steps into the company, he starts working like crazy! Also, when he was writing this book, it was always in the evenings, and I know that because I'm only his imaginary character coming from his *Imagination*. What is the time that you have the most energy? Do then your most important and creative work.

Focus

While you are working on many things throughout your day, stay focused on each one of them because your focus will determine your level of production and efficiency. When you're working out, how often are you looking at your phone? Are you texting somebody? When *Serge* is working out, he is focused, he's not looking at his phone, working on one exercise after another, taking a short time to rest between the sets and that's it. When you're at work, are you focused on the task in front of you, or are you looking through the window imagining being somewhere out and having fun with your friends? Being unfocused will put your productivity way down, and that may cause some problems in your work or your relationships. Staying focused is the key to being productive.

Learn how to say "No"

Believe it or not, this is one of the essential parts of learning how to have not just excellent time management skills, but also to improve your life on many levels. Just because you're a nice guy, doesn't mean that you have to say *"yes"* to everyone and everything. Somebody asks you for a favor, and you know that you have work to finish, but just because you're too nice to reject your neighbor, you'll try to help him and later rush to do the work that you were supposed to finish hours earlier. Who knows how many times you've regretted when you've said *"yes"* instead of *"no."* Learning how to say *"no"* will save you trouble later on.

Work effectively with others

If you want to maximize your productivity and time management, you are going to need to work with others and harness the power of synergy. A group of people working on a common cause will achieve more together than they ever would separately. Do not make a mistake to think that any company will depend solely on you; because that's a false belief. Anyone is replaceable. Also, you don't want to overwhelm yourself and get overworked and exhausted. Learn to trust others, and teach them to do work that will take less time, be more productive and effective.

Be intentional

This is what this book is all about; *to be intentional before every interval of your day.* Use this technique that is so eloquently described in the chapter **'Intentional moments'** and apply it to manage your time appropriately and effectively. Trust me; there's no better way to use your time wisely than to know what exactly you want from each interval of your day; whether it is working out in the gym, spending your time with family, having an important meeting at work, or simply walking through the park. Knowing what you want will make you more intentional, effective, and productive.

These are some pathways that can lead you to develop your time management skill. There's nothing new to say about this because it has been said so many times, and you can find a lot more information on the internet. There are many books written specifically to describe the whole subject of managing your time properly. Would you like to add something?

Serge: No, I think this is more than enough for now. We have come a long way and covered many subjects and many things that will be of value to anyone who reads this book. Although, I believe that we have covered some of the obstacles in connecting our whole being with our *Imagination* throughout the other chapters, but still I would like to go one more time through them in a separate chapter, so readers will know what they have to deal with in order to use the full potential of their limitless *Imagination*.

Obstacles in connecting your whole being with your Imagination

F*uture:* It's a good idea to put the obstacles all in one separate chapter; although, everyone that has come this far must have probably noticed them throughout the book. Your *Imagination* is linked to your *Soul* and connected to the *Universe*. Connecting your whole being to your *Imagination* will have some obstacles until it becomes part of you.

End result

Remember the very first chapter when *Serge* was giving you the first task of putting yourself in a position of imagining your *Future Self?* That's exactly what you have to do. When you imagine your future ahead of the real experience, you should be able to see it from the end result. Again, you have to know what you want, whether from this upcoming moment or for some future moment. Every time you think about your goals, your dreams, and your future, think from the end. Don't try to imagine what might happen in the process because that is what's blocking your inner desire to stay connected to your *Imagination*. Remember, in your *Imagination*; you can go anywhere, you can be anything, you can be, do or have whatever you want.

There are no limits to your *Imagination*. Expand your views, play with it, enjoy yourself while you're at it. Try to see your goals and dreams with your eyes open. If you're dreaming about giving that famous speech, find some video on YouTube from some speakers that you really admire. Speakers who are your role models. Watch it and while you're watching it, imagine yourself being on that stage instead of them; speaking about the topics that you would like to talk about; feel it while your eyes are open. Or if you want to become a famous singer, turn on some concerts and imagine yourself singing in front of the broad audience. If you want to become a published author, go into the bookstore and imagine your books on the shelves, people buying it and carrying it with them.

Serge: That's exactly what I do when I'm in a bookstore.

Future: Do whatever you think will put you in a state of feeling like you've already achieved that goal or dream. Whatever you are imagining, imagine the end result you want to experience. Of course, imagining the result will lead us to the next possible obstacle, and that is to match your *Intention* with your *Imagination* through your feelings.

Match your intention with your Imagination through your emotions

When you're setting the intention for that moment, for that day, for that goal or dream, you have to be able to match it, or maybe it is better to say to connect it with your *Imagination*. **You have to feel it!**

Serge: While you were speaking about who I can become, I had goosebumps in my whole body; it was like tingling energy that was surging through me. It felt so good!

Future: That's because your dream was matched with your *Soul*. What I was saying was simply the dream that you have inside of you; your *Soul* knows it. That's why you were able to feel it so powerfully because you matched your desires with who you are. By imagining your goals, you're giving them some amount of power to attract them. Imagining and talking about them, you're raising that level of vibration in your body. But when you put enough feelings into your *Imagination*, you'll be empowered, excited, and you'll feel the emotion that will be the signal from your *Soul*. One that will say, *"What you're imagining is about to show up in your life if you keep your focus on it."*

Stay focused

This is easier said than done. So many distractions keep your focus out of your intentions throughout the day. ***You're living in a distraction based world.*** Your TVs, smartphones, video games, parties, sitting with your friends and other external stimuli, will make you unfocused. It's no wonder that you can be easily distracted from the task ahead of you.

Serge: This is so true, I found it hard to meditate and read throughout the day, especially with all the noise around me and that is something that I used to enjoy a lot! Then I realized that the only time I can meditate and read in full silence without distraction is early in the morning between 4:00 am and 6:00 am, and so I've been doing it. And it feels good. When I was writing this book, I used to do it in the night, but I was so inspired that I didn't allow any distractions to take my focus out of this. I know what you're saying, but still, I believe that if we stay aware of this moment, the things we don't want will not get our attention.

Future: That's exactly what I was about to say. Being aware of this moment and being present is the key to staying focused. Yes, your phone will ring. Somebody will text you. You'll have some other distractions, but if you keep your concentration at this moment, and you keep doing it over and over again, through practice, you'll learn how to be focused; and this will lead us to the next thing that is important about staying connected to your *Imagination*. It is not just to be present in the moment but to be aware of every interval of your day that we've talked about it in the chapter *'Intentional moments.'*

Be aware of every interval of your day

Serge: I know that we've talked about this, and while I'm writing this book, I'm trying to implement all these principles in my own life, I do find it hard to be aware of every interval of my day. It's easy in the morning to stop a few times and set my intentions for that interval. However, somehow throughout the day, I lose that awareness, and almost always, I remember it after the interval past, and I would be like *"I should stop and set the intention, I'll be more focused next time,"* and somehow I feel angry at myself.

Future: Don't be angry with yourself. It is normal to forget, you're learning. You're still in the process of growing. It will take some time to develop the awareness of every interval of your day fully, and the good thing is that you're aware that you forget about it sometimes. As long as you're trying, it is okay. It will come to you with practice and continuously reminding yourself of every interval. One of the reasons that you lose sight of the interval is because you spend around 8-9 hours at your day job and probably because you've set your intentions for that period, you forget that there are more intervals after your work. It would be helpful to use your smartphone and set a reminder around the time you usually finish work that you have other intervals to be aware of.

However, the good thing is, once you set up the intention for one interval, it will not benefit you only in that interval but in similar intervals in the future too! You're giving orders to your mind, and you're teaching your body to react in a certain way that will be of benefit to you. When you do that continuously, your mind and body will know how to react by default because you have so many similar intervals today that you had yesterday.

Serge: So, for instance, if I set the intention that I want to feel joy at my work; to be a better co-worker, employee and a leader today than I was yesterday; and I do that repeatedly, will it basically project in the future because I've taught my body and mind to think, speak and behave in that way that will be of best benefit to me?

Future: Exactly. It may happen that you simply forget to set the intention for your work today but because you consistently set your intentions in the last few weeks, months or years, you've already taught your body how to react and behave so now your default is to feel good, be a better leader and grow every single day. You've used your work, for example, but this is true for every other area of your life.

Serge: This is so powerful that I can't even express it in words! I knew before that the key to taking control of my life was in setting intentions for every interval of every day, but now this is one more proof that I believe that my

Imagination has deliberately provided for me to be sure that I'm on the right path.

Future: To you and everyone reading this, be patient! The awareness you're developing through time by constantly reminding yourself to be present in every moment of your every day by doing it, over and over again will surface soon. You'll see the signs of your wakefulness. The last thing that I want you to do to remove or to overcome the obstacles of connecting your being to your *Imagination* fully is to **be the cause of your life.**

Be the Cause of your life

Most of you have lived your life as *the effect of it*. Now, I'm inviting you to *be the cause of your life*. Be intentional. Be aware of every interval, every moment of your day. Everything you want to do, do it intentionally. Whatever your goal or dream is, intend it! Set your focus on that intention and cause it! Learn more about the *Law of Cause and Effect*; there are great teachers amongst you that are alive today. Find them to teach you. If you let yourself be the effect of your experience, then, you'll not be able to keep yourself connected to your Imagination. To change this, you'll need effort and some willpower of putting yourself into the state of constant seeing your life as a manifestation of your greatest dreams. That is my hope for you.

Now, the time has come for you and me to end this interview that you've started.

Serge: It is?

Future: Yes. It is.

Serge: But I don't want to. This is so exciting, and I'm enjoying it a lot! Do we really need to stop here and now? There's so much I want to ask, and so much I want to know; so many subjects, interests, and ideas.

Future: Indeed. I know exactly how you feel. But for now, my work with you is over until you get inspiration for your next book or project. You can quickly call upon me whenever you feel like it. Let's say that you can activate your *Imagination* at will. That's perhaps one of your greatest accomplishments so far because it will allow you to go into the places you were thinking are not possible and create anything you want just because you know how to use your *Imagination* to your advantage. So be happy and grateful for this book and everything that's inside. Also, you'll need some time to absorb all this information, and perhaps it will take you longer than you think to accept this as your work. You'll see what I'm talking about in a few months of publishing this book.

Serge: Trust me; I am grateful beyond you can imagine. There's not a single day that I'm not thinking about this and how grateful I am; because in a way, this is my life's work. There's no better reason to be happy than knowing that this book will change somebody's life; that someone will understand how powerful our *Imagination* is and use it to create the experience they want. Honestly, I'm grateful because I'm going to use it in my life to achieve my goals and live my dreams. There's nothing more I can tell you except - *Thanks!*

Future: No need to thank me because I am you. It was my pleasure to serve you. Now I'll leave you with one more task, and that is to write the last chapter of this book.

Serge: Can you write it?

Future: I can, but I won't. I'll leave it to you. We have discussed many subjects here and went from one point to another. You have so much valuable information that everyone reading this can use to change their life. But in the end, there's one thing that most people don't understand and even you, my *Present* didn't realize it until recently.

Serge: And that is?

Future: Do you know why some of the most successful people in any field are at the top?

Serge: Maybe.

Future: Tell me.

Serge: I believe that I know what you're referring to. You're talking about *the Fundamentals of Life*.

Future: Bingo! How did you know that?

Serge: It's funny; I got a feeling that you would talk about that. Maybe a few months ago I watched on YouTube an NBA TV Show called *"The Open Court"* where they were discussing all kinds of subjects about the NBA through history like the best teams of every decade, super teams, winning the championships, looking to basketball as a way to get out of the street and many more really cool subjects. And I recommend it for everyone who loves the NBA like I do to find this show and watch it.

Through the show, you'll hear so many interesting facts and information from the players that were legends of their era. But to go back to our point, in one of the episodes they were talking about the greatest players of all time and of course, one name was at the top and that is Michael Jordan. I can't remember who was speaking; I think it was Kenny Smith (who won two championships with Houston Rockets), and he asked a question, *"so why was Michael Jordan the best among all others that had ever played this game?"* and the other guys were talking and I believe it was Isaiah Thomas (the legendary point guard from Bad Boys Pistons) who said *"Because he was working on the **fundamentals** every single day of his career."* And he was talking about jump shot, footwork, moving without the ball, ball handling, etc. But I remember clearly, that moment because it hit me so hard and I knew that to change my life I had to go back to some basic life fundamentals that I stopped doing.

Future: I have told you that you know what I'm talking about. Thank you one more time for using me in writing this beautiful piece of art. I can't wait to work with you again soon. I'm leaving you to finish this last and perhaps the most important chapter of this book.

Until we work again!

Fundamentals

Serge: Few days before I started writing this book with the help of my *Imagination*, I watched the show that I described in the previous chapter. I quickly recollect that the reason I don't live the life I want is that I stopped working on some fundamentals that caused me to be a happier person then, than I am now. That was the moment I said I would go back to the basics that were life-changing for me. I must say that each one of us has a different foundation on which our success is built upon, but I will tell you what my foundation is. For some of you, they will be enough to take you to the next phase of your life while others will have to work on their fundamentals to live the life they want.

Think about the *fundamentals* in this way: Imagine you want to build a beautiful, multi-level home (your life). Once the site is prepared, and you are ready to build, the first step is the laying of the foundation (the fundamentals). It is crucial that this foundation is strong; for it is upon this that the rest of the house is built.

This leads me to a few fundamentals of life, and I will note that we have talked about them throughout the book, so here I'll put a small point on each of these fundamentals:

Setting goals and having a clear vision

Everything starts with knowing what you want. If you don't know what you want, how will you know why you are doing whatever you're doing every single day? Why did you wake up this morning? Set your goals daily. Set the short-term as well as long-term goals and track them. When I got back to writing my goals down and regularly holding my vision and thinking about it, other fundamentals came back naturally.

Be aware of every moment and be intentional in all of them

The purpose of this book is *'Self-awareness.'* Be in the now! Be aware of every moment, and through time and practice, it will become part of you. Setting your intentions before every interval of your daily life will lead you to the life you want. You'll be in control of your day.

Always learning and expanding your knowledge

Reading, studying, researching, watching inspirational videos, seminars whatever source of knowledge you can use, go for it. It's been five years now since I started reading every single day. From December 2013 until now, there hasn't been a single day that I didn't read at least a few pages of some good books. In the last three years, there wasn't a single day that I haven't listened to some audiobooks or inspirational speeches for at least one hour throughout the day. Thirst for more knowledge, be consistent in learning every day and apply that knowledge. Don't just accumulate it, use it!

Meditation

This is huge! I can't even express how meditation helped me back in 2014 to calm myself; to become more peaceful and open-minded. I was meditating for seven months every single day, and I believe that I didn't have a single sign of being nervous or anxious. Literally, nothing could piss me off. Then I stopped for no reason, and while writing this book, I went back to meditating, and it immediately gave the result of being more peaceful and less time for sleep.

Imagination (visualization)

Spending at least 10 to 15 minutes daily, putting myself in the highest possible state of being and by closing my eyes. Imagining my future or those specific goals I want to achieve is something that I believe we all need to do because it's so powerful. And only through visualization can we teach our body what the future will look like before it actually happens.

Gratitude

I've never stopped being grateful. I always was. Every morning when I wake up, I say thank you. I'm thankful for waking up every morning. Then I go through a list of things that I'm grateful for, and I feel it. I put my emotions into it. Because the more grateful you are, the more you will attract in your life that which you want.

Workout and diet

I used to go to the gym for a few months and then quit for a few months and repeat that process over and over again. The same went with my diet. I thought I was eating healthy, but I was nowhere close to it. No wonder why I haven't seen the results. When I truly decided to put my whole self into this and to give my all in the gym and be disciplined with my diet that I started to see the results. It's not about the workout or diet; it's about the feeling! And I'm feeling great. Exercising and a proper nutrition plan will lead you to a healthier and happier life.

Be who you really are

One of the most important fundamentals is to be true to yourself! To always and at all costs be who you are in every moment of your life! I truly believe that God's desire for us is precisely this.

Be of service

If you set your mind to be of service every single day no matter how big or small that service might be, you will set yourself into a position of living the life you want.

Be kind

Be kind and have respect for others. One simple act of kindness may not change the world, but it will change the person you're kind to. Also, it will change you.

Discipline

In the end, everything comes down to how bad you want it. How willing are you to be disciplined in all of these? Do you have the discipline to keep going when it hurts? Since I love waking at 4:04 am (first it was 4:14 am then I set the alarm to 4:04 am) to do my morning routine before work. There were times I was tired of not sleeping and had some excuses (valid reasons) that could easily cause me to sleep in, but my goals and my dreams started to dominate my subconscious mind, and I know that I don't want to break my discipline, so I kept going no matter how tired I was. Discipline is your best friend; it will take care of you like nothing else will.

When I was thinking about my fundamentals, I realized that the moment I brought them back, I started to feel empowered, inspired, happy, loved, kind, and many more positive feelings. And I truly believe that when it's all said and done, your success in any area comes down to setting up a proper foundation. You have to enable yourself to be able to apply the fundamentals over and over again each day. Getting up at a specific time, doing certain things that the vast majority of people won't do. When you get up and read or workout, most people are sleeping. When they go to bed, you are still working on your dream.

Keeping your commitments, preparing your healthy meals, reading every day, and always being aware of the present moment. You keep being intentional as much as you can, sit down for 10 minutes to meditate, and set your goals over and over again. Stay true to yourself every single day. Provide the service that most people will not do, and so on. Those are the things that when you string them together, you will start to create a day of efficient actions. The more you string those days together, the more likely it will be that you can set up your own success.

Conclusion

Imagination is your greatest asset. There are no limits except the one you set for yourself. *Imagination* is unlimited. It is a field of all possibilities. Whatever you think of, can be pictured in your *Imagination*. I've seen it at work in my life, especially in the last few months. It took me only six weeks to write this whole book, and I believe that was possible because I allowed my *Imagination* to work at its best. I was passionate about it, and as you know, passion is the fire that drives us to express who we are. My *Future* had said that when I was writing, I was using the most creative side of my *Imagination* and that was because of my passion for writing and my desire to change not just my life but the life of everyone who will lay their hands on this book. Also, my *Future* said that if I can use my *Imagination* consciously daily, I can create the life I want. That means that I can go anywhere, I can be anything, I can do whatever my heart desires. That means that you can do, be, or have anything you ever dreamed of. It is true; we are infinite beings with unlimited potential. ***Our Imagination is limitless. There's no end to it.***

If our *Imagination* is a vast space like the *Universe*, doesn't that mean they are connected? And if they are, does that mean that we somehow have access of every thought that has ever existed from the first moment of this world until now? That the *Universe* and *Imagination* are an unlimited library of every thought that has ever existed?

Honestly, I don't have the answers to these questions. But for whatever reason, I believe that our *Imagination* is connected with the Universe itself; and that's why I have access to some thoughts that I didn't know I had in my mind. I've read this book several dozens of time just because I couldn't believe what I was implying. But now I can understand to an extent. And this is just the beginning. I've just started.

Just because I'm writing about this doesn't mean that I have mastered it. I haven't. Like you, I just caught a glimpse of this power. I too have to learn how to use it in every moment, every day, consciously and to be aware of it. And I can tell you that it is hard, at least until now while I'm writing this (September 2018). It is hard to monitor every thought, word, and deed throughout the day and to be aware of every interval and set the intention by using my *Imagination* to have a predictable outcome and be in control of my life.

But I'll not stop. I can't stop. I will continue to learn and grow every single day and research about this phenomenon to understand more about it. As soon as I get it, I'll come back to all of you who are reading this to share what I have found. For now, let's all together make a promise that we'll do everything we can to use our *Imagination* to live the life that we desire.

We are all in the process of transforming to a higher and better expression of ourselves. It is my absolute hope that this book will do exactly that; to help you transform your life. I also hope that you enjoyed reading this book and that you have learned something that will help you to remember who you are and live the life of your dreams. Like I've said, I didn't know how powerful our *Imagination* was until I tapped into its power by writing this book.

I want to thank every one of you for buying this book and spending your time reading it, studying it, and learning from it.

As my *Future* said to me, I'll say the same to you:

Until we work together again!

About the Author

Coming from a small-town Pozega, Serbia, *Srdjan* decided to go to Canada in June 2014 after experiencing a very critical and hard time in his life during which he lost almost everything valuable to him. Not knowing what to do with his life, he was aware enough to hear that invisible voice that we all have who was whispering *"Go to Canada and start your life all over again."* So he did. Coming to Canada was not an easy task and adjustment to life in Toronto was hard for him because he couldn't speak English, nor did he know anyone in Canada. After a few years of adjusting to a new country, new town, people, culture, he came to a point where he wanted to live his dream. A dream to become a teacher working with people who are seeking improvement in their life situation.

In the late summer of 2017, *Srdjan Bogicevic* created a website where he would put training videos intended to help people to overcome their *loneliness* because he was alone for several years. Alone in his thoughts. Alone in his feelings. Alone in all internal battles that he had to fight. By embracing the loneliness and learning to finally accept himself as who he really is, he was ready to start teaching others to remember who they are. Part of that process was writing inspirational blogs, and that was the first time *Srdjan* discovered his talent for writing. Little did he know at that time that soon (two years later), he'll experience a flash in his mind that will give him the insight to write a book by using his *Imagination* to find the life answers he was seeking. Answers, that an imaginary character, *Future Self*, would provide for him.

And so he followed his insight and after several months of working on the book, the time has come for that dream to come to life. ***The Art of Imagination*** is *Srdjan's* first book he hopes will have a significant impact on anyone willing to read and apply the principles described in tit. Now, he's on the road to creating other projects that are connected to *The Art of Imagination* by using his *Intention* combined with *Imagination* so you can have even more knowledge about how to develop your awareness. With the help of *Future Self*, you can be sure that more books are about to be born.

www.ingramcontent.com/pod-product-compliance
Lightning Source LLC
Chambersburg PA
CBHW061818040426
42447CB00012B/2709